The Dreamer's Way

"This book is a powerful gift for dreamers at every level. Topics like precognitive dreams, PK, and Past Lives Dreams that have been left out of most dream books are addressed here. When you partake in Dr. Rosemary Guiley's Dream Labs, the world around you changes. Life becomes more colorful, interesting, and much more creative." —Marcia Emery, Ph.D., author of *PowerHunch!* and *The Intuitive Healer*

"In *The Dreamer's Way,* Rosemary Ellen Guiley masterfully combines scholarly study with personal experience, grounded and rational discussion with the full embrace of the non-rational reality of the world of dreams. Her writing style is extraordinarily clear, direct, and illuminating, making what could be considered an esoteric and illusive subject very practical and tangible. I highly recommend this book as an excellent guide to exploring the wisdom of the subconscious through dreams." —Alan Seale, author of *Soul Mission, Life Vision,* and *Intuitive Living: A Sacred Path*

"*The Dreamer's Way* is a soulful and practical guide for all who dream. It provides an approach to becoming more fully who we are through the power of our dreams." —Nancy Rosanoff, Ph.D., author of *Putting Intuitive Intelligence to Work*

THE DREAMER'S WAY

Using Proactive Dreaming
to Heal and Transform Your Life

ROSEMARY ELLEN GUILEY, PH.D.

BERKLEY BOOKS, NEW YORK

B

A Berkley Book
Published by The Berkley Publishing Group
A division of Penguin Group (USA) Inc.
375 Hudson Street
New York, New York 10014

This book is an original publication of The Berkley Publishing Group.

Copyright © 2004 by Visionary Living, Inc.
Cover art by Laurie Rubin/The Image Bank.
Cover design by Jill Boltin.
Text design by Julie Rogers.

First edition: April 2004

Library of Congress Cataloging-in-Publication Data
Guiley, Rosemary.
    The dreamer's way : using proactive dreaming to heal and transform your
life / Rosemary Ellen Guiley.
    p. cm.
  ISBN 0-425-19423-X
    1. Dreams. 2. Self-realization. 3. Dreams—Religious aspects. 4. Self-
realization—Religious aspects. I. Title.
BF1099.S36G85 2004
154.6'3—dc22   2003063679

PRINTED IN THE UNITED STATES OF AMERICA

10 9 8 7 6 5 4 3 2 1

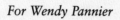

For Wendy Pannier

ACKNOWLEDGMENTS

I OFFER PROFOUND gratitude to my friends in the dreamwork community for their help in bringing this book into being. First and foremost, I thank Rita Dwyer for contributing a wonderful foreword. As cofounder and former executive director of the Association for the Study of Dreams, Rita is the inspiration to countless numbers of dreamers around the world. She is a true visionary dreamer.

I also especially thank Carol D. Warner for sharing her healing dream experience, and for collaborating on a fascinating study to ET dreams; Dale E. Graff for his expertise on psi dreaming; Robert Waggoner for his expertise on lucid dreaming and examples of his own lucid dreams; David Stabley for sharing the role of dreams in his art; Robert Michael Place for sharing the dream experience that led to our collaboration on two Tarot book-and-deck sets; Jean Campbell, Janis Ryalls and Curtiss Hoffman for their contributions to dream activism; Roberta

Ossana, editor and publisher of *Dream Network,* for providing the "Vatican dream"; and Richard Russo, editor of *Dream Time,* for his inspiring experience of dreams and the spirit of place, originally published in *Dream Time,* winter 2002.

I am indebted to Naomi Kosten for her calling dream; Val Bigelow and Tracy Duncan for their animal dreams; Deborah for her past-life dreams; Sylvia G. for sharing her dream journal; and many other individuals who contributed their dreams.

I am especially indebted to two other friends and colleagues. Rev. Toni G. Boehm created the Heart Quest and Seed Ceremony rituals, which I have adapted here. Jo introduced me to the Roman dream temple ruins at Lydney, England and to the dream-inspired healing shrine at Walsingham, England, and also shared her calling dreams.

CONTENTS

FOREWORD

IN THE SEVERAL decades during which I have been studying dreams and actively involved in dreamwork, I've learned much from my affiliation with the international Association for the Study of Dreams (ASD), its conferences and publications, but especially from its members, one of whom is not only a colleague and collaborator, but a dear friend, Rosemary Ellen Guiley. Her new book, *The Dreamer's Way,* is exceptional in its scope, focusing on the reality of dreams and the concrete ways in which they can and do affect our waking lives personally and interpersonally.

Rosemary believes, as do I, that we are all called to be "visionary dreamers," not just passive sleepers who when awake, recall dreams and investigate them for personal meanings, sometimes only on surface or symbolic levels. While these approaches are valid and often helpful and healing, they are merely small tastes of the mystical feast portioned out to us each night. There is so much more to ingest, so much that is whole-some and healing for us collectively, not just individually. This book provides a tantalizing menu.

The dreamer-friendly lessons, labs, and experiments are gifts from a woman who values dreams, who understands the power of love, and who follows the guidance of spirit, just as those of ancient cultures did and today's so-called primitive cultures still do. Rosemary guides us along the dreamer's way with facts and fascinating stories, both historical and personal, igniting our sense of exploration and mapping the journey others have taken in the past to help us in these present times to reach a new level of consciousness, to experience illumined dreaming and enlightened living, and to envision a far more comprehensive worldview than ever seen with waking eyes. We creatures are so wondrously made, not just physically, but psychically and spiritually.

Strangely enough, both Rosemary and I had our interest in dreams piqued through precognitive dreams, hers experienced by members of her family, and mine through those of a friend and fellow aerospace coworker-worker, Ed Butler, who rescued me from burning to death in a laboratory explosion. He came to consider in retrospect that his dreams were like nighttime rehearsals for the hero role he was to play in waking reality. How could this happen? Could we all dream precognitively, or was this just a random fluke?

No science book I ever read addressed anomalous experiences as evidence of human potentials. Instead, when mentioned at all, they were dismissed as superstitious nonsense, unexplored and discounted since they could not be explained, measured, or replicated by the scientific methods of that time. In the years since, I've learned that dreams, particularly those that are labeled by some as "paranormal," are truly a normal part of our dreaming experiences and that altered states of consciousness, precognition, telepathy, and psychokinesis are part of humankind's psychic tools for surviving and thriving.

How I wish that this book had been available to me all those years ago, when I first started searching for answers. What I learned ever so slowly, but what the readers of *Dreamer's Way* will quickly discover, is that we all have innate powers of the mind that dreams open up for us—we can connect with the Divine and our Higher Self, the world of spirit, the past and our ancestors, our personal guides and guardians, our pets and power animals. We can find our true calling in life and improve our creativity, heed warning dreams that alert us to physical danger or illness and provide solutions and healing, preview the future due to the fluidity of dream time, and sometimes change outcomes. We can also join with others, incubating dreams to attain positive concrete goals. This is particularly important during these troubled times in our waking world, when terrorists are creating walls of hatred and fear, nations are warring, innocents are starving or being killed, and our high-tech materialistic society makes many feel like lost souls, rich in possessions, but empty and alienated.

Dreamer's Way offers a new path of peaceful unity, one that encompasses individual growth in wisdom and expansion of the collective unconscious, as well as collective/social consciousness. For example, Rosemary describes how she and I implemented formation of an active alliance of dreamers within ASD called Dream Activists or Awakened Heart dreamers. Other such groups are forming in the United States and abroad, linking dreamers from disparate backgrounds and often separated by long distances, differences that our dreaming minds transcend. We find ourselves connected not only in the web of dreams at night, but through Global Mind. We also link in cyberspace and that huge Web that allows us to quickly relate to each other the inspirations and actions that our dreams bring to any problems we are addressing, whether individual or collective. The expression "brave new world" aptly describes this territory that dreamers are now envisioning and manifesting, through proactive dreaming.

Children in war-torn countries are being helped and peace bridges are being built with dreams as the strands that bind us, spiritual guidance to help us, and love as the power that provides the impetus for change. Though this is a challenging undertaking, it is gaining momentum. As Rosemary writes, "Tomorrow's world is the direct result of today's consciousness." Tomorrow's world is also the direct result of our realizing the interrelation of everything and the responsibility of everyone to awaken their dreaming hearts and make positive changes. The journey can be made with baby steps or giant steps, but what really matters is manifesting the goal of improving our own lives and the world in which we live. This is not a new notion. In the words of writer Adelaide Anne Procter (1825–1864):

> *Dreams grow holy put in action; work grows fair through*
> *   starry dreaming,*
> *But where each flows on unmingling, both are fruitless and*
> *   in vain.*

Early in this book, Rosemary shares a personal experience that was life-changing. In a dream, she meets a "Silver Lady" who teaches her that she can pick stars from the sky. She later comes to the realization that those stars are the creative ideas that she has manifested in her teaching and writing throughout her highly successful career. Last night, I had a dream in which Rosemary WAS the Silver Lady. We dreamers owe her great gratitude for her starry dreaming, which leads to inspiring books such as *Dreamer's Way*.

June 21, 2003

Rita Dwyer, Past President (1992–1993) and Executive Officer (1994–1999), Association for the Study of Dreams

DREAM LABS

CHAPTER 1

The Call to Visionary Dreaming

MY CREATIVITY IN writing began in childhood. By the time I was nine I was in full swing. Material poured out of me: articles, short stories, poems, scripts, skits, and more. I started newspapers at school, which I edited, designed, typed, and filled with mostly my own copy. I created lecture presentations on subjects that interested me, complete with posters and visual aids. I wrote, produced, and performed one-girl variety and comedy shows. I wrote so many papers voluntarily that one teacher asked me to stop; she simply didn't know what to do with all of them. By age fifteen, I had completed two novels and had started several more, and had created several board games. Decades later, I am still at it full tilt, in both nonfiction and fiction.

The headwaters of this constant stream of ideas and creativity originates in my dreams. Ever since I can remember, I have often awakened with my mind flooded with words and ideas, as though I have been somewhere at night gathering in a waiting harvest to bring back into the world of waking consciousness.

I was in my early teens when I became seriously interested in dreams, thanks to precognitive dreaming experienced by members of my family. I became a proactive dreamer—I began experimenting with my dreams to will myself to make dream visits to places and to send and receive messages. Not all my efforts were successful, but enough were, and they fueled a lifelong interest in the power of dreams.

At the time my interest in dreams began, I had a dream that I have never forgotten. It was imbued with an atmosphere of mystery and magic. In it, I was with a woman dressed in a long white dress. She had long white hair that was rather wavy, and she seemed young despite her white hair. In the dream it seemed we had gone somewhere, but suddenly I was in a space that was dark, like night, and I was looking up into a beautiful starry sky. The woman told me that I could take stars home with me if I wanted them. I reached out, and it then seemed like the stars were very close, right in front of me, and I could pick them out of the dark sky as though I were picking dots off a bulletin board. I held several in the crook of my arm and hand and thought, "I have stars now."

Years later in retrospection, I developed ideas about the meaning of this dream, which was more like a dreamtime adventure than an "ordinary" dream. I associated the woman with a muse, a spiritual guide, and an angel—she did resemble an angelic presence I called "Silver Lady," a faceless being in a long silver garment who paid numerous visits to me in dreams much later in life. I associated the stars with creativity and manifestations. The stars are ideas, dreams, hopes, and goals. In the lore of angels, stars are angels themselves. Perhaps most significant, especially in light of the theme of this book, is that the dream pointed to dreams as a place where creativity, manifestation, and magic are accessible to us.

I have paid attention to my dreams and recorded them and worked with them for most of my life now. They have remained an important part of my creative process, and they have provided invaluable help in weathering the inevitable emotional upheavals of life. They have aided me in healing. And my dreams have illumined my spiritual journey. The more I have worked with my dreams, the more they have nourished me.

Dreamwork begins with attention to dreams. We record them and interpret them by examining their symbolic meanings and the associations the symbols have to our thoughts, feelings, and experiences. This level of dreamwork serves as a good compass for navigating daily life. Soon we become ready for the next stage of dreamwork.

The increasing familiarity with dreams leads to the unfoldment of a higher level of dreamwork: visionary dreaming. The essence of visionary dreaming is this:

> Dreams have symbolic meaning *and* are experiences
> that have creative and transformational power.

Visionary dreaming goes beyond the symbolic in dreams to the *reality* of dreams. Our dreams do give us messages in the form of symbols, and most of these messages pertain to our emotions and the subconscious. But many dreams are much more than that: They escort us into a different dimension where we have experiences just as real and as valid as we do in waking life. They leave us transformed; they make their imprint on the physical world by prompting us to follow new directions.

In visionary dreaming, we become proactive dreamers, directing our dreams to work for our goals. We see our dreams as spiritual experiences that reach deep into the soul's interior. Our horizon broadens, and we begin to understand dreams as more than personal experiences, but part of a vast network of consciousness that connects all things.

If you have picked up this book, you are, like me, experiencing the call of visionary dreaming. The chapters that follow explore different aspects of visionary dreaming. I have included throughout "Dream Labs," exercises and experiments for pursuing your own exploration of dream terrain. Visionary dreaming is "the Dreamer's Way," a path of illumined dreaming that unfolds into enlightened living.

CHAPTER 2

Tools for Visionary Dreaming

"VISIONARY DREAMING" GOES beyond traditional dream-work to an understanding of dreams in a more intuitive, even mystical or magical, way. Our dreams inspire waking meditations, reverie, daydreams, intuition, invention, creativity, and spiritual peak experiences. Our dreams connect us in powerful ways to others and become a force for change in the world.

Our dreams are not separate from waking life. Our dreams are part of a flow of life that embraces a multitude of experiences in different states of consciousness. Waking life affects dreams, and dreaming life affects waking life. When we view our dreams as part of a continuum of expression and development of the soul, dreaming takes on new meaning and new dimensions. Dreams become more enriching. We stop trying to draw boundaries between our experiences—this is a dream, that is waking life—and see the interrelationship of everything as a whole.

Our dreams can dramatically change life by showing us that

what seems to be impossible is really possible and within our reach. Our dreams have tremendous power, but this power goes untapped in many people because they do not pay attention to their dreams, or make an effort to understand them. Even when they do, they experience only reactive dreaming: dreams that react to past or existing situations primarily to correct imbalances in life.

We can only realize the full power of dreaming when we shift into visionary dreaming. Visionary dreaming is proactive, in which you can use your dreams as tools to help shape a different and better future.

The following are techniques and tools we will use to experience visionary dreaming.

DREAM INCUBATION

Visionary dreaming makes use of the time-honored practice of incubating dreams to create, perform, or learn something in a novel way. Dream incubation has been used since ancient times to look into the future, to obtain inspiration, to reveal knowledge, and to heal. Dream incubation is a way of directing your dreams to respond to specific needs. If you need guidance, an idea, or an answer to a question, you can put it to your dreams and obtain answers quickly. You can navigate outside of time and space to see the future and experience otherworldly realms. Not only can you change your own personal circumstances, you can also dream with others to affect large-scale events, perhaps even help to alter the course of humanity.

Instructions for dream incubation are given at the end of this chapter.

DREAM JOURNEYING

Dream journeying is having a dreamlike experience in an altered but not sleeping state of consciousness. It is a popular technique used in dreamwork groups for accessing intuition and the dreaming mind without having to go to sleep first. In a relaxed and meditative state, we can obtain benefits similar to sleep dreaming. A guided meditation can take us on a specific journey, or enable us to finish dreams that are incomplete. Dream journeying is similar to shamanic journeying.

DREAM LABS

Throughout the book are Dream Labs—exercises designed for the topics addressed in different chapters. Most of them are incubations for dreams during sleep and dream journeying for waking dream meditations. Many of them can be done either alone or in a group; some are designed especially for group dreamwork.

To avoid repetition, I do not repeat the incubation steps every time, but provide the focus of the incubation exercise. The more experienced you are in dreamwork, the easier it will be to incubate dreams, and without having to move deliberately step-by-step.

DREAM JOURNALS

The dream journal—a record of your dreams and your interpretations of them—cannot be underestimated in any kind of dreamwork. Without a record, our dreams vanish from memory. In visionary dreaming, the journal takes on additional importance as a repository of the soul's secrets, intimate reflections, and inner searching. The dream journal is a private experience that helps you to grow, transform, and get to know yourself better. It becomes a diary of life.

Dream journals are useful for:

• **Personal inventory.** Write down your thoughts about yourself, aspirations, goals, strong characteristics, and things you need to work on. You might want to learn or improve a skill, overcome a fault, or modify your behavior in certain situations.

• **Unfinished business.** Your dreams will show you where you have left unfinished business, whether with another person, an ambition that was never realized, or something that was not brought to closure. Use your journal as a mental and emotional clearinghouse. Once you see your thoughts on paper, many times the "charge" behind the emotional response becomes lessened and new ways to deal with the issues behind the reaction come to light.

• **Milestones.** After you have kept a dream journal for awhile, you will see patterns not only in your dreams but also in your behavior and the events that play out in your life and career. The record of your dreaming and waking life will help you honestly assess what is happening and why, and help you discover possibilities for improvement.

• **Observation of rhythms.** Life contains periods of ebb and flow, ups and downs, highs and lows. Your dream life also moves though a rhythm of intense activity and lulls, during which it seems difficult to remember dreams. Journaling allows you to relate the rhythms of waking and dreaming life.

• **Redefinition.** By reviewing your recent or distant past, you can reinterpret significant events and see them with new eyes.

• **Self-dialogue.** Dream journaling is a good way to ask yourself questions and then let the answers come from the center of your being—in intuition and dreams—rather than just from your rational self, which always wishes to direct and control. This opens opportunities for self-dialogue between you and your Higher Self, creating new insights into old problems and conditions. Thus, you get to know yourself and your world better.

You should review your dream journals every now and then. The details of most dreams, and even the dreams themselves, are forgotten, even after they've been recorded. Our attention is demanded in many arenas. Dreams are highly alchemical, in that they are part of a spiritual process that unfolds over time and in its own time. Sometimes an old dream takes on new significance in light of more recent dreams and events. Sometimes the *real* meaning of a dream only reveals itself much later. Sometimes a dream makes sense only when we've had another dream at a later time. And sometimes we make the uncomfortable discovery that we're still stuck in an emotional place as evidenced by a dream theme that keeps recurring over the years.

For much of my life, I kept my dream journal in notebooks.

About a decade ago, I switched to keeping them in a computer file. Periodically, I do searches for key words and see what patterns show up. If I travel and do not have my computer with me, I record dreams on tape or in a notebook and then transfer them to the master file when I get home.

SACRED DREAM SPACE

Visionary dreaming requires no special environmental trappings; however many people find special effects conducive to changes in states of consciousness. Meditating with a lit candle and soft music prior to retiring is one easy way to set sacred dream space. (Caution: Do not leave the candle burning after you go to bed!) You can also create sacred space with a small altar of objects that have spiritual significance to you, wall hangings, incense, and other items.

Ritual also creates sacred space and prepares body, mind, and spirit for engaging in the realm of dreaming. Ancient dream incubation practices put the power of ritual to work by prescribing purifications to take prior to incubation: fasting or a very light diet, bodily cleansing, prayers and affirmations, perhaps the ingestion of an herbal tea to help induce sleep.

I do find it helpful that on nights when I wish to incubate visionary dreaming, I set my intention to do so early in the day. I have my purpose in mind throughout the day. I eat lightly, especially in the evening, and avoid things that might disturb the sleep cycle, such as alcohol or caffeine. I take adequate time to relax prior to sleep. Light inspirational reading and meditation music are beneficial. All of these actions contribute to the setting of sacred dream space.

Writing down your incubation intent—a question or an affirmation—also helps to set sacred dream space by impressing intent into consciousness. I think it is especially helpful in the beginning. Over time, you may feel you don't need the written prompt to accomplish your objective.

My good friend and dreamwork collaborator Rita Dwyer gave me a little dream pillow that I keep on the bed. On one side is an affirmation, "My Spirit leads the way, and I am successful," with a white bird flying over mountains as it is guided by a star. On the other side is a heart into which one can slip pieces of paper with dream incubations written on them. It creates a lovely little ritual and is a nightly reminder of the majesty of dreaming.

A friend of mine who feels a special affinity with angels has an angel figurine by her bed. When she wants help from her dreams, she writes her request on a piece of paper and places it beneath the angel as her way of turning the matter over to angelic help.

THE INTUITIVE BREATH

We can use our breath to relax the body, still the mind, and circulate chi, the universal life force, throughout our entire being. In *Breakthrough Intuition* I introduced the "Intuitive Breath" as a simple, fast way to prepare for inner work, including visionary dreaming.

Take three long, slow and deep breaths. Breathe in through your nostrils. You can breathe out either through your nostrils or your mouth. As you breathe, focus on these:

1. Breathe . . . *slow down.*

Our thoughts run in all directions. The first breath is to rein in that distraction.

2. Breathe . . . *center.*

Pull in your energy and focus the breath in the body. Be fully present in the moment. The second breath is to gather your inner resources.

3. Breathe . . . *release and expand.*

As you exhale on the third breath, be aware that the Higher Self is now in charge. Space has been made in your consciousness for intuition and dreams to reveal what you need to know.

In three breaths, you will find yourself remarkably composed and in a different state of consciousness. The Intuitive Breath employs a little esoteric magic as well. In numbers mysticism, three represents the ascent of consciousness to higher planes. It's a door-opener to the realm of the gods. When we use the number three with a mindfulness in meditative exercises, we are seeking higher wisdom. This is why we find three so often in tales of mysticism and magic: Charms are recited three times, we are given three wishes, and so on.

Think of the Intuitive Breath as represented by an upward-pointing triangle that rests on the earth (the physical plane) and points to the heavens (intuitive/dream wisdom). The breath brings our mind, body, and spirit into harmony and balance so that the heavens can be reached.

THE DREAM GUIDE

On your journeys through the dreamscape, you may acquire, or wish to acquire, a Dream Guide. The prophets of old had angelic guides on their mystical dream journeys to heaven; similarly, we have figures who are guides in dreaming. You may notice that the same figure or being shows up in certain kinds of dreams. You can also ask, in incubation, for a Dream Guide to present itself.

The Dream Guide witnesses the life/soul experiences you had during dreaming. It can take any form, such as a person or spiritualized being or an animal who travels with us in dreamtime and communicates with us. However, I have met people whose Dream Guides are magical objects: for example, a mirror that reflects Truth and acts as a gateway to dream journeys. Some call their guides the Dream Master, Dream Angel, or Dream Weaver. St. John Bosco referred to his companion in his lucid dreams as "the man with the cap."

The Dream Guide is that part of your consciousness that has experiences in dreamtime. It is connected to the higher aspects of soul that guide the life journey and play a role in decisions that affect the course of the journey. The Dream Guide also is connected to the higher aspects of soul that guide the life-to-life journey: the incarnations upon incarnations that contribute to the sum total of the soul's learning and progress.

The Dream Guide is not entirely within us, but is also connected to the Source of All Being, or the Godhead. Part of its responsibility is the maintenance of cosmic balance and order, and it works with the soul specifically in dreams toward that end. Dreams help us to maintain balance and harmony in life, and our individual balance makes a mighty contribution to the balance of everything in the cosmos. We have but an inkling of the power of our own life upon All That Is. If all of us were fully aware of that power and how much we affect all of creation for better or for worse, we would think, speak, and act with greater mindfulness. Every thought, every word, every deed sends out waves of spiritual energy that travel into the infinite reaches of creation. Waves that are made of positive, benevolent energy contribute to cosmic order. Waves that are made of discord, anger, and unhappiness disrupt and tear the fabric of creation.

Dreaming shows us precisely where imbalances are in life and provides insight into how we can restore balance. Sometimes the imbalances are small, such as feeling overwhelmed with things to do. Sometimes the imbalances are great, such as when relationships become destructive or a job ceases to be fulfilling, or we are devastated by tragedy.

Since consciousness is abstract, it's difficult to imagine it in a form with which we can work. That's where the Dream Guide proves helpful. The Dream Guide is a personification of an abstract part of soul and consciousness.

Once the Dream Guide presents itself, we have an effective tool for navigating and understanding our dreams, especially on a deeper level. The Dream Guide can be summoned prior to sleep to get answers to questions, to take you to places, and to provide an overall protective companionship. The Dream Guide actually is always present when we dream, whether we are aware of it or not, but by actively engaging it prior to sleep, we can make our dreaming more productive and rewarding.

Following are the basic Dream Labs that form the foundation of the work in this book:

Visionary Dreaming Incubation

Use the following formula for dream incubations.

1. Set your intention to direct your dreams to answer a specific question of personal importance to you.

2. Frame a clear question. You will get the best results if you ask a question that can be answered yes or no. Once you become accustomed to dream incubation, try open-ended questions.

3. Write the question down in your dream journal; think about it throughout the day.

4. Prior to going to sleep, meditate on the question.

5. As you go to sleep, hold in mind the affirmation that you will receive the answer in a dream that you will remember upon awakening.

6. Upon awakening, immediately capture as much detail as you can about your dream. Repeat it to yourself or to someone else so that it becomes set in memory. Write it down or tape-record it as soon as possible. Be sure to note the emotions you experienced in the dream and upon awakening.

7. Work with the dream. Did it provide a clear answer? What does your intuition tell you?

8. Pay attention for intuitive information throughout the day.

9. When you receive your answer, decide what action you will take.

10. Keep a complete record in your journal.

QUESTIONS TO CONSIDER

1. Did your answers/results surprise you? In what way?

2. Are you able to take action in accordance with the dream?

3. What did you learn about yourself? Your dreams?

You may get your results the very first night. If you feel you do not, incubate the question or affirmation again the following night. If you do not receive an answer after three tries, look for reasons why. Perhaps the answer has been given but is not recognized or understood. Perhaps you are meant to receive the answer at a later time, either in another dream or in an intuitive flash.

Try the dream incubation on a variety of personal questions. The more you practice, the more responsive your dreams will be.

DREAM LAB #2

The Dream Temple and Dream Guide

This is a dream journeying exercise. Allow thirty to forty-five minutes. You can either tape the guided meditation and play it back or have someone read it aloud for you. It is not unusual during a guided meditation to depart from the script and find yourself having a different experience than the one suggested. Go where you are intuitively led. The purpose of the guided meditation is to initiate the journey and provide a framework if needed.

PREPARATION

Set your sacred space according to your taste. Play relaxing meditative music. Use the Intuitive Breath to relax, center, and expand your
consciousness.

MEDITATION

*Visualize a white screen in the mind . . . The white screen begins to
change into colors . . . beautiful rainbow hues . . . waterfalls of color . . .
the colors give way to a great Dream Temple . . . notice its structure and
shape . . . what it is made of . . . the size and shape of the doorway in
its center . . . you are joyous, for to see this Dream Temple is to come
home . . . to familiar surroundings . . . in a happy, loving atmosphere . . .
a place of rest and inspiration . . . of good fortune . . . of solutions and
answers . . . a place of healing. Experience the happiness and joy at
being here, at having this place where you can come anytime in
dreams . . .*

*Enter through the doorway . . . the hall inside is large . . . notice your
surroundings . . . the objects there . . . what is on the walls . . . hanging
from the ceiling. The hall leads to a room . . . a sanctuary . . . your own
private chamber within the Dream Temple . . . it contains favorite things . . .
things you like.*

*Make yourself comfortable . . . and as soon as you have done so,
the Dream Guide enters the chamber . . . the image and form that arise
spontaneously in this waking dream vision present the Dream Guide as the
Guide wishes to appear . . . accept this appearance and welcome the
Guide in. You have known each other for a long, long time . . from the time
before time . . . and you know that the guidance that comes from the
Dream Guide emanates from the Source of All Being and holds your high-*

est and best interests . . . The Dream Guide oversees your experiences in the dreaming world and seeks to help you understand them.

The Dream Guide can be asked to find information . . . can be asked to reveal things . . . to show things . . . to accompany you and take you places in your dreams. The Dream Guide protects your dream travels . . . and serves as a bridge to other spiritual presences who participate in your dreams.

Enter into conversation with your Dream Guide . . . learn what the Dream Guide has to say about your dreams . . . learn more about what the Dream Guide can do . . . convey your wishes and goals that you would like to pursue in your dreamwork . . .

Now ask a question for which you would like insight and answers . . . Remember that what rises spontaneously within you in response is the answer . . . (Allow several minutes)

Finish now . . . thank the Dream Guide and affirm your relationship . . . leave the chamber and depart the Dream Temple . . . follow a path of rainbow light back to the place where you started . . .

Become conscious of your breath moving through your body . . . Use several breaths to recenter your consciousness fully in the body . . . return to wakefulness, fully alert and refreshed.

Record notes about your meditation. Like nocturnal dreams, waking dream meditations can be easily forgotten. Writing down the details will help set the experience in memory and in consciousness. If you are working with a partner or group in this meditation, work in pairs to discuss your experiences.

QUESTIONS TO CONSIDER

1. What did the Dream Temple look like?

2. What details did you especially notice about the temple or the chamber inside?

3. What form did your Dream Guide take?

4. Were you surprised?

5. How can the Dream Guide be of particular help to you?

6. What did the Dream Guide have to say about your dreams?

7. What question did you ask, and what was the answer?

8. Did the answer surprise you? If so, in what way?

If the answer to your question was not clear, record the response you did receive and put it away for reconsideration later. It is likely that more processing needs to be done, or perhaps the question needs to be rephrased. Sometimes the answer is given but not recognized, especially if it takes us in an unexpected direction. We may desire a certain answer, but the Dream Guide, as part of our Higher Self wisdom, sees the true course.

DREAM LAB #3

Additional Work with the Dream Guide

Now that you have laid the foundation, you can do dream incubations for virtually any purpose. The following are ideas for additional incubations. You can do them either for nighttime dreaming or for waking dream meditations. In either case, allow yourself time afterwards to record the experience and do initial dreamwork.

THE ANSWER PLACE

You may wish to use the Dream Temple as a meeting place, resting place, starting place, or point of orientation in dreams. The Dream Temple can anchor the geography of your dream map. It is a place to where you can always go and always return.

The answers to questions may be found in a different location—a dream library, for example—and you can ask the Dream Guide to take you there.

Incubation:

Show me the place where I can go to find answers to the questions I ask my dreams . . .

SIGNS

The waking world, through signs and synchronicities, can provide you with signals that validate your dreams. The Dream Guide is a part of your Higher Self that functions all the time to provide valuable information. The dreaming mind operates in a much different reality than does the waking mind, and so the Higher Self is clothed differently as well. For example, many people have a personal "lucky sign" that signals to them when something is right, good, or on course. The appearance of a penny on the pavement or the sight of a particular (and not common) bird may be such signs. Feelings, such as distinct and peculiar sensations in the body, also serve as signs.

Such signs can also appear in the dream world. You may ask a question of your dreams, and the response will include a particular sign, but perhaps the Dream Guide itself will not be present. Nonetheless, you will know the answer from the sign.

Incubation:

> *Dream Guide, show me a sign by which I will recognize you in the waking world . . .*

Incubation:

> *Show me a sign that will mean good luck and "yes" whether I am dreaming or awake . . .*

DREAM TRAVELING

Meet the Dream Guide and make a request to visit a particular place, either in earth geography or in multidimensional space.

Incubation:

> *Take me to (or show me) the following place: _____.*

CHAPTER 3

Dreams and the Body

THE MEANING OF our dreams impacts more than our thoughts
and feelings—it resonates in the body as well. We can gain important information about dreams by examining them from two
perspectives: the body's energy zones and the body's physical responses to the dream itself.

ENERGY ZONES

The body's energy zones are the chakras, wheel-shaped interfaces in the body and aura that funnel in the universal life
force—known as chi, prana, ki, mana, breath of God, and
other terms—and connect us to our inner and Higher Self.
Chakra is a Sanskrit term for *wheel*. Chakras are shaped like
multicolored lotus petals or spoked wheels of light, which
whirl at various speeds as they process the universal life force.

They are invisible to the physical eye but can be perceived by the trained inner eye in energy healing, meditation, and spiritual practice.

There actually are hundreds of chakras throughout the body, but attention is focused most on seven primary ones that are aligned approximately along the spinal column, from the root, or base of the spine, to the crown, or top of the head. Each chakra governs a different aspect of life, as well as different physical and psycho-spiritual functions. Think of them as filters. When they are functioning well, the entire system functions well on all levels—physically, emotionally, mentally, and spiritually. When they become clogged or closed, the system is impaired on one or more levels. Chakras can become clogged through disease, imbalance, and disharmony. Many of our stresses in life have a negative, clogging effect on the chakras.

Through meditation, spiritual study, energy healing, and even dreamwork, chakras can be opened, balanced, cleansed, and stimulated to improve our physical, mental, emotional, and spiritual well-being.

Each chakra has a color. The lower three are oriented more to our life and concerns in the physical plane. The higher four chakras, from the heart up, become increasingly oriented towards our spiritual nature and what the saints termed "right living": having a relationship with the Divine and living as best as we can according to high moral and ethical standards. Though each chakra has its own area of governance, they interrelate and overlap.

Our dreams register on the chakras, and if we take them into account in dreamwork, we can gain insights in the following areas:

- Spiritual growth

- Healing unresolved issues and feelings

- Stress reduction

- Improve health and well-being

- Restoration of harmony and happiness

- Improved creativity

- Heightened spiritual awareness

- Improved intuition

- Elimination of unproductive thought and belief patterns

You don't have to be trained to "see" chakras in order to do dreamwork with them. In their own way, dreams do the seeing for you. By addressing the imbalances in your life, you will automatically benefit the functioning of your chakra system.

Let's get oriented to the seven primary chakras in terms of the spheres of life that are associated with them. We will then consider how to relate our dreams to chakras. We'll start with the lowest, the root chakra, and move up.

Root Chakra

- Color: red

- Energy zone location: base of spine

- Governs: our foundation in the world, family, home, relationships, physical well-being, material comforts, reproduction

• Issues: upsetting and unhappy relationships, insecure home life, feelings of vulnerability, lack of energy, poor health, money problems in terms of covering essentials

SPLEEN CHAKRA

• Color: orange

• Energy zone location: near spleen on lower left abdominal side

• Governs: personal power and authority, assertiveness, competitiveness, self-esteem, sexual interests and activity

• Issues: egotism, feelings of inferiority or low self-esteem, aggression, disorganization, lack of focus, fear of failure, sexual problems, feeling unattractive, emphasis on material prestige

SOLAR PLEXUS CHAKRA

• Color: yellow

• Energy zone location: below the navel

• Governs: emotions, intuitions, sense of well-being

• Issues: unresolved emotional conflicts, emotional wounding, lack of awareness of intuitive guidance, fear of risk-taking, inability to acknowledge or express feelings

HEART CHAKRA

• Color: green

• Energy zone location: center of chest

- Governs: love, self-love, compassion, empathy, ability to relate to others, charitableness, spiritual awakenings

- Issues: feelings of betrayal, withdrawal of affections, isolation, lack of consideration, feelings of detachment from others or the world, abandonment by others or God, stinginess, cruelty

THROAT CHAKRA

- Color: blue

- Energy zone location: base of throat

- Governs: self-expression, creativity, self-confidence in a public way

- Issues: timidity, fear of humiliation or ridicule, inability to communicate effectively

BROW CHAKRA

- Color: indigo

- Energy zone location: between the eyebrows

- Governs: spiritual development, spiritual vision, psychic faculties, inspiration

- Issues: lack of faith and trust; failure to nurture ideas, goals, and dreams; narrow-mindedness

CROWN CHAKRA

- Color: purple

- Energy zone location: top of head

- Governs: enlightenment, closer relationship to God, humanitarianism

- Issues: self-centeredness, lack of spiritual practice

A good way to get familiar with the chakras is to visualize them in meditation. With eyes closed, focus your attention on the area of each chakra and imagine a ball of colored light there. Moving up the ladder, think of the areas of life governed by each chakra in turn. Take note of the thoughts and impressions that rise up spontaneously within you.

DREAM LAB #4

Chakra Dreaming

Take a written description of a dream and underline the colors mentioned. Make note of them in List #1. Review the dream for objects and landscape features that have a natural color associated with them, even though you did not record the color in your journal. For example, a clear sky would be blue, trees would be brown and green. Make note of them in List #2.

Relate the colors to the chakras. List #1 features the strongest connections, and List #2 features secondary connections.

Consider the "chakra issues" for those chakras and relate them to your dream. Weigh them in relation to other associations you have made. For example, blue may be your favorite color and thus have a host of personal associations because of that. Then consider how blue relates to your dream from the standpoint of the throat chakra. Does the dream point to something you are not expressing?

What follows is an example of how the chakra dreaming interpretation works in a dream:

Mother is living in a foreign country. She calls me on the phone and asks me how much postage she should put on some green envelopes she has. I tell her I don't know without seeing them. Are they heavy? She says yes. I wonder why she wants to mail me something when she could just give it to me in person.

The dreamer was never close to her mother; their relationship was so distant as to be in foreign territory emotionally. At the time of the dream, the mother was suffering a severe health crisis. This raised within the dreamer unresolved guilt and sorrow over the fact that the two of them had not been closer. The color green pointed the dreamer to the heart chakra, helping her to see that she needed to address a complex mix of repressed emotions. She had "known" for years that she needed to do so, but the chakra dreamwork brought the issue into a new focus. She could see how the emotional burden was affecting her "heart center."

If a color is approximate, associate it with the chakra color nearest to it. Here is an example from my dream diary:

I dream I am graduating from high school. I wonder what I will do next, without the familiarity of school. Part of the graduation involves going through a Grail ceremony by myself. In one part, I am in a cathedral-like building, and I go into a dark alcove where there is a golden Grail cup, to pray. Someone else is in the cathedral, but I do not know who.

I did quite a bit of dreamwork on this dream, which holds several layers of meaning for me. The chakra dreaming technique was valuable in that it emphasized a particular point that needed my attention. I related the golden color of the cup to the solar plexus chakra (yellow). The message for me was to trust my intuition more concerning a certain matter—as well as in general. In the dream, the gold of the Grail cup seems to light up the dark alcove. Similarly, our intuition provides a light of direction to us.

The symbols in this dream are quite strong: graduation, "high" school, a cathedral, a Grail cup, the act of praying, the presence of an unknown companion. They might have overshadowed the point about intuition, but the chakra dreaming technique picked it up and pointed straight to it.

Chakra dreamwork does not reduce the meaning of dreams solely to color/chakra associations. Keep in mind that it is only one part of your overall dreamwork and should be integrated with other insights.

DREAM LAB #5
Body Dreamwork

We can literally, physically "feel" our dreams. You're most likely to be aware of the physical impact of dreams when you awaken from an especially ecstatic—or especially terrifying—dream. These should be considered in your dreamwork.

Dreams also register more subtle clues to their meaning in the body. During dream interpretation work, we can be so focused mentally on probing a dream that we miss the body cues related to the dream's meaning.

Body dreamwork helps us in two ways: 1) To gain additional insights into dreams and 2) to identify and release tensions in the body.

Take a written dream and read the dream aloud. Pay attention to how your body responds. Do you feel a heaviness, a lightness, or a tightening anywhere in the body? Does your voice get louder or more tense or fade to a whisper? Make note of physical responses and the corresponding parts of the dream.

Focus on the physical sensations and ask for their meaning. For example, "The tightness in my chest makes me think of _____." Phrase the meaning of the sensation in a metaphor: "I don't have any breathing room." Don't try to force associations—allow them to come freely.

If possible or appropriate, act out the physical feeling. If your legs feel heavy, get up and walk around as though you had to move great weights. What else do you notice about what the body is saying? How can you relate that back to the dream?

Consult the chakra list for associations related to areas of the body. For example, if you have noticeable sensations in the throat, consider the throat chakra issues.

CHAPTER 4

Lucidity and Dream Traveling

LUCID DREAMING IS the conscious awareness that you are dreaming while you are dreaming. Degrees of lucidity vary, from simple awareness of dreaming to the ability to create and manage the dream itself. A regular practice of paying attention to your dreams may enhance your frequency of lucid dreaming.

Lucid dreams enable us to participate in dreams in a much different and more pleasant way. Most dreaming is characterized by passivity: Dreams seem to happen to us without planning or warning, and we are at the mercy of the dream and the figures in it. Lucidity enables us to exert more influence over the events in a dream. We can determine whether or not we will subject ourselves to something unpleasant; we can create dreamscape action we desire to have; we can purposefully look into the future, share dreams with others, and communicate with others in dreams.

The ability to do these things, however, varies considerably by individual. Some people seem to have a natural affinity for lucid dreaming and learn how to direct the course of their dreams. Others achieve limited control, even with repeated practice of lucid-inducing techniques. They may be able to improve their ability to dream lucidly, but not to the degree enjoyed by some others. Perhaps lucid dreaming is an artistic talent; anyone can learn a certain degree of competency, but not everyone will be a master at it.

Lucid dreaming has been recognized since ancient times. Aristotle commented on it in *On Dreams*. Tibetan yoga has techniques for inducing lucid dreams. Lucidity occurs during both REM and non-REM sleep.

The benefits of lucid dreaming remain inconclusive. Some researchers feel that lucid dreams are a key to breakthroughs of creativity and brain power. Some psychotherapists use lucid dreaming as a way to deal with threatening dream images.

However, some regular lucid dreamers feel that too much planned dreaming loses a spontaneous, creative spark. As an occasional lucid dreamer—sometimes spontaneously, sometimes by incubated design—I have no conclusion myself. Lucid dreaming is interesting, fun, and different. I consider dreams in general to enhance creativity and personal growth, whether they be lucid, extraordinary, or "ordinary." Whether or not you decide to pursue lucid dreaming, you should be familiar with it as part of your own visionary dreaming. Many dreams that have significant precognitive, creative, healing, and spiritual content feature elements of lucidity.

ARE LUCID DREAMS OUT-OF-BODY EXPERIENCES?

Beliefs that the soul can leave the physical body and travel about during dreaming have existed worldwide since ancient times. The soul—or a part of it—travels about in a special body or vehicle, such as the astral body or etheric body (often perceived as a diaphanous, or semisolid, body that duplicates the physical one). Beliefs that dreams are out-of-body experiences (OBEs) are well documented in anthropological literature. Dream travels are viewed not as dreams, but as real experiences of a part of the soul during sleep.

OBEs also can occur during waking consciousness, especially in meditation. In either dreams or wakefulness, we may have the feeling of being out of the body, or may look upon it from a distance as evidence that we have separated from it.

Dream researchers distinguish OBE dreams from lucid dreams; Stephen LaBerge's studies have indicated that about 9 percent of lucid dreams also are OBE dreams. However, it is often difficult for many dreamers, myself included, to draw a line between the two: OBE dreams can be lucid and lucid dreams can involve OBEs. The feeling of being out of the body may be more pronounced in some lucid dreams than in others. For example, you may be specifically aware of leaving and reentering your body. In other cases, you may simply know you are out of your body at the same time you become aware you are lucid.

The late Robert Monroe was one of the most famous OBE/lucid dreamers in the modern West. Monroe discovered on his own that in the hypnagogic state—the borderland between wakefulness and sleep—he could induce OBE/lucid dreams in which he traveled about the dreamscape and other dimensions in his astral body, a glowing outline of his physical form, which recorded the sensation of touch and moved according to his thought. Monroe felt it was important to maintain lucidity as long as possible. He called the ideal state "mind awake body asleep." His strange dream experiences are recorded in his three books, *Journeys Out of the Body, Far Journeys,* and *The Ultimate Journey*.

"Dream traveling" is the visiting of distant places while asleep. The places may be on earth, or, as in Monroe's experiences, in other realms. Dream traveling may be marked by sensations of flying and varying degrees of lucidity.

SIGNS AND CHARACTERISTICS OF LUCIDITY

Lucid dreams feature tip-off characteristics that tell us we are conscious in a dream. You may experience one or more of these whenever you dream lucidly.

FALSE AWAKENINGS

You wake up in the dream only to discover you are still dreaming, as in the following dream of mine, which occurred in a hypnagogic phase:

> I wake up from my nap to find myself in a long and dimly lit hallway. There are doors on both sides that are closed. I start walking down the hallway. It has an eerie feel, and I can't see the end of it. Suddenly it occurs to

me that I am still dreaming. As soon as I think I am still dreaming, I wake up for real.

False awakenings may be accompanied by sleep paralysis, which in a dream manifests as the desire to move or speak but the inability to do so.

ECSTASY AND SEXUAL ENERGY

A prominent characteristic of lucid dreaming in general, ecstasy ranges from intense feelings of exhilaration (such as during flying) to sexual orgasm. Psychologist Patricia Garfield said of her own lucid dreams that approximately two-thirds of them featured sexual energy, of which half featured orgasm—either with Garfield's husband or others. Partners included other men, a male angelic figure, a woman, a half-man/half-woman being, and even Garfield herself. In her book *Pathway to Ecstasy*, Garfield said:

> I believe it quite possible that in lucid dreaming we are stimulating an area of the brain, or a chain of responses, that is associated with ecstatic states of all sorts. Sensations of flying, sexual heights, acute pleasurable awareness, and a sense of oneness are all natural outcomes of a prolonged lucid dream.[1]

Monroe discovered that heightened sexual energy often facilitated his OBE/lucid dreams. He experienced a kind of astral intercourse, which he described as a sort of merging of energies with a sexual partner.

Flying and Unusual Powers

In some of my lucid dreams, I can fly around the room, fly high over the earth, and go through walls. Dream flying also may be to otherworldly realms.

Lightness or Buoyancy

Buoyancy—rising up into the air—is a common phenomenon of lucidity. Many of my own lucid dreams involve buoyancy, as well as sexual energy. One theme that repeats in my lucidity is being with a man (who may or may not be known to me) with whom I share sexual attraction, and we are dancing. He lifts me high into the air, or I rise high into the air on my own, as though gravity can barely hold me down.

In some of my lucid dreams, I become buoyant as soon as I realize I am lucid. I simply start floating up into the air.

Light-headedness and Electrical Feelings

For Garfield, lucidity sometimes is preceded by a feeling of light-headedness. Other dreamers report feeling electrical surges through their dream body, vibrating or tingling sensations. Vibrating—as well as buzzing and rushing noises—also are associated with out-of-body experiences. Monroe would experience a buzzing and vibrating in hypnagogic sleep, and then a sensation of being lifted out of his body. Here is one of my lucid dreams in which body vibrations were strong:

> I discover the secret of wormholes and transport myself to
> K's house [a real place in a foreign country]. The dream is

lucid, and I say, "This is really a dream." It feels real. Everything is very vivid. I materialize in K's laundry room. She has laundered some of my clothes, and they are in the dryer. I take them out and start folding them. She comes in and is startled to see me. I like the surprise. I say jokingly, "I just thought I should fold up some of my clothes." We go out of the laundry room, and I start explaining how I got there, through this wormhole. I can see a reddening in the sky out the window. It looks like dawn, and I ask what time it is. I want to have breakfast before I go back. At some point my whole body starts to vibrate strongly, to the point where I am shaking from head to foot. I am concerned that this means I am about to lose lucidity and involuntarily return home. "It's like Robert Monroe," I say, explaining that Monroe would start to vibrate before he went out of body. I concentrate on staying where I am, and then the vibrating stops. But the dream ends after that.

Unusual Atmospheres

A frequent characteristic of my lucid dreams is a strange atmosphere, as though the air is very thick, almost like water. Two terms I often use to describe my lucid dreams are that they have an *intoxicating* or *opiated* atmosphere. The lucid dream featuring the dimly lit hallway that was mentioned previously had an unusual, eerie atmosphere.

Vivid Colors

Most of my lucid dreams are exceptionally vivid in color and detail. Everything, including my senses, seems sharpened and heightened.

WHAT TO DO WHEN YOU RECOGNIZE LUCIDITY

The ability to remain lucid in dreams varies with individuals. Many people find that they lose lucidity almost as soon as they become aware of it. The practice of incubating lucid dreams tends to prolong the periods of lucidity.

Lucid dreamers have a variety of techniques for establishing and holding lucidity. As soon as I realize I am lucid, I say, "I'm dreaming" or "This must be a dream." I try to touch an object to register sensing something solid. Sometimes lucidity, as well as the dream, come to an end involuntarily. However, sometimes I can prolong lucidity through concentration of sheer will to remain in the dream and conscious.

The presence of a deceased person in your dream may be a trigger to lucidity: You know they are dead, and therefore you must be dreaming.

Modulating emotions will help the retention of lucidity; try not to get carried away in the excitement of finding yourself lucid.

Be sure to validate that you are indeed lucid and dreaming before you attempt to direct the course of your dream.

INCUBATING LUCIDITY

There are various techniques for incubating lucidity. Here are some of the most popular:

INCUBATION AFFIRMATIONS

You can train yourself with affirmation and intention to recognize lucidity, such as:

> *Tonight I will be lucid in my dreams and I will be able to maintain lucidity.*

As you fall into sleep, try to maintain awareness as long as you can.

THE HANDS HAVE IT

Many people report success with a method popularized by Carlos Castenada in his Don Juan books. First you concentrate on your hands prior to sleep; then in the dream, see your hands and raise them to your face. Looking at your hands or touching them while dreaming can help to anchor and maintain lucidity. Lucid dream expert Robert Waggoner recognizes lucidity by saying in the dream, "This is a dream," and also using his hands in front of him as a visual anchor to help him remain lucid.

MEDITATION VISUALIZATIONS

Visualizing blue lights at chakra points aids lucidity for some dreamers. I have had success with presleep visualizations of a blue light at the throat chakra at the base of the throat and at the brow chakra between the eyebrows.

SLEEPING POSTURES

Some techniques call for sleeping on either the right side or the left side, combined with affirmation or visualization. Monroe's technique, called "rotation" or "peel-off," calls for lying prone on your back. As you drop into the hypnagogic state, slowly turn over without using your arms or legs for assistance. When you have turned 180 degrees, think of floating up and away, as though backing up from the body.

Monroe's technique, as well as other sleeping positions, work for many people. In my own experimentation, however, I have discovered that sleeping position makes no discernable difference in whether or not I dream lucidly, or in the nature of a lucid dream.

HERBS

Lucidity can be facilitated with herbs, especially mugwort, which has a long history in folklore of inducing prophetic dreams and astral travel. Mugwort has various medicinal purposes and once was used in the brewing of beer before the introduction of hops. One of its main active ingredients is thujone, similar in properties to THC, the intoxicant in marijuana and hashish, and which is associated with visual and auditory hallucinations when taken internally. It is related to wormwood, used in the making of absinthe, a liqueur with narcotic properties.

I have had success with mugwort myself, both with vivid dreaming and lucid dreaming. Some people report that they experience nightmares or restless sleep, however. I do not take it internally, but use a small "dream pillow" filled with the dried herb, which I place inside my pillowcase.

Lucid dreamer Ed Wirth has reported in a paper presented to the 2000 conference of the Association for the Study of Dreams that mugwort not only increased his dream lucidity but also increased the number of precognitive and synchronistic dreams, from 1 percent of his dreaming to 10 percent. Wirth obtained dramatic results after placing one ounce of mugwort in a paper sack inside his pillow. His paper is published on-line; the URL address is given in the appendix of resources.

Some herbal sleep teas facilitate lucid dreams and also dreams that are unusual in their vividness, content, and intensity, such as this one reported to me, which occurred in the borderland state, coming from sleep into wakefulness:

> As I was waking up from this deep sleep, I seemed to pass through this layer of intense information. It seemed as if I went through it in about a quarter of a second, but the information that I encountered was very rich, very dense, and very detailed. My first thought upon awaking was that I have a lot of brain power, but somehow my waking conscious dumbs me down. Now I think maybe I went though some universal consciousness. Either way that quarter of a second blew my mind.[2]

Caution: Herbs, like drugs, can interact with other drugs and medications. Dried herbs in sachets, or commercial herbal teas, are the best bets.

TOUCHING AND OBSERVING DREAM OBJECTS

Once you realize you are lucid, try touching objects to feel their solidity. Another technique is to see a clock, look away, and then look immediately back at the clock. If the clock or its time has changed, you are dreaming.

LUCID DREAMING WITH OTHERS

Lucid dreams may also involve other phenomena of visionary dreaming, such as mutual dreaming, which is sharing the same dreams with one or more persons. In lucid mutual dreaming, one or more persons involved may simultaneously experience lucidity, as in the following case:

> My girlfriend and I decided to try an experiment to be lucid together in a dream. Before we went to sleep, we meditated together that we would both have the same dream and would be lucid in the dream.
>
> We had different degrees of success. We had several dreams in which we shared some common ground, but not exactly the same dream, and one of us would be lucid. Once we were both lucid in the same dream. We were in a strange place standing along a long road. The ground was flat, and the road seemed to go off into infinity. I felt very strange, and suddenly I realized that I was dreaming. I said to G_____, "Are you dreaming too?" and she said, "Yes." I said, "Let's fly." As soon as I said it, we started to fly up in the air. Then the dream ended.[3]

LUCIDITY AND PRECOGNITION

Lucid dreaming may involve spontaneous precognition, in which we see or experience in a lucid state something that then happens in waking life. We can also set our intention to use lucidity as a way to know the future.

Waggoner has been able to interview people in lucid dreams to ask them questions about what they will be doing in the future, as in the following example from one of his lucid dreams:

> I asked two questions of the same brother; the questions were, "A year from now, will you be married?"—he responded, "No." Then I asked, "A year from now, where will you be living?"—he responded, "In Los Angeles." The responses given to both lucid dream questions were correct one year later. At the time of the lucid dream, he had been making plans to move away from Los Angeles, and had a serious relationship that could have led to marriage, but did not.[4]

Lucidity expert E. W. Kellogg III has used the incubation technique of asking a question and setting the intent to find the answer in a certain medium. For example, you might open a drawer and see a document with the answer written on it. Kellogg has used a silver bowl—he asks a question, then turns over a silver bowl to see the answer revealed.

The following dream labs will help you explore different aspects of lucid dreaming.

DREAM LAB #6

Mugwort Dreaming

Take an ounce of dried mugwort (obtainable at many health food stores), place it in a cloth slipcase, and insert it into your pillow, or hang near the head of the bed.

Prior to sleep, incubate a question or intent, such as:

Tonight I will be lucid in my dreams.
Tonight I will be lucid in my dreams and will meet so-and-so.
Tonight I will be lucid in my dreams and will receive the answer
to my question, _____.

Follow through with dreamwork.

D R E A M   L A B   # 7
Lucid Q&A

Prior to sleep, incubate a question and your intention to receive the answer via a certain method in a lucid dream. For example, one technique discussed in this chapter involves opening a drawer. Your incubation might be:

Tonight I will be lucid in my dreams. My question is
_____. While I am lucid, I will open a drawer and find
the answer. I will read and understand the answer. I will remember my dream.

Follow through with dreamwork.

Dream Traveling

Incubate a lucid dream in which you will travel somewhere, such as to a distant city or country. Ask to be shown something you know nothing about—such as a remarkable building or geographic feature, or little-known name—that can be verified by research later.

Follow through with dreamwork.

Lucid Dreaming with Others

Work with a partner and agree on an incubation for dreaming lucidly with each other, such as:

Tonight we will share the same dream and be lucid together in it.
Tonight we will share a dream in which we _____, and we will be lucid together in it.

Do the incubation at the same time. If you are separated by distance, agree on a time when you will both do the incubation.

Follow through with dreamwork.

Dream Interviews about the Future

Incubate a lucid dream in which you will be with a person whom you will interview about future events. Prepare one or two questions about events that can be verified by you later, to determine the accuracy of the precognition.

Keep track of your success record. Look for patterns of characteristics in successful precognitive lucid dreams. Are there certain elements, objects, colors, or "feel" to these dreams? If so, they may serve as signs to you in other dreams with precognitive content.

CHAPTER 5

Experiencing God in Dreams

MANY DREAMS ARE highly charged with spiritual content—
as though God is speaking directly to us with guidance and instructions. We may be visited by God in the image of a religious
figure who imparts a specific message. Sometimes the "word of
God" is obvious to us because certain dream images are religious in nature or have strong religious associations for us, such
as objects of devotion or faith. In other dreams, the spiritual
content is intuited in the context of the dreams related to situations in daily life.

All dreams have a spiritual component, since dreams by their
very nature are concerned with our overall well-being. Some seem
more spiritual than others. These spiritually charged dreams often
are "big" dreams that come at times when we are being tested or
stressed, or are at the crossroads of major decisions. But dreams
with spiritual content can come to us at any time as part of our
personal growth, especially if we pay attention to our inner life.

For me, spiritual dreams are those that provide insight into my life's purpose and the Great Mystery, or those that expand my consciousness to other levels of awareness about who I am and what I'm doing in this life. Spiritual dreams bring a feeling of transformation, growth, and enlightenment. They are full of power. Spiritual dreams can change us more dramatically and more quickly than many "real" experiences that we have in waking life.

In discussing God in dreams, the term *God* shall refer to a broad range of perspectives on the divine: God, Goddess, Creator, Universal Mind, individual deities, and so forth.

IN THE PRESENCE OF THE DIVINE

Our spiritual traditions agree that God is ineffable—unknowable and mysterious, beyond the comprehension of human consciousness. One of the best portrayals of God's ineffability comes from Jewish mysticism. God resides in the innermost hall of the highest heaven, and his throne is surrounded by a curtain or veil called the *pargod*, which shields his brilliance from incinerating lesser beings, even angels, and also symbolizes his mysteriousness. Not even the highest angels, save one who is elect, are permitted to go inside the curtain. On the curtain is written the entire history of creation, from beginning to the end. The "Angels of the Presence" and the mystics who make the ascent to the throne of God are only allowed to be outside the curtain. The core mystery of God remains shrouded.

We attempt to understand and participate in a minute part of God through our religious and spiritual beliefs and practices. Certain individuals, such as prophets, saints, shamans, and other adepts, are recognized as attaining a greater understanding than the average person.

Dreams are democratic: They allow anyone and everyone to have a deep, transcendent, spiritual experience. Dreams happen outside of physical reality and transport us to a landscape beyond our known physical space and linear time. Dreams are mysterious in their own right. In fact, the very nature and mystery of dreaming itself may be the best medium human consciousness has for approaching the divine.

OUR HERITAGE OF DREAM VISIONS

Our spiritual dream experiences today have evolved from a long and rich history of diverse cultural experiences. Dreams were especially important for divination and prophecy in ancient Egypt, Babylonia, Greece, Rome, and the Middle East. The divine will was held to be constantly revealed in dreams, and incubation procedures were followed to obtain dream answers to questions. In those times, attitudes towards dreams were different than they are today. Dreamers were "seen," not "had;" that is, they originated outside the dreamer, implying that dreams are under the direction of supernatural or divine forces. And, dreams were far less democratic: God/the gods spoke in dreams only to important people such as kings, priests, and prophets, who in turn conveyed divine will and instructions to the masses. There were concerns about "false" dreams that came from evil sources and masqueraded as divine dreams, but nonetheless, dreams were viewed as a mode of direct communication from supernatural sources. Other modes were techniques of divination and prophecy, oracular trances, prayer, and waking visions.

In waking visions, the percipient entered into an altered state of consciousness without going into dreaming sleep. However, language used in ancient descriptions often makes it difficult to discern whether an experience was a night dream or a waking vision—or perhaps even a hypnagogic experience or lucid dream in which a false awakening occurs, giving the experience the feel of a waking vision. The term *dream vision* is the most apt to cover the range of such experiences.

Important dream visions are told in the Bible in both the Old and the New Testaments. The first book of the Bible, Genesis, demonstrates the importance of dreams as a link to God. In Genesis 15:12–16, the prophet Abram (Abraham) is told by God in a dream about the future enslavement of the Jews in a foreign land, followed by their liberation and return to their own land. This dream foretold the enslavement in Egypt.

God personally endorses dreams as a communication medium in Numbers 12:6, when he tells Moses, Miriam, and Aaron, "Hear my words: If there is a prophet among you, I the Lord make myself known to him in a vision, I speak with him in a dream."

JACOB'S DREAM LADDER

One of the most significant dream experiences in the Old Testament is Jacob's dream of the ladder of angels, told in Genesis 10. After stealing his twin brother Esau's birthright with the aid of his mother, Rebekah, Jacob leaves to escape his father Isaac's shame and Esau's wrath. Rebekah suggests that Jacob go to her brother. On his way to his uncle Laban's country, Jacob stops for the night, taking a stone as his pillow. He dreams that "a ladder was there, standing on the ground with its top reaching to heaven; and there were angels of God going up it and coming down" (Genesis 10:12). Jacob hears the voice of God explaining his high spiritual destiny: This land will be the dwelling of his innumerable descendants, and God will never desert him. When he wakes up, Jacob calls the place Bethel, meaning the gate of heaven. He anoints the stone pillow with oil and sets it up as a monument, with which he promises faithfulness and to give a tenth of his wealth to God in return for his preservation and safe return to his father.

Jacob's dream has inspired a considerable body of commentary for centuries. The ladder has been interpreted as a symbol of the angels' constant interventions and frustration with the previous patriarchs from the beginning of creation up until this point, when Jacob at last is found worthy; a prophecy of the ascent and descent of Israel that was to come; a symbol of the hierarchy of celestial intelligences and virtually every kind of correspondence, system, and parallelism between worlds and planes of being.

One or more of those may indeed be the message(s) of the dream. Dreams can have multiple layers of messages. Perhaps the most significant has been overlooked.

I interpret this dream as validation that dreams are a means of communication with God. Angels are messengers, and one of their primary purposes is to carry messages back and forth between humanity and God. The dream is showing Jacob that he has direct contact when he sleeps, represented by the angels going up and down between the earthly realm and the heavenly realm. God tells Jacob he will never desert him. In other words, the line of communication will always be open.

ENOCH'S DREAM VISION

The apocryphal literature—texts outside the canon—also contain many dream vision recitals. Many of these are apocalypses that feature angel-guided tours of heaven and sometimes hell, a revelation of the future (the Last Judgment), and instructions on repenting sin and leading a righteous life.

One of the most significant dream visions in the apocrypha is 2 Enoch, also called The Slavonic Apocalypse of Enoch, a text that probably dates to the late first century C.E. It is written by an anonymous author or authors and attributed to the prophet Enoch, who receives scant mention in the Old Testament. Enoch was a righteous man who was "taken" by God, implying that he translated directly to heaven. The heavenly tour described in 2 Enoch may have actually been experienced by the real author, or may simply be an accepted device for imparting spiritual teachings. Either way, the dream is presented as a valid means for having contact with the divine.

In the beginning of 2 Enoch, the prophet relates that he is home alone one day, sleeping on his bed:

> And while I slept, a great distress entered my heart, and I was weeping with my eyes in a dream. And I could not figure out what this distress might be nor what might be happening to me. Then two huge men appeared to me, the like of which I had never seen on Earth.
>
> Their faces were like the shining sun; their eyes were like burning lamps; from their mouths fire was coming forth; their clothing was various singing; their wings were more glistening than gold; their hands were whiter than snow.

> And they stood at the head of my bed and called me by my name. Then I awoke from my sleep and saw those men, standing in front of me in actuality.[1]

The two huge, winged "men," who are angels, tell him not to be frightened. They take him up into the heavens. Enoch is shown ten different heavens, some of which are hells where wicked angels and people are punished. God instructs the archangel Michael to "take Enoch from out of his earthly garments, and anoint him with my sweet ointment, and put him into the garments of my Glory." The oil is like sweet dew and smells like myrrh and is like the glittering rays of the sun. Enoch takes on a shining appearance like the angels around him.

God summons the angel Vrevoil (Vretiel or Pravuil), "whose knowledge was quicker in wisdom than the other archangels, who wrote all the deeds of the Lord," to bring out the books of knowledge for Enoch to read, and a pen for "speed-writing."

Vrevoil teaches Enoch all the cosmic secrets, talking for thirty days and thirty nights without stopping. Enoch writes 366 books in thirty days and thirty nights with his speed-writing pen. He tells the creation story, the Fall and that the world will end on the eighth day of creation (or after 8,000 years), when time will cease and the righteous and the wicked will be judged. He tells all the rules of morality and righteousness for humans to live by.

When Enoch is done passing these teachings on to his sons and all the people, angels come and carry him to heaven for eternity.

This type of visionary dream still happens today, though the trappings have changed to fit cultural trends. Apocalyptic tours of space, visions of the future (usually negative), and warnings that people must change their ways occur to many people in different formats, such as near-death experiences and extraterrestrial encounters.

DREAMS IN MONOTHEISM

Dream visions lost their importance in the expansion and development of Christianity. The church sought to discourage practices associated with competing religions and also practices that took power away from the priest as the prime mediator with God. St. Jerome, who translated the Bible into the official Latin Vulgate edition, lumped dreams with "witchcraft."

Dreams and visions were acceptable for the divine inspirations of saints and martyrs, and in the practice of sleeping at churches and shrines in order to be healed—a form of dream incubation. But for the average person, divine experience through dreams and visions was discouraged. The Church preached against dreams as dangerous instruments of deception caused by Satan and his demons. (However, in the Middle Ages, dreams of the unhappy dead were useful for promoting the doctrine of purgatory and the necessity of praying for the suffering souls there.)

In the nineteenth century, the emergence of psychotherapy returned importance to dreams, but not from a religious standpoint. Carl G. Jung's work delved into the spiritual dimensions of dreams in terms of "individuation," or growth toward wholeness. Dreams as a way to experience the divine still remain outside of mainstream Christianity. From my own experience in lay dreamwork, however, an increasing number of people are being attracted to working with their dreams because they have had one or more deeply significant dreams of a spiritual or religious nature.

In Islam, dreams are accepted as one of the ways God speaks to the faithful. Dream visions played an important role in the founding of Islam. The prophet Muhammad was initiated in a "Night of Power" ascent to heaven. According to tradition, the soul goes to Allah every night. The true and righteous are favored with good dreams containing good tidings from Allah. In "true" dreams, Allah transmits wisdom, knowledge of the future, and tidings of reward. In "pleasing" dreams, a step lower than true dreams, a person is satisfied and happy. There are two other main classes of dreams: those arising from one's fantasies and desires, and nightmares caused by Satan.

Dreams receive no special emphasis in contemporary Judaism, but are reaffirmed as a valid source of divine inspiration in the mystical Kabbalah text the *Zohar*: "Nothing takes place in the world but what had previously been made known, either by means of a dream, or by means of a proclamation, for it has been affirmed that before any event comes to pass in the world, it is first announced in heaven, whence it is proclaimed to the world."

WHEN IS A DREAM "GOD-GIVEN"?

Sometimes the content and impact of a dream make it clear to us that God spoke to us. Such dreams may feature religious figures or objects meaningful to us, or portray a religious or spiritually significant activity. Other dreams are more difficult to interpret as "God-given." So, how do we know when God *really* speaks to us in a dream?

Many people feel they are too unimportant for God to speak to them in dreams. Or, they think that God speaks only occasionally in "big" dreams and that most dreams are far too mundane to involve the mighty Creator.

If you've entertained such doubts, you are not alone—but I strongly urge that you let go of them in order to move your dreamwork to a deeper level. All dreams are experiences of God, for when is God *not* a part of life? Are some trees made by God and others not? Is one moment God's and another moment not? God is present in all aspects of life, including dreams, from the small and mundane to the big and impressive. A dream about seemingly mundane matters has just as much God in it as a dream that addresses life from a broader perspective. If we regard all our dreams as divine gifts, they take on an entirely different and more meaningful role in life.

Nonetheless, certain "big" dreams do stand out as packing more spiritual muscle than others. These are the dreams that we will be primarily concerned with here.

UNIVERSAL DREAM IMAGES OF GOD

We are most likely to dream within the context of our own culture and upbringing. For example, a spiritual dream for a Christian may have obvious Christian images in it. However, our dreaming mind can pull images from any religion or mythology— even one unfamiliar or completely unknown to us—in order to make a point and best convey a particular message.

In his book *The Unconscious Christian: Images of God in Dreams,* James A. Hall, a noted Jungian psychologist, gives the example of one of his own dreams, which features "a large mother animal, somewhat like an elephant." In reflecting on the dream he realized that the animal looked more like a giant tapir than an elephant. Much later he discovered while casually reading an article about the Cuña Indians of Central America that one of their traditions concerns a giant tapir who is the spirit of the Earth Mother's placenta. His dream tapir had acted in accordance with the mythological characteristics of the Cuña tapir—a striking parallel and a meeting of two different worlds. Hall had known nothing about Cuña mythology. He concluded that somehow his Self had known that this imagery was the right one to express something within his own psyche.

Jung found the same phenomenon happening to some of his patients. He believed that Westerners are deeply influenced by the Judeo–Christian heritage whether they are aware of it or not. However, he found that their dreams sometimes used imagery from the East. According to Hall, there is an unconscious religious impulse deep within the human psyche, and this impulse is not concerned with an individual's conscious tradition.

The ability of the dreaming mind to access any image from the data bank of the entire human collective unconscious is validated by research in parapsychology, alternative healing modalities, and consciousness. Though we have little understanding of exactly what our consciousness is, we do know that it is not limited by time and space or the body and the mind. It exists beyond the body and can travel to distant places and times and can observe and take action.

Dreams often reveal different levels of meaning with the passage of time, and so we should remain open to new information from unexpected sources that sheds additional light on them. Dreamwork engages the intuition and encourages synchronicities that help us better understand our dreams. Consequently, we don't necessarily need to be experts in everything—we will be automatically guided to discover what we need to know, just as Hall was guided concerning his dream of the giant tapir.

INTERPRETING RELIGIOUS IMAGERY

In working with dreams that have spiritual content, it is important to consider one's own traditions and beliefs first, for these are likely to have the most significant associations with the dream images. Then we should look at other traditions with which we may have some familiarity and see if we have any intuitive resonances concerning a dream. If you have an ecumenical approach to religion, have converted from one religion to another, have lived in or studied a culture very different from the one in which you were raised, or have undertaken a wide-ranging spiritual study, then your dreams will contain images from all of these sources.

Our dreams also may contain religious images that are not personal to us but are widely familiar. For example, one need not be a Catholic—or even a Christian—to have Mary in a dream, perhaps as a symbol of healing, peace, or nurturing. Similarly, one need not be a Buddhist to dream of Buddha, perhaps as a symbol of enlightenment or a tranquil state of mind. The meaning of the image will depend on the context of the dream and the free associations that you apply to the image itself. As one dreamer told me:

> I lived in Japan for nine years, and it's been seven years since I returned home to the States. I still occasionally have dreams that feature Buddhist imagery, even though I never practiced Buddhism. You can't help but absorb

some of another culture when you live in it for a long time. Sometimes a dream might have both Buddhist and Christian images. How I interpret them depends on what's going on in the dream and in my life. There are dreams where the Buddhist symbols don't convey a lot of religious meaning, but represent that time period in my life when I was in Japan. Sometimes they do carry a religious or spiritual meaning. It all depends.[2]

Another dreamer said:

My dreams can be a real mix of symbols from different religions and traditions. I've studied so many paths, and I take what is meaningful from each of them and incorporate it into my life. When I was deep into Native American traditions, I had a dream in which a medicine man gave me a gift. He looked like a Native American and was dressed in appropriate ritual clothing—but somehow I "knew" he was Jesus! I took the dream to mean that all spiritual paths lead to the same place. Of course I knew this intellectually, but the dream carried a "heartfelt" power that made me feel this truth deep within me.[3]

The next dream features Eastern and Western religious symbols in the form of the Maitreya and Christ. The Maitreya is the anticipated incarnation of Buddha—2,500 years after his death—in which Buddhist dharma, or philosophy of life, will be restored. Theosophists and others have applied the term to Christ or his proxy on earth. The dream occurred two days before Christmas:

I was sitting with some other people at the table. I was mentioning that Maitreya will come and will benefit all living creatures of the world on December 25 from 3 to 4 P.M. A lady asked me who the Maitreya was. "The new Christ," I answered. Nobody believed me. Another person asked me if I was going to meditate. I explained that yes I was meditating, but I was able to do it even while I was in their company. At this point a bright light appeared in the sky, and running out with great joy I was shouting, "Maitreya, Maitreya." Outside at the horizon a sun most luminous was shining.[4]

INDIRECT SYMBOLS

The presence of the Divine may be more implied, felt, or intuited rather than portrayed by an obvious image. This dream occurred to a woman undergoing chemotherapy for cancer:

I'm in a huge building with lots of long halls, sort of like the hospital. I'm lost, and no matter which way I go, I can't find my way out. Nobody pays any attention to me. I'm starting to get very frightened, when suddenly a woman appears and offers to help me. She has a kind face and a kind of a glow around her. I feel like I know her, even though she doesn't look like anyone I do know. I don't remember many details about her appearance, except she has ordinary-looking clothes on. She takes me by the hand and shows me the way out. I go out on my own.[5]

The dreamer, who professed to be "not real religious," had the strong feeling that the woman was Mary, or "Mary-like."

She felt the dream was a message from God telling her not to be frightened, and that she would find her way out of her illness. "It was telling me that I needed to lean more on God, or could learn more from him. I needed that message. I was trying to be self-sufficient, and I was scared."

VOICES

Authoritative voices are prominent in some spiritual big dreams. They are clear, sometimes loud, and they make statements and give instructions with great force. Sometimes the voice is disembodied, seeming like the literal "voice of God" booming from the heavens. Voices also are ascribed to angels, spiritual guides, and religious figures.

I am often asked, how is it possible to know for certain whether a voice comes from God or an angel, or from one's own mind?

The answer lies in the interconnectedness of all things. We can't separate ourselves from everything else in creation. The dream voices, like dreams themselves, are connected to the Source. The label matters only in the nuances and meanings that are important to the dreamer and appropriate to the dream. If two people had the same voice dream and one person said the voice was God and the other said the voice was his own Higher Self, they would both be right.

In my own experience, a direct voice dream presents a truth that I especially need to hear and understand—a sort of "Get the message *now*?" dream.

Upon awakening, you will immediately know or have an intuitive feel for the source of a voice of authority. Don't question it, but use it as one of the starting points in free association.

ANIMALS

Like angels and religious figures, animals can act as instruments of God in dreams to deliver big messages of spiritual import. Animals that have the gift of speech, and animals that pursue us, often have significant messages for us. In the case of pursuing animals, the message may be something the dreamer is ignoring or has failed to recognize. Here is a dream of a speaking and pursuing wolf:

> During a certain stage in my life, I started having dreams with a white wolf. They would repeat, not necessarily exactly the same, but in similar form. The general theme was the white wolf chased me through a forest and finally got me cornered. I was always terrified it would tear me limb from limb, but it snarled a lot and then started talking to me. The wolf said it would have to destroy me if I didn't do what I was supposed to do.
>
> I knew right away what the dreams meant. I wasn't following my heart about what I wanted to do in life. I'd taken a "safe" job. The white wolf was my medicine power, and I needed to accept it. I tried to ignore the dreams, but they got more and more frequent, and the wolf got bigger and more threatening. I would wake up very disturbed. I knew on some level that denying my heart would ultimately mean some sort of destruction or death of spirit, but I still lacked the courage to do anything about it.
>
> I finally got the courage to take the plunge. When I did, the dreams stopped. Not long after, I had one

dream in which a glowing white wolf was running toward me at great speed, and just before it got to me, it launched itself into the air right at me. But it didn't hit me—it went right into me. When I woke up, I felt that somehow I had "taken in" the white wolf medicine in the dream. It was a part of me.[6]

Here the white wolf—which was appropriate to the context of the dreamer's life—served the same function as religious figures, angels, or even the hand of God: to steer the dreamer, forcefully if necessary, onto the right path.

WHEN THE RELIGIOUS IS THE MUNDANE

Sometimes religious and spiritual imagery is used by dreams to convey more mundane messages. For example, a stressful and threatening situation might be symbolized by crucifixion in a dream. Since we dream in settings familiar to us, people who work in religious settings understandably will have more religious images in their dreams than others. The following dream was had by a woman who is active in her church, managing bookstore sales on Sundays and leading some prayer and meditation groups:

I am to lead a large meditation prayer circle at the church. I have done this before with these people, and I'm not sure I want to keep doing it, but I go ahead. There seems to be a processional, or somehow people assemble. The participants sit in a semicircle several rows deep, and I am at the head of it. They give me a large overstuffed brown chair to sit in. It is throne-like and so big that I feel like a child in it—my feet don't even hang over the side of the seat. I am wearing inappropriate clothing for ritual—jeans and a T-shirt.

I close my eyes and try to connect mentally with the audience. I can't connect very well but decide to start the centering prayer anyway. I say, "Dear God" and begin the prayer. Just then a woman in the back starts talking to the woman next to her, just chatting about nothing. For a moment I try to ignore it, and then I just blow up. "That does it!" I shout at them. "You don't talk during meditation!" I berate them, and the circle starts breaking up. People get up to leave and put chairs away. I go out among them thinking, "Well I will never work with *these* people again." I mean it as a consequence of my actions, not because I don't intend to.[7]

The church and the prayer circle setting are comparable to an office or to her workplace, and, like any work setting, can be places of frustration and tension. The dreamer interpreted this dream as showing her growing feelings of frustration that she was not sufficiently appreciated. She had tried to repress her feelings by reprimanding herself that it was "not spiritual" to think so, but the dreaming mind could not ignore them. In the dream, she feels very out of place (the jeans and T-shirt) and she is treated like a child (the huge, throne-like chair). She also is treated with disrespect (the talking while she is trying to conduct the circle). The dream reveals her fear that if she stands up for herself, it will be the end of her relationships. The dream helped the dreamer to see that she needed to acknowledge her true feelings and also be bolder about seeking recognition.

DREAMING FOR WHOLENESS

A general theme of many spiritual dreams is unification of opposites. This is the basis of the alchemy of the soul in its journey towards wholeness. The opposing forces can be anything in life: conflicting desires within us, circumstances that pull us in two directions, an awareness that we need to let something go in order to move on to something new. Both external conditions and our inner feelings about them must be resolved and brought into balance in order for us to move forward. Spiritual dreams often show us very clearly the forces that are in opposition.

Another theme found in spiritual dreams is unity, which goes beyond the unification of opposing forces within the dreamer to concern the grand, harmonious cosmic order. Deep within human consciousness is the idea or knowledge that the unity of all creation is a state of perfection. We have somehow fallen away from it—but we have the ability and resources to reestablish it. Like the prophets before us, we can be shown this perfection in our dreams and also be given information illuminating the achievement of it. The following dream addresses this theme:

I was conscious of a white submarine named *Unity*. I also was conscious that all humanity had to work at the realization of the submarine. I was seeing a multitude of people sitting and waiting for something to happen. Some of them got up and walked into the submarine.

Slowly others started to go toward it until almost all of the people found themselves working for the submarine.[8]

As a ship that travels deep in the water, the submarine symbolizes both the underlying unity of all things and the hidden and elusive nature of unity. God is unity, and we seek unity with God. Unity is peace and harmony among all the peoples of the earth. The desire for unity lies within the depths of consciousness, symbolized by the water (unseen in the dream) in which submarines travel. The white of the submarine symbolizes purity, especially of a spiritual nature. All the people of the planet must work for the "realization of the submarine"—the realization of unity will not happen of its own accord, but must be worked at by everyone. Yet we sit on the sidelines waiting for others to do the work. In the dream, some people finally take the initiative, and then slowly others do the same. The dream points out that each of us must act. Its message is hopeful, for the dream ends with almost everyone "working for the submarine," or working for unity.

This dream mirrored a stage of spiritual growth in the dreamer, who was delving into a variety of religious and spiritual teachings. It was a powerful reinforcement of the importance each individual has in creating reality. The dream became a reminder to her to continually strive for "right living" in her own life, doing her part for Unity.

UNDERSTANDING SPIRITUAL DREAMS

The experience of God in dreams can be interpreted only by the dreamer. It's important not to measure your dreams against arbitrary standards—such as the idea that only "important" people get messages from God. Pay attention to the resonances that are struck deep within you. Dreams address Truth, the discovery of which is unique to each person.

Sometimes the most productive way to approach big spiritual dreams is to examine them as whole, real experiences, rather than parse them in traditional dreamwork. Imagine that the dream is like an experience in waking life. In that way, the dream is understood more on an intuitive level, a level of "knowing," than on a rational level.

What action does the dream prompt you to take? Dreams without follow-up action are dreams unfulfilled. The real power of the dream lies in the change and transformation that result from it.

Is it possible for spiritual dreams to simply impart a feeling of contact with the Divine as their purpose? In some cases, spiritual dreams may be best left as an "experience" that is meaningful. The following dream of white birds descending from the sky as angels imbued the dreamer with a tremendous feeling of love that was unforgettable:

I was with many people who felt like neighbors. I don't know them, but we were celebrating New Year's Day. The neighborhood didn't look familiar. It consisted of large homes with huge front yards, slightly on a hill. The children were playing, and I had gone outside and met with the people celebrating next door. After meeting them, I went out on the front lawn. I was watching a film crew tape individuals performing a skit on the front porch, which reminded me of the guys from *Saturday Night Live*. The men messed up and were laughing and then looked over at a distance down by the neighbors' yard at their producer, who was a small woman. They seemed to be worried that they would upset her.

I then looked up at the sky and was in pure awe and delight! The sky was a beautiful blue with many small, wispy white clouds. Each of them depicted a swirling motion in the sky, and then out of the center flew a beautiful white bird. As the bird descended, it turned into a glorious white angel as it approached the ground. There were hundreds of these all throughout the sky! I was filled with love and excitement! I ran and called for my oldest daughter, who is four. We got together and started going up to a covered deck with the rest of the group and began shouting, "The angels are coming!!!" The neighbors kept saying to me, "You are right, I can't believe it, you are right!" It felt like we had known this for a long time and shared the coming with others who didn't quite believe until the day the angels flew down.[9]

Birds especially white ones, are symbols and messengers of the spiritual, and angels are messengers from God. The dream seems to be an announcement or awakening—perhaps symbolic of a spiritual awakening. There are plenty of details in the dream to fuel traditional dreamwork, but for the dreamer two things stood out as significant: the feeling of love and the fact that the dream occurred on a certain day of the month, a number that marked many important happenings in her life. Sometimes big spiritual dreams allow us to experience emotion in a more profound way than we have before; the effects are often permanent. Perhaps the sole purpose of this dream was to awaken that feeling of deep love within the dreamer. If dreams connect us to God, and God is unconditional love, then we should expect some of our spiritual dreams to be primarily the experience of the essence of God.

DREAM LAB #11

Dream Prayer

Spiritually saturated dreams happen on their own timetable, but we can fertilize dreaming consciousness to be more receptive to spiritual messages. Turn your dream incubation into prayer; the messages in your dreams are God's guidance and answers.

Ask for God to make use of your dreams. You can ask for something specific, such as dreams to be used to further healing or open creativity. Or, you can ask for dreams to be used according to Divine will.

Dream prayer will seed dreaming consciousness for a productive response and will train the waking mind to pay more attention to dreams.

DREAM LAB #12

Finding the Presence of God

Revisit your dream journal and earmark dreams that conveyed big spiritual content or import. How was the presence of God made clear in the dream? What symbols and imagery appeared?

Look for patterns and consistencies, which will be useful to you in working with all your dreams.

CHAPTER 6

Spiritual Turning Point Dreams

CONFLICT, CRISIS, AND inner struggle are often addressed by big spiritual dreams. The dreams may feature religious figures or authorities, or even God in either masculine or feminine aspects. It is not unusual for such a dream to instantly resolve the difficulty or sort out an answer—even if resolution has proved elusive in the face of massive thought during waking time.

One possible explanation is that the dreamer actually is on the threshold of resolution, or perhaps needs inner permission for a decision, and the religious authority dream figure provides the breakthrough or permission. Another explanation is that in times of need and crisis, we are indeed visited in our dreams by manifestations of the Divine, who help provide clarity in a dramatic way so that we can move forward. In either case, the dreamer credits the resolution to the dream.

Other spiritual turning point dreams occur as part of a dramatic shift in life, including a breakthrough in personal growth, a change in worldview, or an emotional healing. Sometimes it seems that the dream itself causes the change. More likely, the dream is a reflection or demonstration of a change already taking place within the dreamer. The dream presents the change in a bold and unforgettable picture or drama—an initiation into a new awareness.

AN ENCOUNTER WITH CHRIST

Danielle's turning point revolved around finding answers to religious questions and coming to terms with conflicting ideas about God: hers versus what she encountered in churches. Her searches left her unfulfilled; finally a dream made everything fall into place.

"I've always been very interested in dreams, and have always understood them to be spiritual messages," said Danielle. She explained the background of her situation:

> As a young girl between the ages of about eleven and twenty, I often struggled with the ever-imposing questions of life's realities. I had always believed in God but chose to believe that he was all-loving and could not understand why so many were allowed to suffer. I was very confused about where to turn for the answers. I was not religious, and still do not consider myself religious (I do not attend church, nor is there a name for my faith). At my young age, I was struggling to become closer with my God but felt lost because I did not agree with any of the religions at my disposal. I wasn't sure if there was a heaven or a hell. I only knew there was a God.

At age seventeen, in the midst of this profound inner struggle, Danielle had this dream:

I was standing in a hotel lobby. The entire decor of the hotel was done in the color red . . . the carpets, wallpaper, even the lights shone red. Around my neck was a rather crude necklace. It was a leather chain with a rectangular ceramic charm on it. The charm was about two inches long and an inch thick, with something inscribed in it (I could never recall what was carved into it). It was not painted or otherwise decorated. I can recall thinking in the dream that it had been given to me by someone very special and that I had to guard it . . . no matter what, I must *not* lose it.

At one point I reached up to touch it, and it was gone. I panicked and began hurriedly searching the floor and halls of the hotel. I came upon a bureau in one of the halls, which had several jewelry boxes on it, each one different. There must have been a dozen or so. I thought to myself, "It isn't possible that it could be in any of these boxes," but I decided I had no choice but to look through them. I could leave no stone unturned.

After looking into only a few of the boxes, I suddenly stopped and turned around. I was overcome with relief and joy and peace when I found myself looking into the face of Christ. I was thinking that he was the most beautiful man I had ever seen in my life. He was dressed in a long red robe with a thick black border on it, which was decorated with gold embroidery. He actually smiled at me and held his hands out to me and said,

"It's okay." Yes—those were the exact words of Christ when he spoke to me.

That was the end of the dream. I immediately awoke at that point and sat straight up in my bed, smiling. I sensed that a burden had been taken from me in that very second. I still remember this dream as clearly as I did on the morning I woke from it.

Danielle described the emotions she felt both in the dream and upon awakening:

In the dream, the mood was very panicky throughout. As I was searching the hotel, it was that feeling of despair, like the feeling you might get when you turn around in a grocery store and your small child is nowhere to be seen. When I came upon the bureau in the hallway with all the jewelry boxes on it, I regarded them with scrutiny, knowing that I wouldn't find my necklace in any of them, and yet I felt I had no choice but to look through them. Even as I did, there was no feeling of hope—only the knowledge that I was wasting time. It was at that point in the dream that I turned to see Christ with his arms outstretched and smiling. I remember feeling relief and complete happiness. When he spoke, telling me that "It's okay," I woke up.

Upon awakening, I distinctly remember a feeling of pure contentment, as if a weight had been taken off of me. I even felt lighter, literally. I was smiling when I awoke. I felt as though I had truly been blessed—that something holy had happened to me.

The dream accomplished quickly what Danielle had been unable to do in waking life: resolve her inner struggle and the tension created by it. The resolution was clear, and the relief was immediate and profound. The dream marked a turning point for Danielle in her spiritual beliefs. The effect was permanent, and years later Danielle could still recall vividly the power of the dream:

I had been struggling with the idea that in order to please God I needed to find the one "true" religion. I have always believed in a God of Love, *no conditions*. And yet it seemed that every religion known to me at the time was full of conditions. I was all but tormented by the notion that without a religion, I would be without my God. I had attended a few different churches with friends but always walked away feeling unrequited.

After the dream I learned to ask for guidance when I prayed, and ask for nothing else. I believe it was this new approach to "seeking truth" that helped me to find my own spirituality without seeking truth through the beliefs of others, and instead, by looking for the truth in what I had always seemed to believe innately.

The outcome is evident to anyone who knows me. I'm a very positive person now and have an endless amount of faith and strength that just wasn't there before. Perhaps my subconscious mind was only painting a picture of my fear of not finding the truth, and that it was a pointless search because I already knew.

To this day, I am not a religious person. I have not attended church since that dream, but my spirituality and faith have only grown in the past years, and I feel as though I grow closer to God with every life experience.[1]

Danielle said she felt the misplaced necklace symbolized the "truth" she was looking for. It was precious and not to be lost; she felt she wouldn't find it in the limited options of the jewelry boxes, but felt obliged to look inside them, anyway—just as she had felt limited in religious options. The necklace retained an aura of mystery to her, which is appropriate for a symbol of Truth and the mystery of God. A deeply transformative experience, especially of a spiritual nature, yields an intuitive, heartfelt "knowing."

Jesus's robe is a powerful symbol in itself. Red symbolizes blood, vitality, passion, sacrifice, and baptism—all hallmarks of transition. Black embroidered with gold speaks of "enlightened authority."

MEETING JESUS ON THE CROSS

The dreamer of this next dream described it as a powerful healing experience and the most powerful dream she had ever had:

In the dream, I was back in Upstate New York, where I grew up. I was in a car driving on a cold and snowy winter's day. As my car tried to drive up _____ Street, I felt my tires slip and realized that I was on ice. I quickly tried to negotiate the wheel while I fishtailed backwards. I panicked, since there now were cars parked on the sides of the little street and I feared I would smash them.

Just that moment, in the dream, I had a flash of "Oh, I get it." I knew my dream was telling me that I was feeling like I was sliding back in my life's progress. I did feel as though I was "slipping down" or "slipping up" with my responsibilities.

Then I was given a gorgeous site. I saw this fabulously carved wooden Jesus—dead on the cross. I walked up to Jesus and stroked his wooden face with my left hand, when I realized that Jesus was no longer wooden. He opened his eyes. They were brilliant and loving. His stiff wooden arms became flesh, and he hugged me.

I felt all this warm emollient pour over me. I saw fantastic soothing lights and felt so loved. Then Jesus gave me this vision of a pretty country-white lattice with vines woven all over it. Moments later it was like the Fourth of July. He let all the flowers bloom like fireworks. There were roses and lilies and so many blueish and purplish blossoms. It was intoxicating. I was overwhelmed with appreciation. I realized that Jesus loved me more than I could ever guess. I knew that he was not mad at me for messing up.

When I woke up, I just knew that I had enjoyed the most powerful dream of my life.

About a month later—my husband and I had been house hunting for over a year—I saw in the real estate guide this bungalow house with a porch that matched the one exactly in the background of the lattice flowers that I experienced in my dream. We immediately made an appointment to go see the house the following Saturday. I ended up not being able to make the appoint-

ment because I had a car accident. My husband and
kids did make the appointment, and they told me the
side of the house had a neat rose lattice. When my husband got inside, he knew he felt it was the house for us
since the wooden stair railing was exactly like one *he*
had seen before in a dream. A week or so later, I saw the
home and I knew it was the one for us, since it had been
the exact porch I saw in my dream and it just felt like
home. I knew it was meant to be for us since I had that
healing dream of Jesus dead on the cross and then he
came to life.[2]

Not only did the dream bring a profound sense of healing, it
also presaged the finding of the house. The dream seems to be
precognitive about the car accident as well. There is no actual accident in the dream, but one is implied by the dangerous fishtail-
ing of the car. The wife's dream also dovetails with an apparently
precognitive dream that the husband had concerning the house.

The wooden Jesus who comes to life is an interesting image.
Often our religious symbols and images can seem "wooden";
we accept them on faith but at times they nonetheless seem remote and hard to reach. The dream vividly restores life to the
dreamer's faith and sense of connection to the Divine.

MEETING GOD IN HEAVEN

The following dream, from a woman named J. R., is similar to
the dream-vision heavenly ascents ascribed to the biblical
prophets. It features transport to heaven, a tour of certain features there, being in the presence of God, information about the

meaning of things earthly and cosmic, counseling and instruction, and a return to earth as a changed person.

> My dream was that I was transported to heaven. Met God. He showed me a river. And a wall of rain. He said everything on the left was earth and on the right was heaven. He showed me that heaven and earth are very similar. The rain was like a wall. I put my hand and head into it and could see earth and people that I knew. I was given a glimpse of heaven. It is very much like an oriental garden with water/trees/animals and people. I was counseled by other beings while there. I was then returned back to earth and to this life. This dream made a very large impact on my life. I now live each day as though it were the last.[3]

Like many big spiritual dreams, this one had a profound and lasting effect, helping J. R. to integrate a turning point in her approach to life.

COMFORT FROM AN ANGEL

Starr L. had this "vivid and real" dream of comfort during a stressful time. She took it to be a sign of calmness and reassurance. In it she and others are assigned guides:

> I am outdoors lying on my back and watching the sky, which is violet-blue velvet. The stars are electric blue. There is a timbered hill to my right and a dwelling of some kind with two people inside. This is not in town.

Inside, I am feeling great energy all around, and I hear the sound of music; *no,* I *feel* the music. Unearthly beautiful music. I feel fear, which is not scared but *awe* and the most extreme peace. A feeling of *absolute* peace and love.

In that velvet purple-blue above me, were the most beautiful colors of the prism, which had the shape of a keyhole, from which the energy was emanating, more like pulsing.

Further to the right of the rainbow colors was a cluster of florescent ruby colored dots. I shouted at the two people in the dwelling to hurry and come look. (Hurry! Hurry! A UFO!) I knew the ruby dots were not a UFO, but used the term because it grabs attention. They and many others did come and gathered all around. Everyone was looking upward with beautiful expressions, and there was that feeling of total awe, peace, and love around all who were there.

Some time later, everyone was at another place, which was like an airline or railroad terminal. I was outside on a flat mesa-like area, and near me are great numbers of happy excited people all around. All of this is on the mesa area.

Everyone was being "assigned" a person, a being, and were to be guided by that same person or being.

My "guide" was a man about my own age, who limped on his left leg, as I did. I asked why he limped. Had he been hurt? He answered, "Only One is perfect," and he said, "We must go to the top of that hill."

The hill was steep and slippery, with a hard surface, but he led the way, and we never slipped one step. He said, "You have to have ultimate faith to climb this hill."

We got to the top and were looking up into the constellations. There was a large body of water off to the right of the hill . . . All signs of the Zodiac were displayed in the sky from horizon to horizon (like a great dome).

It looked like "connect the dots." The "stars" were the same ruby red of the previous red dots. The outline of the figures were lines of electric blue color. It was SO very, very beautiful, and the music . . . I could still feel it.

That sense of peace, total peace and love and awe was still with me when I awoke. I was crying. There was more, but it started to fade. *The beauty of it all.*[4]

The electric blue and other vivid colors, the beautiful, unearthly music, and the intense emotions of love and joy are characteristic of lucid and other "real" dreams.

Starr's interpretation of the guide was that he was an angel. She has a sympathetic connection to him, because they both share the same condition, a limp. He demonstrates to her, she said, that "being different doesn't matter." He tells her she must have faith in order to climb to the top of a hill, symbolizing overcoming adversity. The sky above signifies unlimited vision. The "UFO" seems like a mysterious harbinger of something good.

Starr also felt that her dream might be a preview of earth changes. The most prominent stars in the sky were the constellation Orion. A possible day residue link was her recent readings about the associations between Orion and the Great Pyramid, as well as her readings about prophecies of earth changes. Her dream reflects a positive outcome, a connection of humanity and higher consciousness in the form of angels. The adversity then takes on a larger-than-personal symbolism to embrace adversity facing all people in a time of crisis.

Months later, the dream still evoked powerful emotions about the beauty, peace, and love in the dream—which may be the most important message of all.

LOVED AND CHERISHED

This next dream is another example of dream imagery evoking Divine presence, which includes a starry sky. It occurred when the dreamer, D. M., a woman, was thirty-seven years old and in the midst of deep emotional turmoil. Seven years later, she said she still felt the dream "powerfully changed my life."

At that time, I was going through a particularly rough time. I was grieving my father's death, my marriage was in trouble, and I was suffering severe panic and anxiety attacks that led to a deep depression. I had difficulty sleeping and had nightmarish dreams when I could sleep. All this occurred toward the end of a very cold and dark winter, and I began wondering if I was losing my sanity.

I reached a point one night where I just gave in. I wanted to experience joy again so badly that I thought: "Okay, if this is how my life is going to be, then I will be happy right here, right now instead of waiting until I 'feel better,' which might never happen." I went to bed feeling that resolve and also believing that I could withstand the worst that my "dark side" could throw at me while sleeping.

As I fell asleep, I heard several musical voices calling my name, and I felt a sensation of floating in complete comfort. I saw a beautiful star field, and then a strand of stars separated from the rest, coming toward me. I felt many hands place this beautiful necklace around my neck in a gesture of blessing. I felt a profound sense of love, encouragement, and acceptance. I slept well through the night and had the best rest I'd had for many weeks. The depression was gone the next morning, and with it the fear and anticipation of panic/anxiety attacks: I have not had one since that night.

Everything in my life did not become "perfect" overnight, but I have regained my self-esteem, and a sense of real security and peace. I often think about that dream and feel certain that I am loved and cherished by the creator of that necklace. I know I am wearing it even now—a billion carats worth of stars.[5]

The stars, the musical voices, the hands, and the feelings of being loved and blessed speak to a heavenly experience. D. M. associated the necklace with God, its creator. The dream transmitted a tremendous healing power with the instant relief of the severe panic/anxiety attacks, a healing that remained permanent.

Although D. M. had had other significant dreams and also many lucid dreams, this one stood out above all the rest. "Since that dream, I pay attention to whatever my subconscious has to say," she said. "I love the subtle language of symbols and layers of meanings and consider my dreams to be a very important part of my spiritual life."

DEATH BRINGS A WAKE-UP CALL

The literature on near-death experiences (NDEs) is full of accounts of people who feel permanently changed as a result of a close brush with physical death. Their brief glimpse of what life after death might be like shakes up their worldviews and values and sends many experimenters on intense spiritual quests.

Can a dream have the same effect as a physical NDE? For Stephanie G., the following dream was as vivid and intense as many descriptions of NDEs:

This life-changing dream was so real, part of me believes it actually was more than just a dream.

I was back in my hometown of _____. It was very dark out, but I don't think it was nighttime. Things were very disastrous and chaotic—people were looting all the damaged buildings. It was very dangerous to be out alone, but for some reason, my car was at the _____ restaurant, about a mile away and I had to go get it. I was very afraid, but I went ahead and walked down there to pick it up, anyway. When I got to the restaurant, I realized that it was now oceanfront property! The new coastline was now ten miles or so inland. A very large portion of the coastline had literally been swept out to sea. I wasn't sure what had caused it, but I remembered thinking it was a massive earthquake and/or tidal wave. Mass damage was everywhere.

I drove back home along with three friends. I was almost home when my brakes failed. As I tried to stop the car, I was thrown out of the car as it went down an embankment. I was killed instantly when my head was nearly decapitated. This was all so vivid, I can remember it as if it just happened. The people who witnessed the accident came over to try to help.

The most interesting part of this dream is how I felt after I died. It was the most wonderful feeling!!! Words don't come close to describing how loving and carefree it was, even amidst all the chaos and destruction. I remember feeling no regrets, no sadness, absolutely no pain, no worries, and no fear! I wasn't even concerned about the people I'd left behind, because I knew everything would be okay. If you can imagine having only positive feelings and emotions and being in complete peace, that's how I felt. It was so all-encompassing and strong! In spite of it all, I still felt like me. I remember feeling only curiosity about my mangled body and studied it briefly. I even joked with the people who were trying to help. Oddly, they knew I was dead, but they could see me.

As I woke up, it was like nothing I'd ever experienced before. It felt like I was passing through a tunnel that was sucking all those wonderful feelings away, replacing them with my usual "earthly" concerns and problems. The whole thing was *so* real and vivid!

I haven't been the same since. My husband called it my "wake-up call," because I've been on a strong spiritual quest ever since. I've never been afraid of death but am even less so now. I know there really isn't such a thing as an ending for us, or anything else, for that matter. I sometimes wonder if I got a glimpse of one possibility for our future.

I don't know if it was a dream or some sort of out-of-body experience. Maybe they're one and the same.[6]

The dream has the same characteristics of many NDEs: lack of regret at leaving life, elation, sense of freedom, observation of one's body and the scene around it, and a return back through a tunnel. The scenes of destruction and chaos are also found in NDEs, in which the experimenters feel they are being shown a future earth. Similarly, Stephanie wonders the same thing upon awakening.

Day residue for this dream was ruled out; Stephanie had not been exposed to any media about NDEs in the time frame near the dream. However, the NDE has had so much media exposure that its "framework" can certainly exist in the subconscious and in the collective unconscious, and thus serve as the staging of a symbolic dream pertaining to major life changes.

Nonetheless, Stephanie was left with profound feelings of having undergone a real experience, not "just" a dream; it, like a physical NDE, prompted her onto a more spiritually centered path.

Dream NDEs have a significant advantage over physical NDEs: One can have the entire, full experience and transformation of consciousness without bodily harm. Now that NDEs have moved into mainstream awareness, more of these dreams are likely to occur.

READING AN ANCIENT MANUSCRIPT IN THE VATICAN

In May 2001, Roberta Ossana, publisher and editor of *Dream Network* magazine, was sent a dream with a spiritual message and was given permission to disseminate it. I was impressed with the message and tone of the dream and saved it in my files. It seemed like a message straight from God, an ideal for us to hold.

I then forgot about the dream as my attention went to projects and other things. More than a year later, I was going through my files when I came across the dream. It still carried the same energy and power, perhaps even more so in light of the terrorist events that had taken place in the meantime.

The dream has a message of faith and hope that is timeless:

I wake up this morning (05/05/01) from a dream in which I am reading a document to the world from an office in the Vatican. I am aware of the date and time, it is 4:44 P.M. on 04/04/04.

I had just prepared a meal for a voluminous crowd who were destitute and searching for answers to their state in life. I had opened the two large ovens in front of me and began pulling out food of all kinds. Whatever the person desired to fill their hunger was produced and given to them without ever depleting the contents of either oven.

I was explaining that God always provided for his children—one just needed to have faith and believe in him. It was at this moment of understanding that I was suddenly reading the document to the world.

The document had been locked away for two millennia in a vault by the early fathers of the Christian movement. A copy was also found in several other places around the world, each in a locked vault of the center of a major religion. The documents were all written in Aramaic in the hand of Christ. The document explained how we are all God's children and our differences were to be set aside as we enter into a new millennium of peace and love. As the documents were opened and read throughout the world, a great glow of love hugged the inhabitants of the earth and hatred was abolished. The multitude of religious beliefs merged into one foundation of sharing God's peace. All weapons of destruction were destroyed, and the desire to kill was replaced by an inner desire for peace.

I felt a great sense of inner peace, greater than I had ever felt before. I knew that God had finally gifted humanity with total awareness of his love for his creation. No single religion was raised above the others as the one true religion. All humanity was being told that the inner feeling of contact with God was God's gift, *not* the outer pageantry of pompous church leaders. All of humanity was one with God, and all will be one with God in the end of time. I awoke from my dream hopeful of a brighter future for all of humanity.[7]

The 444 in the dream has an association with God and angels. In *The Messengers,* Nick Bunick relates his experiences with angels and his past-life memories of St. Paul. Angels tell Nick that the number 444 represents "the power of God's love." Nick's Web site, "The Great Tomorrow," (see Appendix) features a 444 Forum in which visitors from around the world record their own 444 experiences and synchronicities.

ANGELS AND THE CRYSTAL DOVE

Musical voices are firmly identified as belonging to angels by the receiver of this dream:

> I was standing in space with no shoes and wearing a blue-gray flowing dress. There was near me an incredible bright light from which my body was absorbing some kind of powerful energy. At the same time I was hearing a most beautiful choir. I knew that they were angels singing, because never on earth have I heard such divine chanting. At one point I extended my arms with my hands formed in a cup, like I was going to receive something. It was with a shout of joy that I exclaimed, "The Crystal Dove!" Next I was flying away.[8]

This dream marked the first spiritual dream since the dreamer commenced both spiritual work and dreamwork. The lack of shoes can symbolize pilgrimage or readiness to "walk" in a new way. Her entire being is full of energy for this transformation. The dreamer is ready to receive the gifts of spirit by holding her hands in a cup, a symbol of receiving, renewal, and inspiration. The dove is a symbol of purity, innocence, faithfulness, love, and peace. It also represents baptism, or rebirth: The dove of the Holy Spirit appeared over the head of Jesus when he was baptized in the river Jordan by John the Baptist. In the dream, the angelic choir seems like a witness to this initiation or rebirth.

THE PRESENCE OF SPIRIT GUIDES

In times of trouble, we may have figures come into our dreams who seem to be spiritual guides or companions. They may seem angelic or otherworldly, as in this dream of a woman named Karina:

> In regard to spirit guides within dreams, I have them often. The most vivid one for me was when I separated from my husband (a decision I had been making for six years, believe it or not). I had been married at nineteen, and six years later was very unhappy. I was married partly because I had a baby and everyone told me to do it, even though my intuition or whatever you want to call it told me not to. I struggled with these feelings for years and ignored my inner voice completely.
>
> I was at the time [of separation] afraid I had done the wrong thing. One night I dreamed I was in a bar with many people and I began to rise off the floor to the roof. I looked beside me, and there was this woman who I could only describe as angelic-looking floating beside me. She had long, black, curly hair and a white gown flowing past her ankles. She had big blue eyes and smiled at me. She began singing to me. I do not recall the song, but she held my hand and kept smiling. I don't think I've ever felt so at peace before. To my left was Elvis Presley, dressed up in that white famous outfit he had with all the studs on it. He, too, was singing to me. It was a strange dream, but strange in a wonderful way.
>
> I believe the lady was a guide telling me I was going

to be alright; she was looking after me. I'm not sure
about Elvis—I assume he may have been there for a reason, though I'm not sure why. I do love Elvis, though.

Celebrities in dreams often represent qualities or characteristics we admire. There are numerous associations with Elvis
that one could consider here. He was an artist who freely expressed himself, traveled, was the center of attention and ado-
ration, and led a glamorous life—things probably missing from
the dreamer's life. In the dream, he lavishes attention on Karina.
The white outfit imparts a spiritual quality to him.

Despite the peace and reassurance in the dream, it did not
immediately help Karina overcome her conflicting feelings of
guilt. In the end, however, her decision to leave was reestab-
lished, and was bolstered by additional dreams:

I ended up going back to my husband, as I felt guilty for
breaking up the family, but then recently I left for good.
I moved out into a place of my own and since have had
the most amazing dreams, which I believe to be because
I'm listening to myself and being honest with myself.

In one dream, another guide figure—a man in white, which
evokes the white suit of Elvis Presley—provided comfort and reassurance:

I was standing in the pouring rain, and I was afraid, and
this man dressed in a pure white suit came up to me and
put his arms around me and just held me for ages. I was
feeling a bit vulnerable and very alone, and he made me
feel safe and cared for. The dream confirmed my deci-

sion in leaving my husband was indeed correct. I woke up feeling really good.

The next day I went to a New Age festival, which was fun. My friend was having her aura taken, so I sat down next to a lady while I was waiting. She turned to me out of the blue and said, "My God, you have a lot of guides around you." I just smiled and said, "Really?" She said, "Yes, they are all around you." I thought that was a sign that maybe I am being looked after.

Thus Karina received both confirmation of her original intuition and her decision, and also received a synchronicity in the external world that confirmed her feelings about guides in her dreams.

I do believe in spirit guides and that they come to you when you allow them to. Many of these dreams have included flying with a guide and swimming in the most beautiful water with a sense of peacefulness I cannot explain. If one is open to advice they will give it. When they are in dreams, you know that's who they are because of the feeling you get when they are with you. It's almost an instant calming sensation.

I find dreams a fascinating subject, and I believe they are a bridge between the conscious and subconscious minds. It is up to the dreamer whether they are willing to see the warnings or signs that are often given while asleep, or whether they choose to ignore it.[9]

Dreams are one of our primary voices of intuition. The spirit guides may serve as a way for the intuition to be heard as well as serving as messengers of divine guidance.

White garments, unusual lighting, mysterious figures, musical voices, unusual eyes, and sensations of electricity often are associated with spiritual guide and religious figures in dreams. Here is another example of a guide figure who appeared in the dream of a woman undertaking spiritual study:

> I was sleeping in my bed, when suddenly I was woken up by the appearance of a bright light at the entrance of my bedroom. Coming toward me and smiling was an elderly man. He was wearing a long white tunic made of raw wool or cotton. His hair and beard were long, silky white. He came very near me, not saying a word but just smiling at me. I felt like all my body was being charged by a marvelous energy.[10]

The false awakening, or dream within a dream, is a characteristic of many spiritual dreams and was documented in ancient texts such as Enoch's dream vision, as we saw in the previous chapter. The false awakening increases the feeling that the dreamer is having a "real" but dreamlike experience in waking consciousness. In this dream, the man in the white tunic is reminiscent of the "man in linen" seen by the prophet Daniel; the figure is often interpreted as an angel. Daniel's figure is more dramatic: "a man clothed in linen, whose loins were girded with gold of Uphaz. His body was like beryl, his face like the appearance of lightning, his eyes like flaming torches, his arms and legs like the gleam of burnished bronze, and the sound of his words like the noise of the multitude" (Daniel 10:5–6). Daniel's various visionary experiences came in dreams and "visions in his head as he lay in bed," according to Daniel 7:1.

Long white hair and especially a long white beard are esoteric symbols of wisdom. The charge of energy is characteristic of spiritual initiation dreams, in which a master or guide infuses a person with power. This transmission of power is a genuine tradition in spiritual work, called *shaktipat* in Eastern practices.

The dreams in this chapter demonstrate the depths of healing, peace, comfort, reassurance, and clarity that come from big spiritual dreams. Not all big dreams about problems, crises, and turning points have religious and spiritual elements, but many do, for the spiritual reaches into the deepest parts of our being.

DREAM LAB #13

Finding the Lighted Path

When a dream leaves you with a profound feeling of healing, love, reassurance, calm, clarity, or empowerment, use that feeling as the starting point in dreamwork. In meditation, review the dream and then connect with that feeling as deeply and intensely as possible. See it as a brilliant light within you that gradually expands out into the space around you. Ask to be shown a path leading out from that light. The path shows you what action you need to take to fulfill the dream.

CHAPTER 7

Calling Dreams

BY AGE FORTY-FOUR, Susan had achieved most of her career goals. She had worked her way up the corporate ladder to a high-paying job in senior management in financial services. She was married to man who also had a successful career in business. They had two children who were doing well in school. They had good health. They lived in a luxury home and enjoyed a second home in the mountains. Susan even found time to do a little volunteer work. Susan's friends liked to tell her that she lived a charmed life, that all her dreams had come true. Susan herself felt blessed, even though the job was stressful.

In her forty-fourth year, a shadow began to nag her in her dreaming sleep.

I kept having this dream in which I found myself in a hospital. Sometimes the details would be different, but the theme was always the same. Usually, I would suddenly find myself standing in a long, white hallway. I was dressed like I was going to work, and carrying my briefcase—only in the dream it was my "griefcase." I knew the hallway was in a hospital, because nurses and doctors in white uniforms would be rushing around, carrying trays and instruments. They would look at me strangely but not stop to say anything. I would start walking down the hallway, feeling both lost and in familiar surroundings at the same time—sort of like I was in the right place, but out of place, if that makes sense. Then suddenly a tall, very imposing female who seemed to be a nurse would come out of a doorway or come around a corner and stop in front of me, making me stop, too. She would say something like, "You're late" and then walk off. The dream usually would end there.

Susan would awaken from this repeating dream "knowing" what it meant, but not wanting to acknowledge the answer: It was time for her to honor a calling she had felt much earlier in life but had not followed. When she had been a little girl, Susan had envisioned herself as a nurse. But as she got older, she was influenced by a variety of factors to seek a career in business, to prove her worth in a male-dominated work climate. For years she had been fully occupied with marriage, children, and advancing her career. Now, in midlife, it seemed that her earlier ambition was reasserting itself, wanting also to be fulfilled.

The dream increased in frequency to the point where it became distressing, and Susan decided to seek some counseling. The dreamwork clarified what she already knew from the dream: She needed to honor her "first calling." She admitted that for quite some time, she had been feeling increasingly worn down by her job. It didn't offer the satisfaction it once had. The dissatisfaction was not just a temporary low period, but a growing emptiness inside of her. She acknowledged that for some time she found herself daydreaming about "what if" she had followed her first heart's desire.

How did Susan know that the dream related to her career and was not a forewarning of a health crisis? Her answer:

> I simply knew what the dream meant when I woke up. I did consider—and worry about—other meanings, especially since I was always in a hospital, dressed like I had just come from the office, and was carrying a "griefcase." The nurse's words "You're late" could have been taken to mean I wasn't there in time for a decision. I couldn't even begin to think about the prospects of someone I loved dying. But none of these possibilities felt right.[1]

Susan validated her interpretation of the dream after considerable dreamwork, soul-searching, and discussion with her family. At age forty-four, she felt that she was not in a position to start over again—going back to school as a nursing student was "not an option." However, her business and financial skills could be translated into the health care industry. After study and retraining, Susan took a position in hospital administration. It was not the high-profile, high-prestige career she'd had, nor did it pay as much, but Susan felt as though she'd "come home." She also increased her volunteer work as a lay caregiver. "Between the two," she said, "I feel like I've fulfilled my childhood dreams. If it hadn't been for the repeating dream, I probably would have kept on working in business and tried to cope with it all. The dream definitely captured my attention, and the fact that it kept repeating more or less forced me to do something about it."

GETTING THE CALL

Calling dreams are vivid, powerful dreams that have a great emotional impact on us. They can leave us shaken and upset. They can impart an urgency to take action. They can fill us with ecstacy and love. Calling dreams usually happen at turning points in life when we need to be motivated to make a change. They also occur in childhood, imparting a sense of destiny that must be fulfilled. The detail, emotion, power, and impact of calling dreams stay with us for years—even a lifetime. Whereas most other dreams fade quickly upon awakening, calling dreams remain etched in memory.

Carl G. Jung had calling dreams that profoundly changed the direction of his work. In fact, his entire life was guided by significant dreams. He relates in his autobiography, *Memories, Dreams, Reflections,* that the first of these came at the remarkably early age of three or four years. He dreamed he was in a meadow, where he suddenly discovered a dark, rectangular, stone-lined hole in the ground. A stairway led down. He descended to a curtained, arched doorway, behind which he saw what he later realized was an enormous, one-eyed phallus on a throne. Many years later, he realized the dream had initiated him into the mysteries of the earth and the realm of darkness. The dream marked the beginning of his intellectual life.

From 1926 to 1928, Jung had a series of dreams that led to his study of alchemy, which in turn enriched his insights into dreams and psychology. Most notable were dreams in which he became trapped in the seventeenth century, the time period in which alchemy was in its fullest flower, and another in which a mysterious new annex to his home contained sixteenth- and seventeenth-century works filled with mysterious symbols. Jung then began acquiring alchemical texts, which were filled with mysterious symbols, just as in his dream. Alchemy provided a bridge he sought between myth and psychology. He observed these symbols appearing in the dreams of many of his patients, who had no knowledge of alchemy.

Paying attention to his dreams, especially significant ones, was natural and important to Jung, and he urged his patients to do likewise.

ANSWERING THE CALL

A big calling dream is impossible to ignore. We must act; usually we know what we must do, at least as a first step. Sometimes calling dreams are heralds of changes already in motion, which will proceed to carry us along with tremendous momentum. The choice is ours whether to struggle and flail or find a way to ride smoothly with the flow.

Answering the call may be a long process, even a lifelong process. We may be plunged into introspection and soulsearching that is difficult, even painful, but necessary for our growth. In her book *Recurring Dreams: A Journey to Wholeness,* Kathleen Sullivan describes a soul-shaking dream that initiated an inner quest of many years. In the dream, she is on a field trip with her class of schoolchildren. They find an enormous spider's web that at first seems exquisitely beautiful, but then becomes horrific because it has entrapped a majestic female eagle, splayed wing to wing. Overcome with a devastating grief, she falls to her knees and sobs from a place within that she has never before accessed. Sullivan awakens in hysteria, at 3 A.M.

The experience "feels much more potent than a dream," Sullivan says, something she has never before experienced. The anguish and despair will not go away.

> Clearly, the psyche had other plans. How grateful I am today for the power of that single image because it pulled me, kicking and screaming, past the resistance of my intellect and the defenses of my personality. I soon realized that I had to resolve the horror of the eagle image which had slammed into me with wordless force.[2]

About sixteen years passed before the eagle was able to soar free. The journey involved deep introspection and dreamwork, during which Sullivan addressed the transformation of her "inner darkness" and experienced an improvement in her health and quality of life.

> I know that when we go beyond the limitations of our conscious selves into the broader, deeper, and higher spiritual domains of the dream, we become more whole, more satisfied, less frightened and controlling, more giving and loving.[3]

In order to answer a call, we must trust in our dreams to give us unfailing guidance. It may not be easy, especially in the beginning; only through our own experience can we validate the inner voice that speaks through our dreams.

In her book *Dream Weaving: Using Dream Guidance to Create Life's Tapestry,* Emily L. VanLaeys recounts her life story from the perspective of guidance dreams. The dreams emanate from various sources of wisdom—her subconscious, her Higher Self, divine messengers, and perhaps even God—which she pulls together in the concept of the Dream Weaver. When VanLaeys has a dream that is "particularly vivid, or full of fascinating imagery, or one in which the Dream Weaver speaks to me in audible words laden with meaning, I pay attention," she says.[4]

We may often think we know where we are headed, but as VanLaeys notes, sometimes life just has other plans. When VanLaeys feels steered by dreams, she acts accordingly, not always knowing how things are going to work out in the long run, but trusting in the process to unfold according to her highest good. She often prays for guidance before going to sleep and is richly rewarded in her dreams.

We never have an end to calling dreams, because our spiritual growth continues throughout life. VanLaeys says:

Whether a dream encourages contentment with the present or promises a new and exciting stage of life, I will know that this does not indicate the end of my life's quest. If still another dream suggests that I'm backsliding into complacency or imbalance, I'll know that it's not an ultimatum, but a gentle hint that it's time again for renewal. Dreams are among the many guideposts that God gives us to direct our paths on the journey of life. As with any guidepost, it takes faith to follow, even when we don't know what we'll find around the next bend or up the hill. There is one thing I'm certain of, though: Each night presents me with another dream.[5]

REPEATING DREAMS

If we try to ignore calling dreams, they will not leave us alone. They will recur, whether in the same theme, with the same or similar images, or with the same emotions, sometimes with variations. As in the example of Susan's repeating dream at the start of this chapter, calling dreams may recur frequently as the Dreaming Mind attempts to get our full attention. If we persist in ignoring them, calling dreams may eventually stop—but only for a time. They will reappear again, even years later, if we have not fulfilled what we are called to do.

In their book *Working with Dreams,* Montague Ullman and Nan Zimmerman observe that repeating dreams "deal with some recurrent issue in the life of a dreamer that has not been set to rest. Although the dreamer borrows images he has used in the past he arranges them in ways that reflect where he is now and what changes, if any, have occurred. Once the issue has been resolved, either in reality or through the successful working out of the dream, the repetitive dream ceases."[6]

NATIVE AMERICAN CALLING DREAMS AND VISIONS

Dreams and visions are important among Native Americans, especially the societies of the Plains. According to tradition, young men undertook formal vision quests involving solitary time in the wilderness, fasting, and praying for a vision that would unfold their life's calling. The vision imbued the recipient with power; without it, one could not be successful and would even be considered a "nobody." Vision quests were undertaken throughout life, and through them spiritual powers were accumulated.

Native American terminology makes it difficult to distinguish between "vision" and "dream" and different states of consciousness (awake or asleep). According to Lee Irwin, chair of religious studies at Chesterton College and an authority on Native American spiritual traditions, the terms *dream, vision,* and *visionary dream* can apply to:

> receiving a gift of unusual or extraordinary ability in a heightened state of awareness, usually from a humanlike dream spirit or ancestor (while either awake or sleeping) and usually accompanied by specific direction for actions, dress or songs. This power, when enacted and demonstrated to others, confirms and validates the experience, regardless of the state of the dreamer in which the power was first revealed . . .[7]

Joseph Epes Brown, professor of religious studies at the University of Montana, describes the vision quest as a retreat of four days and four nights. The individual prepared for the vision quest by fasting and praying. Dreams might be considered a lesser type of vision, but the overall experience was rated on the nature of what took place in the vision, the form of the visitors, and the powers conferred upon the recipient. Messages might be delivered from animals and powers of the natural world, as well as from ancestors and humanlike spirits. These might become the recipient's guardian spirits.

In order for the power to be realized, it had to be shown to others in the community. The power was kept alive through medicine bundles. For example, the skin or parts of an animal that came in the vision would be carefully wrapped in the bundle.

Vision quests and visionary dreaming are still experienced

in contemporary times, though they have lost much of their communal eminence.

VISIONING FOR WOMEN

Native American women experience calling dreams, but in more spontaneous ways than the formal structure of a man's vision quest. According to accounts, the power conferred by the visions sometimes remained latent for long periods of time, until the woman reached a stage in life where she could express it. In other cases, visionary dreams gave women permission to undertake activities beyond the social boundaries imposed on women.

Plains women traditionally were not expected to undertake visionary quests in order to acquire power and status. Sometimes they had spontaneous calling dreams at the start of menstruation, and occasionally during menstrual periods, when they withdrew from communal contact. Visionary experiences might occur at pivotal times, such as childbirth or during the mourning of a death, or during illness. These are typical circumstances for visionary dreams in general.

Empowerment might concern how to do certain healing techniques, make arts and crafts, acquire social skills, or provide personal help for difficult times or circumstances. Calling dreams might even be rejected if the dreamer did not want to accept the power. (There is little information on whether or not rejected calling dreams became recurring dreams.)

THE CALLING OF BLACK ELK

The famous Oglala Sioux medicine man Black Elk (1863–1950) had numerous "power dreams" throughout his life. In many, he was transported from earth into otherworldly settings, such as in this dream:

> I was taken away from this world into a vast tipi, which seemed to be as large as the world itself, and painted on the inside were every kind of four-legged being, winged being, and all the crawling peoples. These peoples who were there in that lodge, they talked to me, much as I am talking to you . . .[8]

Black Elk received his powers of healing and prophecy at an early age. Born in 1863, he was about age four when he began to hear voices, which frightened him. At age five, he had his first vision, heralded by a kingbird that spoke to him. In the vision, he saw two men coming towards him from the clouds. When they drew close, they wheeled about, turned into geese, and vanished.

Black Elk's "great vision," in which he was empowered by the Grandfathers, or Powers of the World, occurred at age nine, when he fell ill and was unconscious for twelve days. The two men came down from the clouds again, bearing spears that flashed lightning. He was taken away by them into the clouds. There he was greeted by formations of horses at the four quarters, and by the Grandfathers, who were the Powers of the World, representing the four quarters, the sky, and the earth. The Grandfathers took him to the center of the world, showed him the universe, and bestowed upon him the tools that would give him the power to heal and the power to destroy. He was named Eagle Wing Stretches. The Grandfathers showed him the sacred hoop of his people (representing their collective soul or spiritual unity); in the center bloomed a holy stick that was a tree. The tree stood at a crossroads; one road (red) was the scared path and the other (black) was the path of materialism and hardship.

The Power of the Earth revealed himself to Black Elk as an old man and said that Black Elk would need great power, for times of great trouble were ahead. He was shown his people, starving and in distress, their sacred hoop broken. A voice told Black Elk that he had been given the sacred stick and his nation's hoop, and in the center of the hoop he would set the stick and make it bloom into a flowering tree (the World Tree). Toward the end of the dream vision, he stood on the highest mountain—he later identified it as Harney Peak in the Black Hills of South Dakota—and saw the whole hoop of the world. "And while I stood there I saw more than I can tell and I understood more than I saw; for I was seeing in a sacred manner the shapes of all things in the spirit, and the shape of all shapes as they must live together like one being," he later related in his autobiography, *Black Elk Speaks*. This intuitive, mystical comprehension that defies words is characteristic of visions and visionary dreams.

Black Elk saw the sacred hoop mended and many sacred hoops of all peoples joined together in one circle and one great flowing tree sheltering all. The sacred hoop and World Tree remained at the center of Black Elk's life, and its meaning became clearer to him as he grew older.

Black Elk told no one of his vision, but the medicine man who was credited with curing him saw him shining with light. His parents and others felt him changed after his recovery—he was withdrawn and seemed like an old man. He continued to have visions, especially of the two messenger-like men from the clouds, and to understand birds and animals. Whenever he had a prophetic vision, he felt lifted out of himself.

In 1876, he had a vision of a disaster the day before the Battle of Little Big Horn occurred, in which General George Armstrong Custer and his men were massacred. The next day, he witnessed the battle, then rode among the dead and dying soldiers, killing the wounded and taking scalps.

His family joined Black Elk's second cousin Crazy Horse in resisting being placed on a reservation. After Crazy Horse was killed by soldiers, Black Elk, his family, and others retreated to Canada, where they joined Sitting Bull. The harsh winters and lack of food eventually drove them back to the United States.

According to tradition, Black Elk could not use the power of his vision until he reenacted it for others. In Black Elk's eighteenth summer, he began reenacting parts of his great vision, which enabled him to start practicing as a medicine man. He was an effective healer. He described the process as being a hole that the "power from the outer world" came through.

Although he put his power into action, Black Elk ended his life feeling that he had not fulfilled his vision. He became increasingly discouraged by the continuing oppression of the Indians by the whites. He felt their sacred hoop had been broken, and he kept recalling his vision of making the hoop whole and the tree in the center bloom. In 1886, he joined Buffalo Bill Cody's Wild West Show, thinking that if he could see and understand the world of the white man, he could fulfill his vision. He spent three years in the show and traveled with it to England, where he performed for Queen Victoria in London during her Diamond Jubilee in 1897. He also performed in Manchester and Paris. In Paris, he fell ill and had a vision about his people that compelled him to return home in 1889.

He found many of his people caught up in the Messianic

Ghost Dance Religion, which prophesied the demise of the white man and the restoration of a pristine world for Indians. At first skeptical, he attended a Ghost Dance and was surprised to see how much of it fit his great vision. He believed the movement would restore the sacred hoop. He performed and then led the dance, went into trances and experienced visions out-of-body; in one, he was given instruction for making the sacred shirts of the ghost dancers.

Black Elk did not fight in the battle at Wounded Knee Creek on December 29, 1890, when Indians were massacred and the Ghost Dance Religion was squelched. However, he witnessed the aftermath and the heaps of bodies. He participated in fighting that followed, and was wounded seriously in the abdomen. He favored continuing the fight against the white man, but the leaders, seeing their people starving and facing great odds, surrendered. Black Elk was among those sent to live on the Pine Ridge Reservation in South Dakota.

In 1930, the American writer John G. Neihardt sought an Indian who had lived through the Messianic period who could retell the days firsthand. He was sent to Black Elk, who lived at Manderson, South Dakota. Neihardt found a dispirited old man who received him as one "who has a strong desire to know the things of the Other World." Through Neihardt, Black Elk hoped to salvage his great vision, which he said had been given "to a man too weak to use it." Black Elk relayed his recollections in Sioux (he spoke no English), which was translated by his son, Ben. The story, augmented with the recollections of others whom Black Elk knew, was published in 1932 as *Black Elk Speaks: Being the Life Story of a Holy Man of the Oglala Sioux*.

Black Elk expressed a desire to make a trip to Harney Peak

so that he could address the Six Grandfathers one last time. He said that if he had any of his power left, the Thunder Beings of the west would answer him with thunder and rain. Neihardt and others arranged the trip, which took place during a drought season under a clear blue sky. Black Elk painted and dressed himself as he had been in his great vision.

In addressing the Grandfathers and the Great Spirit, Black Elk recalled his vision and said, "With tears running I must say now that the tree has never bloomed. A pitiful old man, you see me here, and I have fallen away and have done nothing." Though the tree was withered, he expressed hope that some little root of it still lived and asked the Powers to nurture it. As he spoke, clouds gathered and a thin rain fell. After a few minutes, the sky cleared.

Black Elk died in 1950. Later observers have felt he did succeed in realizing his vision; his humility in the face of the Powers was in accordance with Native American tradition. The contemporary renewal of Native American interest in traditional ways is seen as a fulfilling of his vision. His tradition was carried on by Wallace Black Elk, a Lakota Sioux medicine man who was acquainted with Black Elk as *grandfather,* a term customarily applied to respectful relationships with an older and wiser person.

DREAMS CALL THE SAINTS

Calling dreams appear often in hagiographies, the biographies of saints that contain legends and lore of their feats and experiences. Many of the dreams came early in life; some in times of illness and crisis. The individuals recognized God's instructions in the dreams and acted accordingly. Their experiences illumine a number of themes that characterize all calling dreams in general.

The following are examples of the calling dreams of saints:

ANSELM (CA. 1033–1109)

The eminent Doctor of the Church and archbishop of Canterbury dreamed as a child in Piedmont, Italy, that he sought heaven in the mountains and there received the bread of the Lord. By age fifteen Anselm knew he wanted to become a monk and was received into the Benedictine order in 1060.

BERNARD OF CLAIRVAUX (1090–1153)

Another Doctor of the Church, passionately devoted to Mary and known as "the Honey-Mouthed Doctor" for the sweetness of his spiritual teachings, was called to the religious life by a dream he had at age eight and a vision he had at age twenty-one. In 1098, Bernard of Clairvaux dreamed he saw a young woman praying in a stable, who suddenly held a radiant baby in her arms. He recognized the baby as Jesus. Mary smiled and allowed Bernard to caress him. He prayed often to Mary and felt a close bond to her. Bernard found himself equally attracted to the reformed Benedictine community at Citeaux and to a career as a writer and scholar as his family wished. In 1111, he prayed to God for direction. He had a vision of his own departed mother, whom he understood to be sent by Mary. He knew instantly that he was to become a monk.

CATHERINE LABOURÉ (1806–1876)

Catherine Labouré was a mystic who conceived the famous Miraculous Medal of Mary in a vision. At age eighteen she had a dream that foretold her destiny in the church. In the dream, she attended mass said by a saintly old priest. She then met him again when she visited a sick person. The priest told her, "My daughter, it is good to nurse the sick. Now you avoid me, but one day you'll be very glad to come to me. The good Lord has plans for you—do not forget it!" In 1830 she joined the Daughters of Charity, founded by St. Vincent del Paul, in Paris. When she saw a picture of him, she was astonished to recognize him as the saintly old priest in her dream.

FAUSTINA KOWALSKA (1905–1938)

The originator of the Divine Mercy movement had a vision at age twenty in which Jesus chastised her for her spiritual sloth and instructed her to join a convent. Faustina Kowalska soon entered the Congregation of the Sisters of Our Lady of Mercy in Warsaw and took the veil. Toward the end of her novitiate, St. Thérèse of Lisieux appeared to her in a dream and foretold her final perseverance, her future heroic sanctity, and her canonization, thus confirming her calling and sharpening her focus and resolve.

FRANCIS OF ASSISI (1181?–1226)

The stigmatist and founder of the Franciscan Order was the carefree, spendthrift son of a wealthy businessman in Assisi, Italy. Francis joined the Fourth Crusade as a knight. But en route, he fell ill and either had a dream or an audition in which

God told him what he was doing was wrong and that he should "serve the master and not the man" and go home. He did so.

Upon returning home, he began visiting the sick and poor, giving them whatever he had. He spent more time in prayer, even removing himself to a cave, where he wept and prayed about his sins. One day in prayer in the church of San Damiano (St. Damian), a voice emanated from the crucifix and told him three times, "Francis, go and repair my house, which you see is falling down." Francis took one of his father's horses and a large amount of cloth, both of which he sold to rebuild the ruined church. Francis took a vow of absolute poverty and traveled about preaching and helping people in need. According to lore, Pope Innocent III granted approval to Francis's rule because of two dreams had by the Pope.

JEROME (347–419)

The Doctor of the Church and translator of the Latin Vulgate Bible was an esteemed converted pagan scholar when he had a life-changing dream. Despite his conversion, Jerome had continued his study of pagan classics. In 375, he fell seriously ill and had a dream or vision in which he was called up before God on the judgment seat, ringed by angels. Asked who he was, Jerome identified himself as a Christian, but God accused him of lying and ordered the angels to scourge him. As he was lashed, Jerome begged for mercy, and finally the angels also begged for mercy on his behalf. He vowed to remain faithful to God. He was suddenly returned to "the upper world" and woke up, his eyes drenched with tears. Jerome made good on his promise, becoming one of the greatest and most influential scholars of the Church. Of his dream, he said, "And that this was no sleep nor idle dream, such as those by which we are often mocked, I call to witness the tribunal before which I lay, and the terrible judgment which I feared . . . I profess that my shoulders were black and blue, that I felt the bruises long after I awoke from my sleep, and that thenceforth I read the books of God with a zeal greater than I had previously given to the books of men."

JOHN BOSCO (1815–1888)

The founder of the Society of St. Francis de Sales is called the "Dreaming Saint" because of his frequent lucid dreams, many of which were prophetic. John Bosco's lucid calling dream came at age nine. In the dream, John was in a field with a crowd of children. They began cursing and misbehaving. Shocked, John jumped into their midst and shouted at them to stop. A man with a radiant face appeared; he was dressed in a flowing white tunic. The man (later thought to be Jesus) told him he would win people over with gentleness, not with blows, and he would send John a teacher. A majestic lady then appeared (perhaps Mary), wearing a beautiful mantle, glowing as if bedecked with stars. The children vanished and were replaced by wild animals. The Lady told John this was his field where he must work and to make himself humble, steadfast, and strong. The animals turned into gentle lambs. The Lady said, "In due time everything will be clear to you." John began studying for the priesthood at age sixteen and was ordained at age twenty-six.

JOSEPH (D. 1ST C.)

The husband of Mary and the father of Jesus had a calling dream that profoundly influenced the course of not only his life, but of religious history as well. According to the Gospels, after Joseph's betrothal to Mary, he learned she was pregnant and planned to divorce her quietly so as not to bring shame and punishment down upon her. An angel informed him in a dream that Mary was pregnant by the Holy Spirit, so he married Mary. Later, Joseph was guided by angels in dreams again when he was told to take the family to Egypt to avoid King Herod's hunt for the Messiah, and later when he was told it was safe to return home.

LAWRENCE OF CANTERBURY (D. 619)

The second archbishop of Canterbury nearly gave up on his religious career, except for a harsh calling dream. Working as a missionary and then archbishop, Lawrence became discouraged at severe political turmoil under a pagan king and considered fleeing to Gaul (France). In an experience similar to that of St. Jerome, he had a dream in which St. Peter appeared to him and rebuked him for abandoning his flock and beat him. In the morning Lawrence found wounds on his back and showed them to the king, Edbald. Impressed by the dream, the king converted.

PATRICK (CA. 389–461)

The patron saint of Ireland—born a Roman Briton—was guided to introduce Christianity to Ireland because of a dream, according to lore. As a youth he was captured by Irish slavers. After intense prayer asking for help to escape, he had a direct voice dream in which voices told him that his hungers would be rewarded and that he would soon return home. Startled awake, Patricius, as he was named, heard the voice continue, "Behold, thy ship is ready," and he left immediately. Patricius eventually made it to Gaul, where he lived in a monastery, and then returned to Britain.

One night he dreamed that a man of his acquaintance, Victoricus, handed him a bundle of letters. One was addressed to *Vox Hiberionacum,* the "Voice of the Irish." As Patricius read the letters in his dream, he heard a multitude of voices, which he identified as the people of the forest of Fochlat, crying, "We pray thee, holy youth, to come and again walk amongst us as before." Patricius awoke, determined to return to Ireland and bring Christianity to a people described as living at the edge of the world. He changed his name to the Irish form, Patrick, and returned to Gaul to study and prepare for his life as a missionary. He returned to Ireland in 432.

THEMES IN CALLING DREAMS

Several themes in the aforementioned dreams stand out. If you've had a calling dream, you may recognize one of those themes in your own dream. All of these individuals had an early interest in the religious life, so it is not surprising that their calling dreams contain strong religious imagery. Calling dreams can be equally powerful without these symbols; the dreams use whatever symbols of authority, persuasion, and validation that are appropriate for the dreamer. The themes are:

THE FIRST CALLING DREAM COMES EARLY IN LIFE

A powerful calling dream in childhood or youth can set us firmly on a certain path of destiny. Anselm and John Bosco had their pivotal dreams in childhood; Bernard of Clairvaux and Catherine Laboure were in early adulthood, before their life purpose had fully formed.

THE CALLING DREAM PROVIDES FOCUS OR COURSE CORRECTION

The dream serves to get us back on the right track. Francis of Assisi was wasting his time; Joseph and Lawrence of Canterbury were about to make a wrong decision, Faustina Kowalska and Jerome were not measuring up in their spiritual practice.

THE CALLING DREAM CARRIES GREAT AUTHORITY

Figures or voices of authority who can command the respect, attention, and obedience of the dreamer appear in the dream to deliver the message. Patrick heard voices; Catherine Labouré was instructed by a saintly priest she later recognized as Vincent de Paul; Joseph was visited by angels; John Bosco saw Jesus and Mary; Bernard of Clairvaux saw Mary; Faustina Kowalska saw Thérèse of Lisieux; Lawrence of Canterbury was confronted by Peter; Francis of Assisi heard the voice of God, and Jerome was taken before God himself, the ultimate authority.

THE CALLING DREAM OCCURS DURING CRISIS

Calling dreams often break through when we are at our lowest, such as during illness or turmoil, and thus in our greatest need of new direction. Francis of Assisi and Jerome received their calling dreams during illness; Lawrence of Canterbury was suffering from political upheaval; Patrick was desperate to escape slavery.

THE CALLING DREAM ISSUES WARNINGS

Some calling dreams are stern, warning us of dire consequences if we do not take action. The dreams of Jerome and Lawrence of Canterbury are stark examples. This type of calling dream is likely to occur if we have been ignoring or postponing a course of action. In Susan's dream in the previous chapter, the nurse, who is the authority figure, gives the ominous warning, "You're late."

We may not even be consciously aware that we are putting on hold something that is extremely important. For example, a person settles for a job in the interest of security and maintains the outlook that "someday" he will follow his true desires. As more and more time passes, it becomes harder to change, but he still holds on to "someday." The dreaming mind attempts to get guidance through, but these dreams are allowed to slide by— until a truly forceful one occurs.

In my book *Dreamwork for the Soul,* I tell of a woman's calling dream consisting only of a booming voice that said, "Friends will die. Relatives will die. You will give up everything, and your life will be transformed." The words were followed by a feeling of intense ecstasy. The dreamer subsequently underwent a radical change in life and in worldview, seemingly rolled along by the hands of fate.

THE CALLING DREAM HAS PRECOGNITIVE ELEMENTS

The above-mentioned direct voice dream predicted things that did come to pass, even though the dreamer doubted them upon awakening. The dreams of Catherine Labouré and

Faustina Kowalska were precognitive: Catherine dreamed of a man she did not know and had not yet met; Faustina was told the course of her life and of her sanctification. Sainthood is recognized after death, and a nun or priest would have no way of knowing in life if that would prove to be the case for them.

Unless we are skilled at precognitive dreaming, we are likely not to know if a calling dream foresees particular things in our future until after those events come to pass. However, a calling dream may be permeated with a feeling of "certainty" about an envisioned future, which points to a possible precognition.

THE CALLING DREAM REPEATS

Calling dreams have an intrinsic force and urgency to them, and if we ignore them, they return. We may have the same dream or dreams with the same theme over and over again as the dreaming mind tries to get our attention, sometimes with nightmarish effects.

ALL DREAMS ARE CALLING DREAMS

In a sense, all of our dreams are calling dreams, for every dream calls us to take action. We are called upon to resolve emotional issues and problems in daily life, change our attitudes, discover something about ourselves, express ideas, and become empowered in new ways. We are called upon to grow, mature, and develop. The actions sought by dreams may be small or large. It is important that we pay attention.

Calls of the Heart

When a dream has a powerful impact on you, record it immediately. Do thorough dreamwork for symbolic meanings; then consider what the dream is telling you to do. Does the dream address a "call of the heart"? How can the call be honored? If immediate significant change is not possible, what smaller changes can be initiated?

Recurring Patterns

Go through your dream journal and look for recurring dreams, themes, and symbols within dreams. Do they address a common situation? What are the patterns of recurrence? For example, does a dream recur under certain circumstances in waking life or in response to certain emotional triggers? Examine the dreams from the perspective of what still remains undone on your "Life To-Do List."

The Heart Quest

The Heart Quest is a simplified vision quest for listening to the inner voice of your heart. It helps us to reflect on who we are, where we are going in life, and how we are getting there. It is an excellent tool for self-empowerment and is intended to act as an incubation for productive dreaming.

The Heart Quest has three parts: 1) Preparation, indoors or outdoors; 2) A silent, guided walk outdoors; 3) A return for integration. It can done alone or in a group. You will need a small notebook. Allow at least one hour.

1. Set your sacred space. A group should be arranged in a circle.

2. Discuss or contemplate the purpose of a vision quest. Read over the instructions for the questing walk. For a group, set a point for start and return.

3. Do the quest.

4. Process and discuss results.

5. Set intent for additional insights in dreaming.

THE QUEST

You are going to take a walk. Not an ordinary walk, but one that is meant to open you to another level of being and to introduce you to new or forgotten aspects of yourself.

From the starting point, walk in any direction for about fifty paces. Stop and take a deep breath. Breathe slowly and deeply three times.

While taking your breaths ask yourself, "Who am I?" Take a moment to reflect upon the different answers that float into your conscious mind. Don't negate any thought that comes forth. Follow it and see where it goes. Write down any impressions that come to mind.

Walk a little farther, then stop again and breathe deeply three times. Now ask yourself, "Who am I, as a wife/husband/partner/friend? As a mother/father, coworker/worker, and all the other roles in my life? How do I show up for the people in my life?"

Reflect upon your feelings and awareness as they surface. Become aware of your body responses to each question. Write down your responses.

Walk a little farther, stop and focus on your breath. This time become aware of the sun touching your skin, the breeze on your body, or other sensations. Write down your thoughts and feelings.

Walk again, stop and focus on your breath. Now listen for the sounds and rhythms within and around your body. If there is a place to sit, do so. Listen even more closely. Reflect on the sounds you hear. Birds, whistles, cars, trains, your heart beating—what are you aware of hearing? Write down your reflections.

As you return to the point of your departure, think of a symbol to take back with you. The symbol represents something special that you have learned about yourself in this time. Keep your heart open for this symbol and allow it to appear out of the landscape. If possible, bring it back with you. Do not destroy anything in order to take your symbol.

Upon return, write down any further thoughts or feelings.

Based on what you have experienced, frame a dream incubation for additional guidance.

CHAPTER 8

Calls from the Goddess and the Ancestors

IN THIS CHAPTER, let's look at two powerful, life-changing calling dream experiences. The first involves a single dream featuring Inanna, the Sumerian goddess of fertility and immortality, whose stories date to 200 B.C.E. The second involves a series of dreams that took the dreamer on a journey of mysticism, healing, and magic in a relationship with the animal powers and the ancestral forces of South Africa.

INANNA CALLING

Naomi Kosten lives in Norwich, England, a one-thousand-year-old city still encircled by the ancient remains of Roman walls, about one hundred miles northeast of London. Kosten is the proprietress of Inanna's Festival, a flourishing shop devoted to esoteric and spiritual books and merchandise.

Kosten owes it to a dream that took her quite by surprise. Here is her story:

It was Walpurgisnacht, the night before May Day—Beltane—April 30, 1988. I was in a friend's cottage, in North Wales. My bedroom looked out over the Menai Straits to Anglesey, a magical island off the coast. I was twenty-three and had been let go from my job as editor of a health magazine some four months earlier. I knew I didn't want to go back into that work. I wanted to do something involving people: assisting them in some way, having different days every day, traveling, learning, and enjoying variety in my day-to-day work. But I had no idea what direction my ideas might find themselves heading in. I was drifting, really—working as a legal secretary, a life model, a freelance typist—nothing really meaningful and emotionally involving.

I dreamed I was with a group of my friends, walking around Norwich, where I was living and have lived since commencing my university degree in 1983. We were a group moving around the shops, talking and laughing. The light was dropping as evening approached—it felt perhaps late autumn or early winter—and the shop windows were bright and colorful. We walked around together, and finally stopped for a moment in front of an open shop door. I could smell wonderful, rich fragrances, hear beautiful music, and see all sorts of glittering and sparkling items. I stopped in excitement. The shop was bustling with people and looked fascinating and impossible to walk past.

"Oh! Oh! This looks wonderful! Can we go in? Can we? *Please??!!*" I begged my friends.

"Of course!" one of them said. "It's *your shop!!!*"

I walked into the shop and the girls behind the counter greeted me. I started to walk around the shop and saw all sorts of wonderful interesting things—statuary and jewelry, music, incense, tarot cards and mobiles, greetings cards and candles . . . and I was amazed and astonished.

It was bright, colorful, fragrant, filled with sparkle and sound, music and laughter. It was intensely beautiful and moving all at the same time. I felt amazed that my friends were saying that this was my business—that I had created this setup.

I then walked outside the door again and looked up at the signage over the door. It said "Inanna's Festival."

I turned to my friends and said, "Who is Inanna?" And then I woke up.

I yelled to my friend in the next room, "Quick! Bring me a pencil and some paper!" I scribbled down everything I could remember about what was on the shelves of the shop. I still have that piece of paper.

I looked at my friend and said, "I think I know what I want to do!" I knew Inanna was a Middle-Eastern goddess, but I didn't really know anything else. I started reading some of my friend's books on goddesses.

I learned about Inanna's role as Queen, Goddess, originator of writing, her songs and poems and the wall sculptures dedicated to her. Inanna had a mischievous temperament, and she tricked her father for his rulership. She rejected the princes offered her as consort and instead chose Dumuzi, a loving shepherd, who desired her truly for herself—he saw her as joyous and alive, beautiful and sensual, intelligent and witty—and he was her sexual match. But Inanna was bored with royal living. She desired to know herself inside and out and decided to make the arduous journey to the Underworld, to visit her Dark Sister, her Shadow Self, Ereshkigal. She was made to divest herself of all her seven royal queenly vestments and accoutrements in order to pass through the seven gates of the Underworld to meet with her Dark Sister. Ereshkigal killed Inanna and left her hanging on a meat hook to rot. Inanna's faithful servant and friend, Geshtinanna, rescued her from death by journeying to visit Ereshkigal. Weeping with her, Geshtinanna commiserated with her about the loss of her children. She melted Ereshkigal's heart and was permitted to assist Inanna back to the Living World after her resurrection three days following her death. Inanna then questioned Geshtinanna as to who had missed her presence, who had looked for her, who had searched for her, and discovered that during this time, Dumuzi was busy partying!

Inanna grew angry and was disappointed in his lack of care. She realized he had not valued her fully, in all her roles as Maiden, Queen, and Crone, and he needed to fully appreciate all the aspects of her womanhood and spirituality. Ereshkigal, realizing she had been lulled into releasing Inanna by the sympathies of Geshtinanna, knew that once a soul has entered the World of the Dead, no one can leave without a price being paid—

someone else to take their place. Ereshkigal began send-ing the galli, the little imps of the earth, to find someone who would take Inanna's place. It fell to Dumuzi to take the place of his Queen for six months of the year as penance for his behavior. During this time it is winter, and Inanna grieves; then she welcomes him back for summer.

The Descent to the Underworld story affected me very deeply, and continues to resonate in my life to this day.

A few days after I had the dream, I returned to Nor-wich, my head filled with the idea of this shop, called Inanna's Festival.

Thirty days later, on the first of June 1988, I opened, with two humble tables in an indoor antiques and col-lectibles market in Norwich, as "Inanna's Festival—worldwide sourced gifts and crafts laced with magic and mystery."

Three months on, I moved to a shop premises of my own, and three years on, to the Royal Arcade, a marble-floored and stained glass–filled Art Nouveau shopping arcade, the jewel in Norwich's architectural crown. It is decorated with wall tiles and wrought iron lamp fittings in peacock designs, and each end of the arcade is crested with serene goddess faces. An interior quadrant is decorated with four seasonal-elemental fe-male divinities each holding a sphere of magic like crys-tal balls in her hands. It's been the home of Inanna's Festival ever since.

And now, thirteen years after moving in to the Royal Arcade, I am in the midst of planning a move to a rather bigger, but much more ancient premises—a low-ceilinged, timber-beamed shop with a Georgian interior and a medieval cellar, used as a trading commercial premises for five hundred years.

The dream affected my life in a major way: no more hunting for jobs. Instead, a whole new phase in my life opened, that takes me traveling: sourcing stock, meeting so many people who are in my life now, each event leading me on to the next, and the next. Friends, festivals, shows, fairs, suppliers, accidental meetings, plane seats, catching sight of people who seemed intriguing and talking to them, I constantly seem to encounter people I need, want, and love to know!

I love my dreams! Most, of course, simply reflect day-to-day worries and concerns, but every once in a while—perhaps monthly—a dream of something quite unexpected and deeply affecting seems to happen. I dream fully in color with all senses including pain and deep grief. My dreams can often include abilities I don't seemingly have right now, and occasionally they reveal people, places, conversations, and happenings that later present themselves in waking life.[1]

SUMMONED BY THE ANCESTORS AND ANIMAL POWERS

Our second case concerns a woman named Jo, who also lives in England. Her calling dreams began unexpectedly in 1999. Jo was experiencing a new and complete freedom—she was recently divorced and was able to quit her job. The future looked both exciting and uncertain, and the mix of opposing feelings within her may have created the right psychological conditions for breakthrough calling dreams.

The first dream occurred in February 1999 during a visit to family members in Strachan, Tasmania. One night Jo slept on the edge of the ocean in a large wooden beach house. She drifted off to sleep listening to the soothing sound of the sea and frogs croaking away. Then something happened:

> During the night a young man walks towards me. He may be aborigine, I'm not too sure, but he is dark-skinned, brown. He is not negroid, I'm sure of that. As he comes towards me he holds out a stick. It is probably around sixteen inches in length, curved with a bulbous tip. This tip is more elongated than round. It is covered with studs of some sort. It is surrounded by a radiant white light. Without speaking, he indicates that I should take the stick. I do. At this point I wake up.

The dream was puzzling, for Jo had no idea what the stick meant, or why an aboriginal-appearing man would be giving it to her. In addition to the radiant white light, the dream itself was lit by a strange phosphorescent aura. Jo had paid attention to her dreams for years and recognized these as hallmarks of her "big" dreams. In fact, the episode was more like a nighttime "experience" than a dream. It was strangely compelling, and Jo could not get it out of her head.

In the morning Jo related the dream to a friend, who, like Jo, had no idea what it meant. Two weeks later, Jo left Tasmania and returned home to England. She heard from her friend. The friend had relayed the dream to an aborigine friend of hers. Upon hearing it, the aborigine was annoyed and said, "What on earth is a whitey being given one of those for? That's a message stick—that's *our* business." Message sticks are a tradition kept among aborigines. The bearer of one is able to move with safety among the tribes.

With this revelation, the mystery only deepened. Jo still had no idea why she would have a dream involving a culture and tradition with which she had no involvement; nor did she have much knowledge about them. She did not feel that the dream was simply place/culture residue from being in Tasmania.

There were no further developments for nearly eight months. Jo decided to accept an invitation from friends to come to South Africa, a place she had never visited. She left in October 1999.

While there, Jo was taken by her friends to attend a *sangoma* ceremony. The sangomas are highly respected diviners, initiates who work in trance and shamanic altered states of consciousness to divine the causes of illnesses, including social disharmony, and prescribe remedies. Sangomas are specifically called to their path by their direct ancestors through an initiatory sickness, of which they must heal themselves. This calling through sickness is found in many shamanic traditions. Once the calling comes, the candidate undergoes *twasa,* the training for becoming a sangoma.

The sangomas do not put on ceremonies for public display or for tourists. Jo received a privileged invitation because of her friends' connections to the sangoma community. The ceremony was called "the Finding," in which initiates prove their abilities and connections to the ancestors by finding hidden objects, in this case near the home of the senior teacher where the ceremony was taking place. The ceremony was colorful, with drumming and dancing—a traditional way to alter consciousness and invite spirits to enter the dancers in temporary possession. Just as Jo and her friends were leaving, they were invited to join in the dancing. They accepted.

Immediately afterwards, Jo experienced the manifestations of what may have been, at least in the Africans' eyes, a spirit trying to enter into her. She had tremendous electricity-like shaking in her right arm, which traveled down towards her body. She had a difficult time stopping it.

There were no unusual dreams in South Africa, but odd nighttime experiences began after Jo returned home to England:

> I was woken up by my right arm shaking quite strongly.
> I found a little personage in my room standing by the bed, trying to wake me up. He—for I felt it was a he although his sex was not apparent—was gray green in color and had the appearance of being covered with small pieces of bark. He was very slim and about four feet high. He had a wedge-shaped face and very large eyes, almost owl-like. I say that I "woke up," but I don't think I could have been awake.

In other words, the awakening was a false awakening—a dream within a dream. The little being wanted Jo's attention—but for what purpose?

The little being visited Jo several more times at night. He would always remain silent and would just make his presence known and then disappear.

These dreams came at the same time that Jo suffered a depression. In the sangoma calling, depression is one of the signs.

Jo returned to South Africa in July 2000, but only for a visit and not to resume her sangoma training. One day she was researching rock art in a newly published book, *Stories that Float from Afar*. Turning a page, she was shocked to see a picture of her little dream friend—it was on a piece of rock art found on De Beers land at Kimberley, South Africa. Access to the site is not allowed to the general public. The figure is one seen by San Bushmen in trance.

She had numerous "real" dreams, many involving leopards, one of the major power animals of the sangomas. "These dreams are always entirely different to anything I have ever had in my life before," she said. "They always manifest with the beings glowing with light."

This dream, which Jo had on August 28, 2000, the night of a new moon, symbolizes passage into a new world:

A large man dressed all in white standing in squared arch opening in wall. Get the feeling that the wall may be circular. It also is white. The man is dressed similarly to the Zulus. He has a short spear—an assagai—or club in his hand, which he moves, indicating that I should either move towards him or go through the arch.

That dream was followed on September 4 by another significant dream:

A very large black, red, and white cat comes to me. He seems to glow. He is similar to a leopard and reaches to about my hips. He leaves but returns later in the dream.

Later I find myself on a white road walking with other people who are dressed in white. They are all trying to help me.

On September 9, Jo attended a sangoma ceremony as an observer, and on September 23 attended a major ceremony, the Mandao, or "Going to the River," in which initiates go into the river to meet with a mystical snake from whom they gain their powers.

Other leopard dreams occurred over a period of time the following month:

> This leopard who would come very close to me. He was absolutely beautiful, very large, but not an ordinary leopard. He was red, white, and black, and the colors would shift. He would appear in the distance and then get closer until after about ten days he would actually touch my leg.
>
> The leopard comes again, he is now a glowing orange red and walks around me touching my legs.

The leopard is considered quite significant among the sangomas. Black and white are the colors of traditional costumes; the addition of red indicates a readiness to work in healing. On October 17, Jo had this dream:

> I dream I am in T's office. I walk out through the garden door and begin to walk past the back of the house. Suddenly the ground turns to a sheet of water. From the movement, there are very powerful currents there. There seems to be streams of something phosphorescent in the water. A glowing figure rises from the water and hands me a white coat.

On October 28, Jo was invited to attend the Coming Home Ceremony of one of the initiates, John, who had completed his training and could now establish himself as a healer. During the ceremony, Jo was invited into the *ndumba,* or spirit house, in order to take photos. The senior teacher asked Jo to take a photo of her "throwing the bones," a divination method of reading the placement of sacred objects—shells, bones and so forth—cast from a bag. It is similar to throwing I Ching coins or yarrow sticks. The senior teacher then threw the bones for Jo and astonished her by saying, "You have a lion or a leopard who is coming to you in your dreams, don't you? I think it is a leopard." Jo had not discussed her dreams with any of the sangomas.

Intrigued by this, Jo decided to have a full reading, or *sheya:*

The sangomas told me that I was being called to twasa. I disagreed with them, as I was not sick, totally forgetting at that point the depression I had suffered during the previous winter. However, they laughed and said that I would be shown that I was indeed being called. They said, what greater thing could there be than to become a healer and to help other people?

During this reading they told me to carry a white coat with me at all times, based on their interpretation of the dream in which I was handed a white coat, which they associated with being a doctor.

Later, I was doing some research in the library of the University of South Africa on the sangoma traditions and came across one small paragraph in someone's doctoral thesis in which it was mentioned that "traditionally the appearance of a lion or leopard in dreams signifies a call to twasa, but not from one's direct ancestors but from the 'ancestors of the forest, and the ancestors of the river' who were there ever before mankind walked the earth." I had a very wry chuckle to myself when I read that.

The sangomas suggested to me that as I was going to visit my son in Australia, I should take the opportunity then of seriously considering undergoing twasa.

In November 2000, Jo traveled to Australia as planned for an extended visit with family members. While there, her unusual dreams continued, such as this one on April 10:

I am shown something I have to wear which will protect me. It appears to be a cowrie shell.

The cowrie shell is worn tied in the hair by twasas. Men wear it at the back of the head in the nape of the neck, and women wear it in the front in the middle of the hairline. Jo began carrying a cowrie shell on her person at all times.

She left Australia on April 26, 2001, and returned to South Africa, intending to stay for three months and begin twasa. On May 4, she had this dream:

Black and white turbulence in which creatures live. Quite scary. Feel hair brush my face. A large black snake rises up out of this turbulence and comes to me. It lays across my right arm. Later I am conscious of a spot on my face. A small rainbow-colored striped snake comes out of this.

The snake is a major ancestral figure, important in African mythologies, and has associations to the rainbow creator deity.

According to sangoma tradition, one's power dream animals must be regularly "fed," that is, nourished by spiritual contact and activity. If the animals receive no attention, they are summoned elsewhere and depart. Jo was reminded of this in a dream lesson the next night on May 5:

> I find myself in a very pleasant lodge or hotel. I am taken by a guide to a hide. The guide explains that we have to leave food out and then it will come tomorrow. I look at some photos displayed on a wall. Suddenly, like a film screen, a whole picture image comes up outside the hide and I see a beautiful leopard coming running towards me. Very quick and then its gone. I am told again that I must feed it in the morning and that it will come again.

Jo left South Africa without completing the twasa training, having suddenly had doubts about it. After her return to England, she remained uncertain about whether or not she would resume it. She was concerned about losing her link to the dream leopards. As if in answer to that concern, this dream came:

> I am calling the leopards and asking them not to leave me. The mother turns and comes to me, bringing one of her cubs, which she leaves with me. It is to stay with me until I return to South Africa.

In November 2002, Jo returned again to South Africa but was unable to resume the twasa training due to the dangers of living in the township. Her experiences opened up new doors, however, for her to continue spiritual training with different friends and teachers. She had answered her calling dreams and was richly rewarded:

> I have been totally in awe of the way that doors have opened up for me wherever I have gone and where this type of tradition is to be found. I am puzzled also, because I do not come from this type of tradition. So just what was I connecting to? What force, what power, what knowledge? Why was I being permitted to contact? I know that it is not a bad or evil thing. I found when I visited Australia that their "men of high degree" also have a ceremony similar to the Going to the River. They contact a similar serpent who gives them their power, their ability to heal. The serpent is not demonized as it is for us in the West. I can only conclude that it must be some Universal Source that we may all tap into for guidance, advice, and knowledge. The training permits us to come to this in the correct way, and we are not to misuse this. Humility and reverence are very important within the sangoma training.
>
> South Africa is a kind country for me. I have made many wonderful friends out there, both black and white. I think that we could learn a lot about forgiveness from the black people there. It was a great privilege to live amongst them. They are the most kind, humorous, gracious, and generous of peoples. I admire their sense of family, which we appear to have lost in the West, and also their respect for the older members of society.
>
> I have found a different perspective in my life and thank God every day for the blessings I am fortunate

enough to have. I have found that in committing myself to continue with my training to become a healer that I myself have been healed. I have become alive again, and life is good.[2]

It can only be speculated what might have happened to Naomi and Jo had they not paid attention to their dreams. The road not taken can never be known. I believe that when callings come, they repeat until we pay attention. However, like the animal powers who depart if they are not nourished, callings also eventually change—for circumstances in the outer world do not remain static—perhaps mutating into different opportunities.

Calling dreams alert us to prime opportunities and prime timing. We may overlook them for various reasons: We are too busy, we feel limited by obligations, we fear taking risks. The question to ask ourselves is not what might happen if we answer the call, but what opportunity may be missed if we don't.

CHAPTER 9

Dreaming for Creativity

I'M A PROLIFIC writer, and I am often asked how I manage to produce so many books. At any given time, I usually have from two to as many as six in the works, plus a host of articles, columns, and presentations. In response I like to say that I have a troop of angels or fairies who work for me all night. In a sense, that's true—the angels and fairies are my dreams.

Many ideas for my books, articles, fiction, workshops, and lectures come straight out of my dreams. Some of them come spontaneously and unbidden and take on an energy that I feel I must complete in a creative fashion. Other ideas come as the result of incubation, in which I ask—even demand—that my dreams provide me with a needed creative inspiration. My dreams never fail to respond.

As I mentioned in Chapter 1, I have been writing and speaking to audiences since grade school and have been paying attention to my dreams for almost as long. Dreams and creativity are a natural marriage to me. The creativity that comes through the process of dreaming is another dimension of the creativity that is born in waking states of consciousness. All of the ways in which we get our ideas complement one another. If you are not using your dreams for creative purposes, you are overlooking an important and enriching source.

My own dream creativity is but one small part of a very long heritage. Dreaming ideas into being has been recognized and practiced since ancient times the world over. The dream literature contains scores and scores of examples of artists, novelists, composers, musicians, playwrights, poets, filmmakers, dancers, scientists, inventors, architects, engineers, and many others who experience creative breakthroughs thanks to their dreams. For some, dreams constitute the major source of inspiration. For example, singer and songwriter Billy Joel had stated that *all* of his ideas for songs come in dreams.

The Association for the Study of Dreams recognizes the importance of dream creativity. Every annual conference features a Dream Art exhibit of mixed media, sculpture, writing, drawings, and paintings that have been inspired by dreams.

HOW DREAMS PRESENT CREATIVE IDEAS

INDIRECT IDEAS

Dreams don't always lay out creative ideas in logical fashion, or in plain language. Rather, they are likely to present imagery or action that metamorphoses into more developed ideas in waking consciousness. We have to play with the dream to know and understand it.

When rock musician Sting left his band, The Police, to embark on a solo career, he had a dream that literally shaped his first solo album. Sting had long acknowledged his use of dreams for song material. For his solo debut, he wished to strike out in a new direction—always risky for a successful artist whose fans usually want more of the same. Sting dreamed of being home in Hampshire looking out over a walled and neat garden. Suddenly a group of rowdy and drunk blue turtles appeared through a hole in the wall and began doing acrobatics, tearing up the garden. Upon reflecting on the dream, Sting saw the blue turtles as symbols of the subconscious and unrealized potential. Their destruction of the neat and manicured garden represented his desire to destroy preconceptions and expectations about his artistry. As a result, he reached deep within himself to produce the material for his debut album, appropriately titled, *The Dream of the Blue Turtles*. Several songs became hit singles, and the album sold more than three million copies.

In her book *The Committee of Sleep,* Deirdre Barrett tells of an Indian chemist who was seeking to develop enzymes that would refine crude oil. Finally stumped for ideas, he asked his dreams for help. He dreamed of standing on the side of a road while a big truck full of rotting cabbages went past. The stink was tremendous. At first, however, neither the chemist nor any of his associates could make any sense of the dream. A few days later, the chemist was working in his laboratory when he realized that the bacteria produced by rotting cabbages broke down into just the very enzymes he needed. What was more, cabbages were exceptionally cheap.

Among the many other creativity examples Barrett discusses is an architect who dreamed of a person with outstretched arms, who became a ship and a prow pointed at the same angle, and then turned into a house that the architect saw in detail from the inside. She built a Y-shaped house with the windows exactly as she had seen them in the dream.

Horror author Stephen King—who gets many plot ideas from his dreams—says that he uses dreams the way a person uses mirrors to see things that cannot be seen directly ahead. In other words, dreams reveal something that is not obvious to us. Unless we pay attention and work with the dream, the inspiration goes unrealized.

DIRECT IDEAS

Sometimes dreams present ideas in direct ways. One of the most famous examples is Paul McCartney, who heard the melody for his famous Beatles song "Yesterday" in a dream. The dream was so vivid and the music seemed so familiar to him that first he had to convince himself that he did not dream someone else's music that he had heard and forgotten.

Some filmmakers have lifted their dreams exactly as they had them into dream scenes in their films. Ingmar Bergman put his dream of four women in mourning in *Cries and Whispers,* and a coffin dream in *Wild Strawberries*. Robert Altman's *Three Women* was a story as he dreamed it, though it was not filmed as a dream.

When I work on new material for workshops, I often have vivid dreams in which specific pictures and diagrams are shown to me. For example, for meditation and chakra workshops, I have been shown diagrams of the human body with lines depicting the movement of energy through the chakras in certain ways. I am given to understand that if energy is directed according to the diagrams, it will facilitate certain energetic effects. I always test out dream material like this and then incorporate it in workshops.

In *Dreamwork for the Soul,* I tell about dreaming a twenty-third Major Arcana trump for the tarot, called Truth. In the dream, I am in a class and am shown the card by the teacher. I had my artist friend and tarot collaborator, Robert Michael Place, draw the dream image: a bearded man wearing a triangular auric crown, holding the Truth card, which depicts a seven-layered pyramid capped with a flame. The triangular auric crown was known to us both as a symbol of God the Father, who is Truth. Bob discovered in his research that the image of the flame-capped pyramid strongly resembled an alchemical woodcut that neither of us had seen before.

The Truth card has served as a versatile teaching tool. This dream came unbidden—I had not incubated it, nor was I thinking of creating another tarot (Bob and I collaborated on two, *The Alchemical Tarot* and *The Angels Tarot,* as Bob tells later in this chapter.).

An idea for an inspirational card set came to me out of a multilayered dream. It starts with me in a shop of angel merchandise searching for a birthday present for a friend. I see some carved wooden chivalric figures. I begin to get ideas for a card set involving the figures. Then suddenly I am shown a drawing of another object. It is in brilliant colors, and I can see all the markings on the object in detail. The image, what all the markings mean, and how I am to use them in an inspirational card set all come to me at once in the dream.

I awakened with all of this fully present to me, and I immediately made a crude drawing (my drawing ability never made it much past stick figures). I gave the drawing and my dream notes to my sister, Linda Hope Lee, an accomplished artist, to execute it professionally. The card became another teaching tool for workshops.

SORTING AND FILTERING

Sometimes we don't have dreams containing specific ideas, but the ideas are clear to us upon awakening. This is often the case for me when I incubate requests for creative help, such as ideas for lectures and books and ideas for ways to present and organize information. I may have no recalled dreams at all, but the answers to my needs are in my head as soon as I awaken. I see everything in a sharp, crystal clarity, as though an entire plan has been rolled out in front of me. When that happens, I make certain I write everything down as quickly as possible. I hold in my mind's eye the image of light flowing down from the heavens, entering me through the top of my head and flowing out from my fingers as I write or type.

DREAMS THAT INITIATE AN ADVENTURE

Creativity dreams sometimes show only part of an idea and leave most of it shrouded in mystery. Our ability to uncover the full idea depends on following our intuition in waking life.

As I mentioned earlier, Bob Place and I collaborated on two tarot book and deck sets. The road to this collaboration—and bringing two creative ideas into manifestation—began years earlier with a literal calling dream Bob experienced, which led him on a journey. Here is his account:

> I did not consciously choose the Tarot as my divinatory tool. The Tarot chose me. It started with a dream on a

summer night, in rural New Jersey, in 1982. In the dream, I was walking through a room when the phone rang. The phone was also part of the dream, but its ringing woke me into a state of lucidity while I continued dreaming.

With a feeling of utter amazement—that another being could actually call me in a dream—I picked up the phone. On the other end an international operator informed me that she had a person-to-person call for me from a law firm in England. I accepted the call, and then a secretary from the firm came on the line. She told me that she was sending me my ancestral inheritance. She could not tell me what it was, but only that it would come from England, it is kept in a box, and that it is sometimes called the key. She added that I would know it when I saw it. Then she ended the conversation with some precautions on its use and misuse.

I awoke that morning with a feeling of excitement and expectation. All through the week I eagerly anticipated receiving my inheritance. At the end of that week a friend came over with his new deck of Tarot cards. It was the deck designed in England in 1910, by Arthur Edward Waite and Pamela Colman Smith. Although I was not unfamiliar with this deck, I now saw it in a new light—I knew that this was it.

Within a few days another friend gave me a deck called the Tarot of Marseilles. That was my own first deck, but soon I went into Manhattan to buy the Waite-Smith cards that I had seen.

I began experimenting with the cards. At first I resolved not to read any books on the Tarot. I wanted to communicate directly with the images unhindered by preconceptions. I did remember being shown the Celtic cross spread in college. So I decided to begin with that combined with Jungian techniques of dream interpretation.

In 1987, I was sitting in the living room reading a book on alchemy while a commentator on the radio was talking about the Harmonic Convergence. I had been hearing about this for a few weeks, but thought of it as just another New Age curiosity. However this time it was different, the commentator said that during this period of spiritual transformation sensitive individuals all over the Earth would be experiencing a flood of information on spiritual subjects. Finally someone had an explanation for what was happening to me.

The Tarot had taught me a great deal directly, but eventually I realized that to unlock its secrets further I had to gather more information. I began reading everything that I could find on the Tarot, Gnosticism, alchemy, and related subjects. I soon filled a large hardbound notebook with charts, lists, and notes—this was odd because at that time I was not a writer, and had no plan to become a writer. My reading had become noticeably excessive to my wife and friends, and at last someone was able to explain that this intensity was a product of the time, that in some way the spirit of the Earth demanded it.

Shortly after August 16th I was reading the *Picture Museum of Sorcery, Magic, & Alchemy*, by Emile Grillot de Givry, when I became fascinated by an alchemical hieroglyph representing the philosopher's stone. In a flash, I realized that the symbolism in the design was entirely interchangeable with that of the World card. This realization was like a key opening a lock. I sat mesmerized as it became obvious that the Tarot trumps are alchemical, and that the series of trumps outlines the alchemical opus.

This insight happened in seconds, but it began a long journey that led to these Tarot designs and this book. It led me back into illustration work, and caused me to start writing. It helped me to experience the Western tradition of meditation, and spiritual transformation.

From the beginning the journey was marked by synchronistic events that brought information to me and led me on the right path. Synchronicity led to my first article on the *Alchemical Tarot* that was published in *Gnosis,* and it led me [to] team up with Rosemary Ellen Guiley.[1]

As an artist, Bob is accustomed to following inspirations from his dreams, visions, and meditation. He awakened from the dream with a sense of expectation, which he continued to nurture in waking consciousness. Our dreams open doors for things to happen in waking life. We can unwittingly close them by not paying attention to dreams or by dismissing them as fantasy. Bob's expectation kept the door open, and many synchronicities happened. When he saw the tarot cards, he had an intuitive hit that connected them to the dream.

I was working on my first book on the tarot, *The Mystical Tarot,* when I read Bob's article in *Gnosis*. It struck a chord in me, and I loved Bob's artwork. His address was published in the article, and I was excited to see that he lived not far away from me in the same state. I wrote to him, and thus began not only our collaboration, but also an enduring friendship.

While we worked on the tarots, we both experienced dreams and meditation visions that enhanced the creative process. This was especially true for *The Alchemical Tarot,* for the language of alchemy is archetypal image, the same language as dreams.

AN ARTIST'S VISION

While I was working on this book, my husband, Tom, and I attended the annual winter American Arts and Crafts Council fair in Baltimore, a juried event that features leading artists in many media. We were attracted to a display of ceramic art by David Stabley that seemed very dreamy in nature, especially a wall plaque of a dreamy woman flying over a nighttime landscape. Not surprisingly, we discovered the piece was called *The Dreamer*. We learned from David that he is often inspired by his dreams. Here is his description of his work and how creativity and dreams are intertwined:

> Ceramics has always been a major working force in my life. I am forever fascinated by its endless expressive possibilities as a medium.
>
> All of my pieces are made from an earthenware clay body and fired to 1900 degrees Fahrenheit. I draw my imagery onto the piece in the leatherhard stage and then carve and texture the surface. If areas are to be glazed, I do this in the bone dry stage and single fire in an electric kiln. After the firing, I apply a rubbed on patina to all of the unglazed areas. Even though I use similar forms, all of the imagery is unique to that particular piece.
>
> My work is based on ideas about dreams and their relationship to fantasy. My most recent works deal with

how we remember and perceive dreams in fragmented ways. I am exploring space, texture, surface design, and the overlapping of objects to create this sense of fragmentation. My imagery reflects situations that are comfortable, mysterious, and romantic in nature. I am fascinated by the unknown and the mysteries of the universe. The faces emit emotions, feeling, and energy that create a mood within the surrounding landscape. Each piece does not tell its own story, rather it allows the viewers to discern their own feelings and thoughts. My work is meant to evoke the viewers' senses of idea and content as well as the relationships to space, texture, color, form, and surface.

I have always paid attention to dreams that I have had and I am always trying to figure out why I dream certain things and how they affect my daily life and my artwork. In the past few years I have tried to pay more attention to not only dreams but how I remember my dreams.

For the past fourteen years, my artwork in ceramics and drawing have been influenced by my personal ideas about dreams. I have been very interested in how I remember my dreams when I wake and as the day goes by, how I recall parts of the dream. These "fragments" of dreams have become a part of my artwork. Even though I sometimes use specific dreams in my art, most of the time I am trying to relate general feelings about the dreaming state. I feel that there is a strong relationship between dreams, fantasy, the many mysteries of the universe, and the unknown powers of the mind.

I have not used incubation in the past for dreaming.

More recently, I have been trying to think about ideas about dreaming just before I go to sleep. I find that if I concentrate as long as possible before I fall asleep, that I seem to remember more of my dreams when I wake. I have not really awoken, remembered a dream, and thought that I needed to get to the studio to produce that image. I tend to use parts of my dreams in a more spontaneous way in my work. I am not big on waking and writing down or recording my dreams, so I can't remember any patterns that I see over and over again.

All of my work in clay and drawing has a relationship to dreams. I have some favorites that seem to be more sexual in nature, and they were made within the past three years. As I grow older, my artwork is turning towards more sexual avenues of expression. I guess like most men, I think about sex a lot during the day and also while asleep. Not that my wife and I don't enjoy a good sex life, but there is some kind of draw for me to keep producing feelings about sex and romance. I have been interested in expressing romantic notions through the use of nude floating figures that are intertwined around each other within a landscape. Most of the time they appear to be in a dreaming state. I have dreamt about sex with other women, although my wife is always present in some way or another.

Dreaming lucidly is one area in dreaming that I have not been able to conquer yet. For me, it is the most interesting and I would love to be able to know that I am dreaming. I would probably want to sleep all of the time. I believe that if I could master this technique, that I would conjure up a lot more imagery in my artwork.

I would hope that I would be able to go to other places deep inside my innermost feelings and thoughts. Really stretch out those visual thoughts. I would love to be able to fly over and into some of my landscapes and be able to change shapes, colors, and textures. Meet other beings in the future. I could "dream" up a lot!

I believe that my dreams have made me more aware of the bigger picture in life. To take the time to try and understand my subconscious thoughts and utilize them throughout everyday life. In general, I am a much laid-back person. I look up at the stars a lot and always wonder about the vastness of space and all of the unknowns about time and how we all fit in. I have always been interested in science fiction through books, the movies, and my own imagination.[2]

THE GERMINATION OF IDEAS

Creativity is born in dreams spontaneously, and directly, through incubation or request.

SPONTANEOUS CREATIVITY

Dream ideas that seem to occur "out of the blue" happen spontaneously, but do have a basis in a longer and more involved creative process. Creativity in any endeavor involves devoting time and personal resources to a certain focus. We spend time and energy thinking of ways to do things differently or better; we practice skills; we research and study. This creates a field of energy in which we are immersed all the time, even when we are doing things not specifically related to our creative focus. In this field of energy, we have dreams that strike us with good ideas.

Dreams can seed creativity—even years later. Stephen King relates that a childhood nightmare of a hanged man who came horribly to life and grabbed at him became the inspiration many years later for his novel *Salem's Lot*.

INCUBATED CREATIVITY

Incubation for dream creativity takes many forms. We can frame a specific question for meditation prior to sleep. Maintaining intense creative energy throughout the day serves as a form of incubation for continuing the process during sleep. Concentrating on having meaningful dreams prior to sleep also acts as a type of incubation.

Every artist experiences getting stuck. We can rack our brains for ideas on how to resolve the blockage, sometimes to no avail. But put the matter to dreams and the solution can immediately be known.

Sometimes I have petitioned my dreams for help with a traditional incubation question, "How can I _____?" Sometimes the pressure of deadline has made me demand help from my dreams: "I need an idea *now*!" The pressure of need acts like incubation itself. We may not formally ask dreams for help, but the anxiety of being at a seeming dead end may produce a dream that resolves the situation.

NURTURING DREAM CREATIVITY

Regular dream incubation for creative ideas can help to keep a steady flow of inspiration. Even if your creative work is going well, ask your dreams for additional ideas. Like the mirror metaphor referred to by Stephen King, your dreams may show you something new in your creative landscape.

Expanded Waking Consciousness

The artist knows that everything contains a unique story, and it is the job of the artist to tell those stories. The artist does so by becoming immersed in the energy of the story and giving himself over to the story that must be told.

Creativity in dreams can be stimulated by shifting our consciousness while awake. In his book *The Artist Inside,* artist and shamanic practitioner Tom Crockett describes this phenomenon as "vision-shifting," seeing things from an energetic or spiritual perspective. For example, you take yourself on a walk and pick up objects, sensing what they have to say to you. Crockett observes that there is always an exchange of conscious energy between two things, and the more we practice experiencing the awareness of this, the stronger becomes our ability to participate meaningfully in this exchange. The dream artist is on the job all the time, even when not dreaming during sleep. He says:

> We don't need to make the time to sleep and to dream, but we do need to allow ourselves time to process our dream imagery. We need to arrange protected and sacred time for ritual journeys into the spirit world, and we must give ourselves the gift of time in order to express our visions through creative work. With vision-shifting, we can learn to walk in two worlds simultaneously.[3]

Such shifts of consciousness can happen spontaneously. You've probably had experiences where suddenly you see the environment around you from a profoundly different perspective, as though you could perceive an invisible dimension. These experiences especially can happen when we are outdoors, uplifted by our sensory immersion in the realm of nature, and also after intense periods of meditation or prayer.

Richard Russo, a writer, artist, and editor of *Dream Time* magazine, describes in his article "Dreams and the Spirit of Place" his own spontaneous experience of stone consciousness and its impact on his dreams. While hiking in Yosemite National Park, Russo stopped to rest at a bend along a shallow river. As he absorbed the atmosphere, it struck him that this was a magical spot. Suddenly his attention was drawn to an egg-shaped stone lying in the water, and he was prompted to take it with him. It occurred to him that the river god inhabited the stone; he received an intuitive impression as a voice in his head answering "yes." For about an hour, Russo was in a trance in which he communicated with the voice in the stone. His senses were heightened, and he "felt every shift in the breeze, heard every murmur of the water, every rustle of the leaves." In this waking dream, he sensed being part of something much greater than himself that was unfolding through him.

Russo returned the stone to its original place, and asked the river god to visit him in his nighttime dreams, to teach him the "secret of flowing." As he went to sleep, he hoped for a Carlos Castenada-like experience, but was not visited by any being or spirit:

> I did not even dream in any normal sense of the word. Instead, I half-awoke from a restless sleep to find myself

flooded with memories. It seemed every story I'd ever written, going back to college, passed through my mind as I lay
there, unable to wake and rise, unable to even move, yet
unable to sink back into sleep either. I relieved the writing
of each piece, saw and savored it in its entirety, then moved
on to the next. The river of my own creative history flowed
through me as I lay captive in its grasp.[4]

Russo's experience superbly illustrates the intertwining of
waking and dreaming experiences: They are part of each other
and complement each other. Russo acknowledged that during
his altered-state communication with the river god, part of him
kept thinking that he was creating an elaborate fantasy. This is
a natural reaction whenever we have extraordinary experiences
during wakefulness. He was able to overcome that by allowing
himself to just "enjoy the ride."

We can encourage waking dreaming experiences like this
through mindful awareness and by setting our intent, especially
when we are engaged in outdoor activity. In Chapter 11 of this
text, "Odyssey to a Roman Dream Temple," I describe my own
waking dream interaction with the spirit of place at the ruins of
a Roman dream incubation temple.

BORDERLAND DREAMING

Many artists say their most creative dream ideas happen during
dreaming in the hypnagogic state of consciousness, the borderland between wakefulness and sleep. Hypnagogic dreaming is
frequently characterized by fragments of voices and fleeting images. Salvador Dali received so many ideas for his paintings
from hypnagogic dreaming that he developed what he called the

"slumber with key" technique and taught it to his students. The technique calls for placing a plate upside down in front of a comfortable armchair, and then settling into the chair for a nap while holding a heavy key between thumb and forefinger, poised over the plate. As one falls deeper into sleep, the key is released and hits the plate, causing awakening. This, said Dali, enables one to capture the dreaming before it is lost in deeper sleep.

CREATIVE VARIETY

There are probably as many permutations to creative dreaming as there are artists. Dreaming is one of many ways to access sources of inspiration. Try the Dream Labs and ideas in this chapter to see what works best for you. Adapt as you wish.

DREAM LAB #17
The Dream Mirror

This incubation exercise uses the previously discussed metaphor of the dream as a mirror that shows things that cannot be easily seen.

For the incubation, enter into a meditation state. Visualize yourself standing in front of a three-way mirror in a dimly lit, furnished room. The mirror should be positioned so that it shows periphery and background you cannot see otherwise. Look fully into your face; pay attention to detail. Then look at details revealed to the sides and to the back. Turn so that you can see your back completely in the mirror. Then face forward. While looking into your face, pay attention to details that emerge in your peripheral vision.

Make the affirmation:

Tonight the mirror of my dreams will reveal what is hidden or hard to see.

Follow through with dreamwork.

DREAM LAB #18
Spirit of Place Dreaming

As part of your regular spiritual and visionary dreaming practice, spend time outdoors. Meditate with the intention that you will engage in a meaningful communication with a spirit of place. After meditation, allow your attention to be attracted to the spirit that wishes to communicate with you. Give yourself over to the experience.

Ask for additional information or a visit during your dreams.

Follow through with dreamwork.

Note: Do not remove any objects from the setting of your meditation without express permission from the communicating spirit.

DREAM LAB #19
Creating in the Light Body

Earlier I mentioned that when I record a creativity dream, I visualize light flowing down from the heavens into the top of my head and out through my fingers as I write or type. This puts me into a sort of "light body consciousness" in which I am in touch with an inspired and higher part of myself. This visualization can be adapted to an incubation intended to stimulate creative flow during sleep.

In meditation prior to sleep, visualize yourself effortlessly performing your desired creative activity, emanating light as you do so. Feel lightweight and buoyant. You are in peak performance, supremely happy. Affirm that this is the result of what you will dream that night. Leave your intention open-ended; your dreams will feed back to you what you need.

Do followup dreamwork upon awakening. As you record the dream, visualize light entering into you and emanating from you. Do so even if your remembered dream does not seem remarkable. If you have no remembered dreams, write a spontaneous statement about how wonderful you are and how brilliant your ideas are. Be patient—inspiration will strike in time.

If you do this Dream Lab periodically, it will help you to enter and sustain periods of creative inspiration.

You can adapt this exercise to overcoming blockages. In meditation, make the affirmation:

I have the solution to _____.

Then visualize yourself creating as you are filled and flowing with light. As you fall asleep, affirm that your dreams will work out the solution and present it to you.

Follow through with dreamwork and visualization as above.

DREAM LAB #20
Seeding Ideas

We all have seed ideas: little thoughts that unlock the door to big innovations. Thomas Alva Edison had an innovative idea about how to make electrical light commercially practical and he changed the world by lighting the darkness. We all have great ideas, but we let many of them go because they seem impractical or even foolish. History is full of inventors who were laughed at for their seemingly strange ideas, but who had the vision and courage to allow their ideas to unfold and grow.

The Seed Ceremony is designed to help you recognize the worth of your ideas and allow them to expand and develop. Ideas are like seeds. They only have to do two things: *allow* and *unfold*. The seed allows the elements of the earth to nurture it so that it unfolds into a plant or even a mighty tree. A seed knows its own potential, its own greatness.

This exercise will help bring new creativity into awareness. It is designed to be done in a group, but you can also do it alone. Conduct it like a sacred ceremony, with participants in a circle and a lit candle in the center of the circle (or, if you're by yourself, place a lit candle in front of you). You will need a plate of seeds, such as sunflower seeds, which are big enough to be easily picked up. You may also wish to have soft music for meditation.

Here's how it works. If you are doing this alone, you will assume all roles:

1. The facilitator invites the group to be seated in a circle and sets the atmosphere with a short inspirational talk about seed ideas and potential. Stories, poems, and real-life examples can be used. Participants are invited to enter into the exercise with a sense of expectancy and a willingness to allow their inner creativity to unfold, just like a little seed. If you are working alone, collect some inspirational images, maxims, or short writings to contemplate.

2. In silence, the facilitator passes a plate containing the seeds around the circle. Each person takes one. The facilitator then

asks everyone to close their eyes and reflect silently on the seed, its tiny size, and the tremendous creative force it contains. Can they feel the power and the energy inherent within the tiny seed?

3. The facilitator asks participants to contemplate the mightiness of their own seed power and potential.

4. Pose these questions for everyone to contemplate silently in meditation:

- What is waiting to grow through me?

- What is desiring expression through me?

- What do I yearn to create?

Do not rush this experience, and do not try to hear what you want to hear. Sometimes better ideas are in the shadows waiting for light to be cast upon them. Allow ample time for the seed ideas to come forth. Assure everyone that it is all right if no ideas spring forth immediately—they will come forth at the best and most appropriate time.

5. Record your own thoughts in your journal.

6. End the ceremony with an affirmation to dream insights on the questions:

Tonight I will receive additional information and inspiration from my dreams.

7. Everyone incubates dreaming on their own.

8. Follow through with dreamwork.

9. When the group reconvenes, discuss your dreams. How do they compare to the thoughts that arose during the meditation? What have you learned about yourself? What action can you take now to nurture this new creativity?

VARIATION: DREAM JOURNEYING

After the meditation upon seed ideas, the facilitator conducts a guided meditation for dream journeying, using Dream Lab #2, "The Dream Temple and Dream Guide," as a blueprint. Allow about twenty minutes for the journey. Discuss results as a group. Follow through with individual dreamwork.

VARIATION: SEEDING IN PAIRS

In a group setting, divide into pairs. Instead of meditating on your own ideas, you will meditate for your partner: What is waiting for him/her to bring into being? The answers may come in images that you do not understand, but will make great sense to your partner. As thoughts arise, do not evaluate them, but accept them. Report to each other and discuss the results. You can also do dream journeying or incubated dreams for each other.

Discuss your results with your partner; then discuss as a group.

CHAPTER 10

Healing Power in Dreams

VISIONARY DREAMERS WHO work with their dreams are well acquainted with the power of dreams to heal emotions and stresses. Dreams also are intertwined with our physical health. They serve as early warning systems of the onset of illness and can provide insights into the healing process.

The therapeutic value of dreams has been respected since ancient times. In particular, the Greeks and the Romans were dedicated dreamers concerning their health. They constructed hundreds of dream temples devoted to the gods of healing, of whom the Greeks' Asklepios is the most important. The sick and injured would make pilgrimages to these temples, where they underwent purification rites and then incubated healing dreams in dormitories. The pilgrims hoped to have dreams in which they were visited by the gods and touched—and thus healed—in the dream itself. If such a dream did not occur, they hoped then for dreams that would reveal the way to a cure.

These dream temples flourished for hundreds of years, testifying to the healing power inherent in dreams.

The practice of incubating dreams for healing was absorbed into early Christianity and given over to angels. Though today Raphael is the angel identified with healing, the primary angelic healer in Christianity is Michael. Just as Asklepios (Aesculapius) was petitioned to appear in dreams to heal the sick and afflicted, Michael was petitioned for dream healing by Christian pilgrims to his sacred sites.

HEALING DREAM VISIONS OF ANGELS

As Christianity spread through Europe, Michael supplanted pagan gods of protection, battle, and healing. Apparitions and dream visions of him occurred on or near mountaintops or rocky outcrops, which became the sites of healing springs and miracles. Shrines, churches, and even great abbeys were built at these places and were dedicated to Michael, attracting countless pilgrims.

EUSEBIOS, CONSTANTINOPLE

The church of Michael at Eusebios, Constantinople, became famous as a healing site because of a dream vision reported in the ninth century. The story concerns a candlemaker named Marcianus, who was a pious servant of Michael. Marcianus was never ill. If he felt the slightest discomfort he would go into the church and immediately recover. On one occasion when he felt poorly he went into the church but took with him a medicinal poultice because doctors had convinced him it was necessary to do so. As he slept that night in the church—a customary practice at healing centers—he had a terrible dream vision. The doors of the church suddenly flew open, and in rushed "a fearful man as out of the heaven, descending on a white and terrible steed." The man dismounted and entered the church, escorted by men dressed in the garb of court officials. The church became filled with a strange unworldly odor.

The mysterious man walked to where Marcianus lay on his cot. He examined him and asked Marcianus what the poultice was. He demanded to know who had dared to bring such medicine into his house, thus identifying himself as the namesake of the shrine, Michael. Marcianus told him about the doctor who had insisted on the poultice, and Michael ordered his assistants to find him. Michael then led Marcianus to an icon of himself, which had a lit candle and small dish of oil beside it. Michael dipped his finger in the oil and made the sign of the cross on Marcianus's forehead. He then got back on his horse and rode off into the sky, the church doors closing by themselves behind him. The next morning, Marcianus had a cross on his forehead, which proved to the deacon the truth of his vision. The deacon learned that the offending doctor had become mysteriously and seriously ill during the night. Marcianus visited the doctor and then brought him on his bed into the church and told him to beg Michael for forgiveness and mercy. He then imitated his own healing by dipping his finger in the icon oil and drawing a cross on the doctor's forehead. The doctor was miraculously healed, thus establishing the model for successful healing.

MONTE GARGANO, ITALY

At Monte Gargano in Italy, dreams in which Michael appeared to the bishop of Siponto in the late fifth century led to the establishment of a healing shrine there. Versions of the story date to the eighth and ninth centuries.

According to the lore, one day a bull belonging to a wealthy man named Garganus became lost on a mountainside. After a long search, Garganus found it inside a cave. Irritated at the bull, he shot an arrow at it, but it turned in midair, "as if breathed upon by the wind," and hit him instead. He went back to the town of Siponto and told the story. The bishop undertook a fast of three days and three nights to learn the cause of this mysterious event.

Michael came to the bishop in a dream and said, "Let it be known to you that it occurred because I willed it. For I am the Archangel Michael, he who always stands in the presence of God." The bishop fasted a second time to be worthy of Michael's aid and presence. He had a second vision.

On the third night, Michael appeared in a dream and identified himself. He said he had intervened because he wished "to dwell in this place on earth and guard all." The next day, the bishop and some townsfolk visited the mountain and found two doors cut into its face.

In another dream, Michael told the bishop that the Sipontini and their allies, the Beneventi, would win in a war against their "heathen" enemies, the Neapolitans. The next day, the mountain was full of thunder, lightning, and darkness, which so frightened the Neapolitans that they fled. The locals went up to the doors in the side of the mountain and entered a cave where they found traces of Michael's presence: "a small trace, as if the footstep of a man struck there in the marble." A shrine was begun there and was called "the place of the footprints."

The shrine was completed after a visit by Michael to the bishop. The bishop was uncertain how to consecrate the chapel and was told by Michael in another vision not to consecrate it at all. Michael told him, "I myself have put it in order and consecrated it. You need only come and approach with your entreaties since I am attending as master in that place." Michael told him to return the next day and he would show the townspeople how the place would guide them.

The bishop did as instructed and found a chapel ready made and carved out of the living rock "as if by the hands of the archangel." He knew the angel had made it, because it was too irregular, rough, and full of corners and angles to have been made by human hands. A red cloak covered the altar. A spring erupted nearby, which became known for its healing properties.

The site attracted hordes of pilgrims. In the seventh century, the shrine was at a peak of popularity, due in part to a Lombard victory over the Saracens in 663 that was attributed to Michael's help. According to lore, the Lombards, who went to the shrine to pay thanks for their victory, found the imprint of Michael's foot near the south door of the temple.

MONT ST. MICHEL, FRANCE

The story of Monte Gargano figures in another dream-related event involving Michael, which bears mention because of the fame of the site: Mont St. Michel, an enormous Benedictine abbey built upon a quasi-island rock off the coast of Normandy, France. According to lore, the abbey owes its existence to dream visitations made by the archangel.

In 708, Michael appeared three times in dream visions to St. Aubert, bishop of Avranches, and instructed him to build a chapel on this rocky outcrop. The bishop did not believe Michael and asked him to prove his identity. So, the angel pushed his finger through the bishop's skull. The bishop asked for more proof. Michael told him a stolen bull would be found at the top of the rock; it was. Still Aubert was skeptical. Michael told him to send two messengers to Monte Gargano, where they would be given the red cloak that Michael wore when he appeared there and had left upon the altar, as well as a fragment of the altar on which he had set his foot. The messengers were sent, and they returned with the promised items. Convinced at last, Aubert founded an oratory.

In 966 an abbey was founded there by Richard I, Duke of Normandy. Construction of the abbey was finished in 1136. By the twelfth century, Mont St. Michel was called the City of Books and was a great center of learning. Many of the manuscripts kept by the monks were lost during the French Revolution when the monks were expelled. In the late eighteenth and early nineteenth centuries, the abbey was used as a prison.

Today Mont St. Michel is one of France's greatest tourist attractions. Inside the entrance to the abbey is a large marble frieze depicting Michael pushing his finger through the skull of the dreaming Aubert.

St. Michael's Mount, England

Many other stories have been recorded of Michael's appearances at other sites—in daytime apparitions—which also became famous as healing sites, though dreams were not necessarily incubated at them. A pilgrim might visit to dream, or to drink the healing waters, or to simply absorb the healing energies of the place and pray for healing. St. Michael's Mount on a large rock off the coast of Cornwall, England, is one such place. Michael appeared in an apparition to fishermen there in the sixth century, and a Benedictine monastery was later erected there (and now is a private residence and historical site open to the public).

WALSINGHAM, ENGLAND

Other healing shrines owe their existence to dreams of anonymous angels. England's only shrine to Mary, Our Lady of Walsingham, came into being in the eleventh century because of instructions by angels issued in dream visions. Richeldis Faverches, the lady of the manor at Walsingham, was a pious woman. One day she was deep in prayer and had a dream vision in which angels transported her to Nazareth to show her the home in which Jesus was raised. The dream vision repeated on two or three more occasions, and Richeldis became convinced that she was to build a replica of the house on her own land. She did so, and the little village of Walsingham became known as "England's Nazareth," attracting crowds of pilgrims.

According to lore, Richeldis was uncertain as to the exact spot to build the house. When the spot was chosen and the builders were brought in, they could not work, for things kept going mysteriously wrong. Richeldis spent a night in prayer. The next morning, she discovered that angels had moved the structure about two hundred feet to the proper place.

The original wooden house has since been rebuilt as a brick and stone shrine. Pilgrims still visit Walsingham to pray for healing and to partake of the healing spring waters there.

After the late Middle Ages, the importance of dreams and healing began to decline in the West, affected by the Protestant Reformation and also the Age of Reason, which placed supreme emphasis on science and rationality rather than on dreams, intuition, gods, and angels. Thankfully, the renaissance of the dream in the late nineteenth-century emergence of psychotherapy has renewed dreams as a powerful medium for healing.

DREAMS THAT REVEAL ILLNESS

Sometimes our dreaming mind knows we are ill before we know it consciously, and perhaps even before obvious physical symptoms develop. The diagnostic powers of dreams were known to the ancient Greeks; Carl G. Jung recognized them in some of his psychotherapy cases. "Prodromal" dreams (from the Greek *prodromos,* or "running before") alert people to potentially threatening illnesses, perhaps even saving some lives.

In his book *Healing Dreams,* Marc Ian Barasch tells how his cancer of the thyroid was first revealed in disturbing and bizarre dreams. Barasch had not paid much attention to his dreams until they jolted him with recurring, frightening images. He was chased by an axe murderer trying to decapitate him and was stared at by the figure of Death. A number of dreams had a neck theme: Primitive tribesmen stuck long needles into his "neck-brain"; a World War II bullet was lodged in his neck and removed by a Chinese surgeon; he found himself crawling about a Mayan "necropolis."

But after one terrifying dream—torturers had hung an iron pot filled with red-hot coals beneath my chin, and I woke up screaming, the odor of searing flesh in my nostrils—I couldn't ignore them any longer. I was sure that something inside me had gone drastically wrong. Each successive dream had spelled it out more explicitly until, although the

word was never uttered, it glared at me from a neon mar-
quee: cancer.[1]

But an initial examination by a doctor turned up nothing,
and the doctor opined that the dreams were stress-related. Then
Barasch asked if there was a bodily organ that might be a
"neck-brain." The doctor said it might be the thyroid. However,
a blood test showed normal levels of the thyroid hormone.

The distressing dreams continued, sending Barasch back to
the doctor. This time, a lump was found on his thyroid. It was
malignant.

Barasch's healing journey involved more than curing the
physical cancer: It involved his entire being. The necessity to
heal the inner self as well as the body also was forecast by his
dreams. In response to an incubation question, "What is the direction of a cure?" his dreams responded.

Under the ground a white, snakelike worm is turning in
upon itself in a perfect spiral. When its head reaches the
center, blinding rays of light shoot out, and a voice
solemnly intones: "You have been living on the outer shell
of your being—The Way Out Is the Way In!"[2]

In Barasch's experience, his doctor initially thought his
dreams to be only stress-related. Unfortunately, few Western
doctors question their patients about their dreams or know how
to assess them. Yet our dreams are quite revealing about our
health.

According to Dr. Oliver Sacks, a neurologist, dreams are altered in certain ways by neurological disorders. For example,
migraines are often associated with dreams of fireworks. Pa-

tients with multiple sclerosis may dream of remissions before they actually happen; similarly, stroke patients can dream of improvements in motor function before they actually happen. Many other patterns in dreaming that correspond to neurological conditions have been documented.

Not all disturbing dreams are about dysfunctions in the body, and it is important not to rush to such interpretations of dreams. However, the visionary dreamer is aware that dreams can be a sensitive barometer of our physical health as well as our emotional and spiritual health.

HEALING IN DREAMS

Records left at ancient dream incubation sites testify to experiences of healing in dreams, for example, from chronic illness, blindness, and lameness. The fortunate dreamers awakened free of their afflictions, or knowing what to do to be healed. If the gods or their proxies did not appear in dreams to give healing, then dream interpretation priests gave prescriptions for dreamers to follow on their own.

The famous Greek physician Galen, who lived in the second century B.C.E., had a dream healing that influenced his medical practice. At age twenty-seven he suffered a potentially fatal condition from an abscess under his diaphragm. He went to a dream temple devoted to Asklepios to dream a cure. He had two dreams in which he opened an artery between his thumb and forefinger and let it bleed until it stopped naturally. He awakened knowing this was the cure. He performed this procedure on himself, which drained his infection, and he was healed. During the course of his career, Galen performed many operations on his patients based on information obtained from dreams and said he had saved many lives as a result. His own experience made him a believer in the diagnostic and healing powers of dreams.

Healing within dreams can—and does—take place today, though how and why it happens still remain a mystery. A dramatic case was described to me by Carol D. Warner, a psychotherapist in Virginia and a longtime dreamworker who has held board and officer positions in the Association for the Study of Dreams.

Warner had a client, a teenaged girl we shall call Tina, whom she was treating for problems related to sexual abuse, drug abuse, and depression. Tina had been raped, sexually abused, and beaten by a relative at home. The man was brought to trial, but was acquitted. Tina ran away from home and entered a street life of drugs and more abuse.

After about three years, she made a decision on her own to return home and put her life back in order. But soon after doing so, and while in therapy, she was diagnosed with advanced ovarian cancer. There were three spots on one ovary, so distinct and developed that they could be seen with the naked eye. Tina was given about three months to live.

Warner was in the habit of praying for her clients. One night she prayed for Tina and for guidance concerning how to help her. She did not pray specifically for healing, but for help in accordance with God's will. As she prayed, she felt her heart go out to Tina in a deep and profound way. She so sincerely wanted to help her.

In the middle of the night, something mysterious happened. Warner dreamed a dream that seemed so vivid as to be real. In the dream, the Blessed Virgin Mary floated down from above, surrounded by, and dressed in, the most beautiful blue color. The energy around her was amazing and awe-inspiring. Warner became aware that Tina also was present in the dream, but was invisible. Instead of seeing Tina, Warner somehow viewed what she knew were the girl's ovaries.

As Mary came closer to Warner, she sent out three luminous globes of light. Warner knew that each one of the globes was going to one of the spots on Tina's diseased ovary. She saw each spot surrounded completely by a beautiful, glowing globe.

Warner emerged into waking. She knew with the most profound and inexplicable certainty that she had just witnessed Tina's complete healing. The cancer was gone. Despite her conviction, Warner debated whether to share the dream with Tina. Warner was experienced in working with dreams, which usually have symbolic rather than literal meanings. She wondered if she was interpreting the dream correctly. She also questioned whether sharing the dream might raise false hopes in Tina. She finally decided to tell her.

With hope renewed, Tina went back to her doctor, who was astonished to find no trace of the cancerous lesions. A biopsy showed Tina to be cancer-free. Tina could barely contain her joy. She had no doubt that Mother Mary had indeed healed her.

Relieved and overjoyed herself, Warner nonetheless continued to ponder just what had taken place that night. She believed in miracles and the power of prayer and felt that she had been privileged to witness a miraculous healing within her dream. But why did the dream come to her and not to Tina? The healing figure, Mary, is a universal mother symbol, but identified with Catholicism. Tina was Catholic, but Warner was not. Would Tina have been healed without Warner's dream?

There are, of course, no definite answers to those questions, only speculations and more questions. It is possible that the dream state, free of the conventions of waking consciousness, may be a powerful state for healing to take place. We know from our other experiences in dreams that many things are possible in dreams that are not possible—or at least not likely—in waking life. Praying for healing, help, and guidance prior to sleep may enable us to access powers we otherwise would consider miraculous, but which are available to us with the proper attunement.

DREAMS AND RECOVERY

Our dreams can provide helpful information during the course of recovery and healing. Dreams can dramatize stages of healing and communicate information about remedies and treatments.

While I was working on this book, I had an accident in which I slipped on black ice and broke my right wrist—a devastating injury for a right-handed writer. The initial X ray showed two breaks: The major one went straight across the wrist, and a minor one went perpendicular to it from the wrist into the hand. Although the injury was diagnosed as a "clean break," I was told I might have to have surgery and pins, depending on how the bones set during the first week or two.

Having heard unhappy stories about wrist breaks that were complicated and required surgery and pins, I was anxious to avoid this. The doctor told me that the X ray a week after the injury would probably show whether or not surgery would be necessary. Throughout the week, I held an image of a perfectly healed wrist in my mind.

The night before the appointment for the X ray, I had a

dream in which I looked down at my wrist to find that it was transparent, as though it were a "live" X ray. I could see the bones in detail. I had the feeling that everything looked "normal." A doctor with me—not my doctor in waking life but an unknown dream doctor—looked at my wrist and said, "Your bones are in good position." The dream was quite vivid.

The next morning, the doctor showed me the new X ray and said, "Your bones are in good position. If they stay this way, we won't have to do anything."

The healing progressed well. The bones remained in good position, and no surgery was necessary. I remained in a cast for six weeks and then entered occupational therapy for several months, regaining all of my original strength and, as of this writing, all but a small amount of my original flexibility.

The rest of the period in the cast was devoid of significant remembered dreams, save for one, in which I had a conversation with the cells in my wrist concerning the progress of the bone mending. I attribute the absence of recalled dreams to the fact that I had a great deal of difficulty sleeping due to the discomfort of the cast.

A HEALING TURNING POINT

A physical crisis can bring to the surface a host of emotional issues that are in need of healing and are revealed in dreams. After a hysterectomy, a woman named C. C. had a dream that kept repeating until she understood its message:

The hysterectomy brought up a lot of issues from my childhood, about my mother, about my lack of being a mother, about the limits of physicality, letting go of body, accepting medical help, letting go of fear, having faith in God. On the day of the surgery, when I was wheeled into the operating room, I was completely calm and though the drugs helped, I had a lot of guidance and support from the spiritual realm. I saw hovering above my chest a giant golden star of David, and knew I was protected by Rabbi Yehoshuah (Jesus), and no matter what happened during or after the operation, all was well.

In the dream that began coming to me later, I was at my parents' house, a shabby place, getting ready to leave. But my father has taken away my baggage. I am pretty annoyed at first and search for the bags to no avail. Eventually, I insist my mother must help me leave, which she begrudgingly does, and I set off on my journey.

It finally clicked that the dream was saying God has removed my baggage, meaning psychological baggage, and when I said thank you for freeing me and began enjoying the freedom in many ways, the dreams stopped. My mother represents my feminine side that I have not given up because of the hysterectomy. I insist she is a part of me and must help me find my way. That's my intuition about the dream at this point.

My spiritual work on myself is not done of course, and a labyrinth walk the other day revealed I still have "shit" to get rid of. It was an interesting walk. I went into the labyrinth with the intention of honoring God and being quiet. About halfway through I realized that I needed to go to the bathroom. The funny thing is I already had gone earlier. Anyway, I continued my slow meditative walk into the center, and came back out a little faster aware that there is always "shit" to deal with. Later that day, I saw two dogs taking a crap! They were embarrassed to be seen. And then a horse, a stallion, who was not a bit embarrassed. It was really funny. It made me realize that no matter how free of baggage we are at this moment, things can build up, and we have to be constantly vigilant and practice soul-lessons in order to get rid of the wastes we manufacture within ourselves.

When C. C. made the connection between her father in the dream and "God the Father," the meaning of the dream burst forth. This insight led her to other insights and to a new direction in her spiritual work. Mundane events—the bowel functions of animals—were woven into the process of insights, showing a point from another perspective. It is common for mundane events to play off dreams and dreamwork in syncronicities. The process of dreaming is holistic—it involves our entire being and our waking mind as well as our dreaming mind.

DREAMING OUR HEALTH

How should we use our dreams for healing and health? Certainly it is advisable to seek a medical opinion if dreams recur that involve violence and injury to the body, especially a particular body part. Dreamwork in general helps to maintain and enhance emotional and spiritual health. Dream incubation can be undertaken for guidance in healing. Dreamwork is not a substitute for professional medical advice, but can make an important contribution to the healing process.

DREAM LAB #21

Healing Incubations

Consult your dreams for information and guidance related to health and healing. Possible incubation questions are:

- How can I heal _____?

- What needs to be healed?

- What should I do to improve my health and well-being?

Bear in mind that healing involves all aspects of our being. Physical health cannot be separated from your emotional and spiritual health. Your dreams and dreamwork may point to unresolved negative emotions about events, relationships, or past events that need to be healed. If you interpret prescriptive guidance from your dreams, consult an appropriate health care practitioner first.

CHAPTER 11

Odyssey to a Roman Dream Temple

ONE COOL AND intermittently rainy spring day, I took a journey back in time to a Roman dream temple where pilgrims once had gone in search of healing. Only ruins exist now at the hilltop site at Lydney, England, located in Gloucestershire between the Forest of Dean and the River Severn. Once this place attracted thousands who came in hopes that through their dreams they would meet the god Nodens, who would heal them as they slept. Many went away healed.

As I started my journey at the base of the hill, I tried to send my consciousness back two thousand years to experience what it must have been like when the sacred temple was at its glory.

Lydney has several sites of Roman ruins, including one of the most important Roman archaeological sites in all of Britain: a camp and temple at Lydney Park believed to be the cult shrine of Sabrina, goddess of the Severn. The ruins of the dream tem-

ple are on privately owned land and are open to the public for
brief periods every year. Because of its remote location and private ownership, the site retains a wild, quiet, and pristine atmosphere that may not be much different than it was during the
Roman occupation of Britain.

The Romans built the Lydney healing temple around the
fourth century C.E. Their healing temples were inspired by the
dream healing temples of the Greeks, who believed strongly in
dreams as a medium of contact with the gods. The Lydney temple does not compare in grandeur to some of the great Greek
healing temples, such as Epidaurus, with its huge abaton (dormitory), amphitheater, and other structures, but it offered a
complete healing sanctuary: a temple for the priests; a hydrotherapy center of Roman-style cold, warm, and hot baths; a
dream abaton; and stalls for resident physicians, consultants,
and healers.

The Greek temples were dedicated to the primary god of
dream healing, Asklepios. Lydney was not dedicated to a major
deity, but to a little-known deity, Nodens. The Romans were
great adapters, and Nodens may have been derived from a pan-
Celtic deity Nudd of the Silver Hand.

Now I stood at the base of the hill, facing the footpath that
wound up the hill to the temple, which was out of my sight. In
front of me was a little stream, a significant symbol of the
boundary between worlds. My waking dream journey as a pilgrim follows:

> I step over the stream of water, knowing that I am leav-
> ing the waking world and entering into the world of
> dreamtime and the gods. I start my ascent. Slung across
> my back is a small bundle of offerings and clean cloth-

ing. In one hand I carry a live chicken in a small cage, a sacrifice. Every step up the hill takes me deeper into the realm of the gods. I am entering sacred space, and I have come prepared to pay homage and respect. I come with sincerity for healing deep in my heart.

In silence I climb, slowly, carefully, aware of the stillness and presence of this holy place. Already I can feel the force of the god Nodens enveloping me. Hope quickens within me that this is a sign that I will be graced by the god in my dreams. I have heard that he will, if he chooses, appear in one's sleep and give instant healing.

At the top of the hill I come into a clearing. I am awed by the sight of the temple buildings and the activity I see there. The path takes me to the entrance of the priests' temple, and I wait at the steps. Through the trees I can glimpse the great river Severn, named after Sabrina/Isis.

Shortly a priest comes out of the temple and greets me. I bow and explain my need, and ask for help. I have brought a sacrifice, I say, placing the chicken on the ground at his feet. I unsling the bag of offerings and pour out into his palms the few coins I have in my possession. The priest graciously accepts my gifts and disappears into the temple with the coins. I cannot see him, but I know that he is taking them to the altar in the inner part of the temple.

The priest returns with a large knife. After making the appropriate preparations, he performs a ritual sacrifice of the chicken to Nodens. He and other priests examine the bird's entrails and also look into the sky for other secret signs that only they can decipher. I wait anxiously, for through these signs they will know if I can proceed.

The signs are good. I am elated and very thankful. I say a quick and silent prayer of thanks to Nodens.

The sacrifice is the beginning rite of my purification. I have taken no food this day, and I will continue the fast. I am given some water that has been specially blessed and am allowed to take some rest from my journey. I am dusty and tired. I feel there is a special magic here that is already beginning its healing work on me. To be here is to be healed. I have a tremendous faith that I will leave here cured of my affliction. Nodens will not let me down.

When I am refreshed, I am taken to the hydrotherapy center and am allowed to bathe. The floors are tiled with lovely mosaic patterns in white, coral, and sky blue. I soak in hot water, feeling the heat penetrate deep within my bones. It is quite relaxing. Then I move to a chamber of tepid water and soak there. Finally I move to a chamber of cool water. The shock of it is vivifying.

I emerge feeling much better and put on the clean clothes I have brought with me. But I am still ill, not yet healed. There is a long building of small stalls. I am sent there to consult with a priest and receive instructions for my night in the abaton. I spend a long time with him, discussing my ailment and how it has resisted treatment.

The priest tells me how I am to prepare myself for sleep so that Nodens will come to me in my dreams and perform a healing. He teaches me a charm, or prayer, to petition the god. He shows me the room in the dormitory where I will sleep. It is small, barely big enough for a person. There is a mat on the tile floor and an oil lamp. I am to arise at dawn, take no food, and come straight to him to discuss my dreams.

I memorize the prayer and spend the rest of the afternoon walking about the grounds in quiet and sitting in contemplation. Near a stand of trees I find a huge oak tree with gnarled roots thrust above the ground, and I sit there for a long time. The tree feels magical. I have heard it said that the temple grounds are populated by some sort of *genii,* or spirits of the place, a race of small beings who are part god and part mortal and live in the ground and in the trees and grasses. They are for the most part invisible, but can choose to reveal themselves if they desire. I have also heard it said that they will help Nodens in his healing, but if they do not like you, they will work against you. As I sit beneath the great gnarled oak, I offer a silent greeting to the *genii* and ask for their help. This is their land, too, and I give thanks for their welcome.

At dusk the priests conduct a worship ceremony. Then I and the other pilgrims like me retire to our appointed rooms in the dormitory. A small bowl with a special herb drink has been left in each room. As night thickens, I light my oil lamp and face east, reciting my prayer. Then I extinguish the lamp, drink my herbal potion, and lie down on the mat. At first my mind races with a mixture of expectation and apprehension. But shortly, the special herbal formula of the dream priests does its work, and I find myself drowsy and then slipping off into sleep.

I dream an odd dream, unlike any I have ever dreamed. It is brightly lit with intense light and colors. All of my senses seem heightened. At times I think I am awake, and at times I know I am dreaming.

In the dream I am in the presence of a large, imposing man who seems to alternate between a hunter and some sort of wild man of the woods. He is fierce and carries a bow and quiver of arrows. He is accompanied by a dog the likes of which I have never seen. It is long and lean in body with very short hair, a long snout, a long tail, and flop ears. I think the man must be a hunter because of the dog. The dog is friendly and comes to me and licks me. I pat it on the head. The hunter readies an arrow in his bow. He then shocks me by turning to me and shooting me straight in the heart. I am dizzy and in intense pain, and as I fall to the ground, I think I am going to die.

I awaken from the dream with my heart racing. I am relieved to discover it is "only" a dream. But then I am immediately plunged into disappointment. Surely this was not Nodens, nor was it a healing. I fear I am not healed.

I almost do not want to know the meaning of the dream, but after rising and dressing, I go to the stall where I am to meet the dream interpreter priest. He keeps an expressionless face as I recount my dream. I finish and fall silent, almost dreading that he will shake his head and tell me the god has refused my request.

But the interpreter has other news. In a matter-of-fact, passionless way, he informs me that Nodens has indeed come to me and given me blessings. He pulls from beneath his table a small sculpture of a dog and asks if this was the one I saw in my dreams. I am amazed that it is. The dog, he says, is the companion of Nodens. He licks those the god will heal. Healing is not always instantaneous, but requires time. The healing was shot into my heart with the arrow. The priest interprets the dream to mean that a healing process has begun and will spread through me, but it will take time, and the process will be painful. I will be reborn in the process.

He consults his secret oracle signs and then sends me to one of the resident healers, who prescribes medications for me. I can tell from their appearance, texture, and taste that they are different than the medications I have taken before. They make me feel rather ill, but the healer assures me the side effects will wear off, and I must try to keep them down.

I am allowed to break my fast and have another session in the hydrotherapy pools. Then I take my leave of the temple. In my descent I can feel the withdrawal of the sacred presence. I step over the little stream and reenter the physical world.

In the days and weeks that follow, I stick to the course of medication, prayers, and supplications that have been prescribed. I become completely healed.

The snake and dog were animal totems and proxies of Asklepios, and at Lydney there is evidence that the dog was a totem of Nodens. A small sculpture of a dog such as the one I described was excavated at the site. The dog has on one haunch a marking, perhaps a magical tattoo or brand of some sort.

The site at Lydney is still active with a spiritual presence. If you go with the right intent, you can feel the presence of Nodens, as well as that of the fairy folk who live there.

CHAPTER 12

Dreams about the Dead and about Dying

DREAMS ABOUT THE dead, dying, and death don't receive much attention in many books about dreams. Perhaps that is due to our natural reticence to confront the subjects. Yet all of us have such dreams. We dream of dead loved ones; we dream of the subject of death; and if we die gradually of a terminal illness, our dreams open the way into the unknown.

DREAMS ABOUT THE DEAD

The loss of a loved one can send us into a tailspin of grief and mourning. Our dreams play an important role in healing by reflecting stages of our grief and our ability to come to terms with the death. We may have dreams that close unfinished business, enable us to say a final good-bye, give us reassurance, and leave us feeling peaceful and happy. We may also have disturbing dreams and nightmares that require the help of a therapist. Dreams related to grief can occur over a long period of time. Grief seldom resolves in a straight line from stage to stage; rather, we move in and out of different stages of denial, acceptance, and closure as we come to terms with our feelings about the deceased and our relationship with him or her.

REALISM OF DREAMS

Many dreams of the dead are so lucid, vivid, and realistic that dreamers feel they have had a "real" experience rather than a dream. In some cases, I believe we do have real encounters with the dead—we are able to meet them where the realms of the living and the dead intersect, in the dreamscape. Sometimes a single dream can bring profound emotional relief.

Here is a dream that brought comfort to a man who lost his grandfather:

> My grandfather was a Native American shaman. Two weeks after he died, I had a dream in which I saw him dressed in white buckskin. He was outdoors. It was so real—I could literally smell the smoke of his fire.[1]

Carl G. Jung experienced a profound dream of his dead wife that had so great an emotional impact on him that he could scarcely describe its effects. In the dream, which he described as like a vision, his wife appeared in her prime at about age thirty, dressed in a beautiful dress and looking squarely at him. Her countenance was neither happy nor sad, but "objectively wise and understanding . . . as though she was beyond the mist of affects." Jung knew it was not her but more like an idealized portrait of her that contained the sum total of their relationship and marriage, and also the end of life. "Face to face with such a wholeness one remains speechless, for it can scarcely be comprehended," said Jung.

CLOSURE AND FAREWELL

Unfinished business, especially matters of "making peace," forgiveness, expressions of love, and so on, are dealt with in dreams:

> I had walked down a long, dark corridor and was standing under a light centered in a hub with corridors branching out in all directions. As I looked back from where I had come, I saw a figure wearing a long black robe and hood. A monk. I kept thinking I should go back down there, but could not bring myself to do it.
>
> Then the figure came toward me, and when it was close, the person threw out her arms and smiled at me. I recognized her instantly, for it was my late aunt M., after whom I was named. Her message was that she loved me and forgave me.
>
> For what? For being nice to her when she was alive, because I had an ulterior motive. I wanted to inherit her small estate, and I did.
>
> M. is my spirit guide, my guardian angel, who comes to me in times of need. Strangely, she is my daughter's protector, too. Strange, because during her lifetime children annoyed her, and I didn't know my daughter even liked her.[2]

Dreams also can help us heal grief by helping us see the departed in a new state of being:

The night immediately preceding my mother's death (we had to take her off of life support) I dreamt that she was boarding a plane and I wanted to go along, but she told me I couldn't (very unusual since we did everything together). She was accompanied by a soldier and other people. Interestingly enough, the other people were fuzzy images, lots and lots of them (thousands?). I couldn't see their faces.

After she had died (exactly one month later), I did see her in a very lucid way—she was very bright—and in a cocoon type of thing—I felt like I was in a place I couldn't stay. It was very bright and warm. She was in a white, sleeveless dress and kept telling me (without words—only feelings) that she loved me.

I think the soldier represented a death too soon. I thought my mother, though seventy-four years old, was too young to die.

I had another dream about her in which she was in her bedroom behind closed doors. I tried to open the door, but I wasn't able to—she said that was okay, that I couldn't come in but that I could still talk to her through the door.[3]

The cocoon is an image of gestation for rebirth. Barriers between the living and the dead are common in dreams. Here the two are separated by a closed door. Bridges are common between-worlds boundaries. Sometimes the deceased person announces he or she has made a special effort to visit in dreams and cannot stay long.

Our dreams of the deceased change as we move through grief. Disturbing dreams can hinder the process and should be taken into a therapeutic setting. Repeating dreams may indicate being stuck in bereavement, and also should be evaluated by a therapist. Guided waking dreaming can assist in resolving emotions about unhappy relationships with the departed.

DREAMS OF THE DYING

Individuals who suffer terminal illness experience changes in their dreams as they get closer to death. Marie-Louise van Franz, a psychotherapist and a pupil of Jung, noted:

> The dreams of dying people are not about death, but generally about a journey. They have to get ready for a journey, or they have to go through a dark tunnel and be reborn into another world, or they have to go through a disagreeable darkness or through a dark cloud to come out into another space, or they are finally going to meet their beloved partner.[4]

Dreams of journey, transition, and rebirth help to prepare the dying person for their passage into the afterlife. Oftentimes, people want to talk about their transition dreams. Health care workers who assist the dying should be educated in dreamwork and especially in dreams of the dying, in order to help people process the emotional and spiritual content of their dream experiences. Dreams can be powerful forces to allay fears of dying and validate personal beliefs about the continuation of life in another realm.

STAGES OF DYING

Like dreams of grief and mourning, dreams of the dying move through stages as well. One case in my files concerns a woman's mother who was dying of cancer. Initially she dreamed repeatedly of finding her beloved garden in stages of death and decay; nothing could be made to grow there. Toward the end of her illness, she had begun to dream of finding new shoots of growth in her garden.

Initial dreams of the dying may emphasize images of death and decay, especially of vegetation and animals; things coming to an end and the stopping or freezing of time-keeping pieces like watches and clocks. These images have potent healing power to help the patient come to terms with what is happening to them. The dreams themselves usher in a new stage of consciousness.

THE ELEMENT OF LIGHT

A dominant image in dreams of the dying is light: Darkness is illuminated with light or turns into light; a new light shines. (Light also is dominant in dreams about the dead—the deceased often appear swathed in radiance or seemingly emanating light from within.)

In his book *Dreams: God's Forgotten Language,* John Sanford gives this dream of a dying Protestant clergyman:

> [He] sees the clock on the mantelpiece; the hands have been moving, but now they stop; as they stop, a window opens behind the mantelpiece clock and a bright light shines through. The opening widens into a door and the

light becomes a brilliant path. He walks out onto the path of light and disappears.[5]

Doors and windows are symbols of portals into new worlds. A path, like a river, takes us on a journey through a landscape.

In *On Dreams & Death*, von Franz tells this dream of a young woman with brain cancer. The dream occurred the day before she died:

> I am standing beside my bed in the hospital room and I feel strong and healthy. Sunshine flows in through the window. The doctor is there and says, "Well, Miss X, you are un-expectedly completely cured. You may get dressed and leave the hospital." At that moment I turn around and see, lying in the bed—my own dead body![6]

The dream seems to presage the imminent transition from life into death and the afterlife. In the dream this is heralded by the sunshine that floods through the window. Von Franz rejected the idea of this dream as a wish fulfillment for a cure.

The dream forecasts the transition, and also speaks to a holistic healing on a soul level.

INVISIBLE HELPERS

Not uncommon are experiences in which the dying person spends more and more time in the company of others who are dead, or who seem to be spiritual beings, such as angels, who have come to help them make their transition. Such experiences occur in dreams, borderland states of consciousness, and even waking visions, all of which are very real to the experiencer. Dreams and visionary experiences of the dying should not be treated as hallucinations, but given proper attention. Sometimes as death nears, the patient spends more and more time aware of an invisible world and invisible presences.

THE WHOLENESS OF LIFE AND DEATH

While dreams of the dying do point to certain themes, there are no "definitive" dreams that announce death. Images and symbols are as varied as individual dreamers and relate to personal context just as do "ordinary" dreams. Von Franz said that sometimes a dream of death may relate to our need to confront the subject or to fear of death. Death dreams also may address symbolic deaths, such as the ending of something important in the life of the dreamer.

Jung said that the worlds of the living and dead form a whole. Our physical and psychic energy is the same; during life it is contained in physical form, and then it makes a transformation in death to the psychic, which is unbounded by time and space.

Our dreams of dying, death, and the dead are as important to our wholeness as are the dreams about our stresses, anxieties, emotions, healing, creativity, spiritual initiations, turning points, and experiences of God. Unfortunately, Western society does not like to talk of death and the dead. We consider it frightening and morbid. Certain religious factions link dreams of the dead and death—and even all dreams in general—to the workings of the devil, thus killing any possibility of the healing power of these dreams. As long as we keep death swept beneath a carpet, we deny ourselves full measure of living. Dying is a part of living. Jung observed that our birth is a death and our death is a birth. Our dreams deal with the full spectrum of our existence, of our coming and going in different forms.

Do not be reluctant to work with dreams about the dead, death, and dying. However, since they can raise powerful emotions, also do not hesitate to seek therapeutic help to deal with them. If someone you know is terminally ill and wishes to discuss their dreams, encourage them to do so, and make certain that they have a qualified professional who can help them.

CHAPTER 13

Precognitive Dreaming

IN THE AFTERMATH of the terrorist plane attacks that destroyed the World Trade Center and damaged the Pentagon on September 11, 2001, people came forward with reports of vivid dreams they'd had of these disasters days, even weeks, in advance. Hundreds of dreams were posted on the Internet and shared in dreamwork communities. The dreams were filled with imageries that later took place: planes crashing into buildings, planes crashing on the ground, tall buildings collapsing, flames shooting out of buildings, people running covered in gray ash, and feelings of panic, mass death, and war. These nightmarish dreams were so realistic that many people awoke from them in terror, covered in sweat. Examples of some of the dreams sent to me are excerpted below:

> I dreamed that chaos and destruction had erupted. It seemed like the end of the world. There was a gray film

over everything, like a nuclear winter. People were running all over.

I was in a city where a tall building was on fire. People were screaming in the windows, and some were jumping.

On the night before the attack, I dreamed I was raped by an evil man with dark eyes. We had a violent struggle. I awoke feeling very vulnerable, even sick.

I am in a building giving a presentation, when there is a huge rumbling sound, like an earthquake. Everyone starts to panic. Somehow I get out of the building, because the next thing is, I am out on the street. Things are flying around in the air. I look up and see the building has a giant crack in it, and I worry that it is going to fall. I am amazed that anyone got out.

I'm trapped in a building with some other people. Something horrible is happening. I keep running around trying to find a way out, but everywhere there is something blocking the way. I woke up with a choking feeling in my throat.

A plane fell out of the sky into a city. I seemed to be watching from above and far away. I just knew that there were a lot of people dead. I felt awful.

Other dreamers reported dreams in which they felt a vague sense of dread that "something terrible" was going to happen soon. Still others had dreams that contained something related to the attacks, though in more indirect ways.

While these dreams seem to capture elements of the 9-11 attacks, none of the dreamers knew they were having precognitions. A dream that a tall building is collapsing would not have sparked the immediate connection that terrorists were going to fly planes into the World Trade Center on the morning of September 11, 2001. The dreams simply seemed nightmarish and disturbing and unusual in the course of "normal dreaming." Only after the events took place were the dreamers able to match their dreams to the circumstances. But if so many people dreamed in advance of these disasters, why could nothing be done to prevent them?

In the dreamwork community, interest in precognitive dreaming rose dramatically following 9-11. Of particular interest is proactive precognitive dreaming: being able to dream enough information in advance in order to prevent terrible things from happening.

On February 1, 2003, the Columbia space shuttle broke apart minutes from its scheduled landing in Florida, killing the seven astronauts aboard. The meteor-like disintegration of the craft sixty miles up in the morning sky played on television to shocked audiences. Once again, many dreamers realized after the fact that they had had precognitive elements in dreams concerning this tragedy—but, as with the 9-11 attacks, no one had the whole picture.

Once again, the laments were raised: "If only I'd seen more . . ." "Why couldn't we have done anything? . . ." "What use are precognitive dreams if they don't give enough to take action? . . ."

ARE EVENTS PREVENTABLE?

There are major cases where tragedies have taken place despite warnings in precognitive dreams.

FAMOUS ASSASSINATIONS

According to Shakespeare, Calpurnia, the wife of Roman Emperor Julius Caesar, had a dream in which Roman senators stabbed a statue of her husband with knives and blood flowed from the statue. Unbeknownst to her, several senators were indeed conspiring to kill the emperor. Calpurnia awakened, certain that her husband would be killed that very day in the public Forum. Caesar was skeptical and relayed her dream to Decius, a senator who was among the conspirators. Decius slyly interpreted it as a favorable omen of Rome's future victories under Caesar. Caesar went to the Forum as planned that day—and was stabbed to death by his enemies.

The case of President Abraham Lincoln is well known: Lincoln dreamed he saw his own body lying in state in the Capitol building; later, he was shot to death by John Wilkes Booth at Ford's Theater. The dream only revealed Lincoln's death and gave no information about the time, place, or way in which it would happen.

In 1914, tensions were high in Europe, and many people feared that war would erupt. On June 28, Bishop Joseph Lanyi of Grosswardein, Hungary, awakened from a nightmarish dream that he knew would come true. Lanyi had once been the tutor of the Archduke Franz Ferdinand of Austria, one of the figures involved in the political tensions.

In the dream, Lanyi went to his desk to look through some letters. On top was a letter bearing the seal of the archduke; it was bordered in black. Lanyi recognized the archduke's handwriting and opened the letter. The top of it featured a postcard-like light blue picture of a street with a narrow passage. Sitting in a motorcar were the archduke and his wife, a general who faced them, and the chauffeur and another officer. People were crowded on both sides of the street. The picture suddenly came to life with two young men leaping from the crowd and firing guns at the archduke and his wife. Below the picture was a note from the archduke, addressed personally to Lanyi. It read, "I hearwith inform you that today, my wife and I will fall victims to an assassination. We commend ourselves to your pious prayers." It was dated June 28, 3:45 A.M., Sarajevo.

Layni awakened in tears at 3:45 A.M. He immediately recorded the dream, sketched the scene, and had the drawing certified by two witnesses. He sent an account to his brother and commenced earnest prayer.

The archduke and his wife were shot to death just as Lanyi had dreamed—only there was but one assassin, not two. Photographs published in the newspapers closely matched the scene Lanyi had seen in his dream.

AIRPLANE CRASHES

Perhaps the most famous precognitively dreamed airplane disaster is the tragic crash in 1979 of American Airlines Flight 191. On May 26, a DC-10 jumbo jet with 270 people aboard took off from Chicago's O'Hare airfield, bound for Los Angeles. On takeoff, one of the massive engines fell off the plane, and the second engine shut down. The plane was only five hundred feet in the air when it turned radically on its side with one wing tilted up, and then fell to the earth. Everyone on board was killed. It was the worst air disaster to that date in the United States.

This accident was seen in advance in vivid detail in precognitive dreams of at least two people, who alerted others in advance of the impending disaster. Unfortunately, there was not enough information to avert the accident. In the aftermath, the same questions arose about the purpose of precognitive dreaming as did more than twenty years later after 9-11 and Columbia. If we get advance warning of a future event, why do we not get enough information to change course? If we can't prevent a disaster or undesirable event, what is the purpose of psychic dreaming?

One of the dreamers of Flight 191 was a New York woman who had a history of precognitive dreaming and had accurately predicted other air disasters. In 1978, she had dreamed in advance of another famous disaster that occurred that September. A PSA jetliner with 144 on board, enroute from Los Angeles to San Diego, was near landing when it collided with a private plane and plunged to the ground in flames. Everyone was killed, as were the two people aboard the private plane. In the dream, there was a plane in the sky headed for California; the dream was permeated with a feeling of imminent disaster, one that would be the worst in U.S. air history to date.

The woman, a counselor who made numerous appearances on radio, was on air the next morning in Pine Bluff, Arkansas, where she related her dream. Three hours later, the news of the disaster broke. It was indeed the worst air disaster to date—but would be superseded by the 1979 American Airlines Flight 191 crash.

Less than five months later, she began having dreams of another airline disaster, this time in the Midwest. She felt it was still weeks or months away, but she was certain that it would happen. On March 12, she made the prediction on air in Tulsa, Oklahoma. Off the air, she gave the name of the airlines to the show host. It was American Airlines, and the plane would be headed for California.

The woman dreamed again of the impending crash and gave details on air in Savannah, Georgia, on April 26. It would be a jumbo jet. The accident was less than one month away. However, she was not certain of the exact location where it would happen.

Repeating and disturbing dreams of the accident made her reluctant to fall asleep. She dreamed of being both a passenger on the doomed plane and a spectator to the crash. In the dream, she was a passenger as the plane went down. After the crash and everyone was dead, she walked away as a spectator. At that point, she bolted awake, frightened.

The second significant precognitive dreamer was a man in Ohio, who had no previous experience of psychic dreams. On May 16, 1979, he was jarred awake by a terrifying vision of an airplane crash. In the dream, he was looking out to the right over a field with a diagonal tree line. He looked up into the sky and saw a big jet whose engines were making an unusual noise. He had no sense of danger or impending doom—but then the plane started to turn with its wing way up. It flipped onto its back and dove straight into the ground, exploding. As sound died out, he woke up.

The dream was frightening, unlike any he had ever had. He tried to forget it, but the emotional impact of it and the vividness of the images remained with him throughout the day. The dream repeated a second time. When he awoke, the man found he'd been crying in his sleep. This time he felt a sense of urgency—that he must take action fast. The dream repeated every night. On May 22, after the seventh dream, the man called the local office of the Federal Aviation Administration (FAA). He relayed the dream and said the plane was a big American Airlines jet with a big engine on the tail. An FAA official reviewed details with him. But unfortunately, the dream gave no information as to where and when this accident would happen.

On May 25, he had the dream for the tenth time. He awoke with a different feeling—he knew he would never have it again. Throughout the day, he was upset and distracted, so much so that he left work early at 4 P.M.—the very time when the doomed plane was taking off at Chicago (where it was 3 P.M.). The disaster happened as he had witnessed it in his dream. He did not see or know an engine fell off, but witnesses captured dramatic photographs of the plane turned with its wing up before diving into the ground.

When he heard the news, he knew it was his dream. Understandably, he blamed himself for not being able to prevent the accident. He kept thinking if only he had gotten just a little more information, he could have prevented it. He thought he had been singled out as the only person in the whole world to see the accident in advance. Much later, he still believed the crash could have been prevented.

DREAMS THAT CHANGE EVENTS

Nonetheless, there are cases of record that show that precognitive dreaming does make a difference in averting disaster. Psychiatrist Ian Stevenson collected about nineteen cases of precognitive warnings about the sinking of the *Titanic* in April 1912 on its maiden voyage. The warnings occurred to people in England, America, Canada, and Brazil. Some warnings were as early as two weeks prior to the ship's sailing date of April 10. Between April 3 and 10, several persons, including the financier J. Pierpont Morgan, abruptly canceled their passage. Some people canceled after dreaming the ship was doomed; others responded to a "bad feeling." There is no record of a specific enough warning to prevent the sinking itself, which killed 1,502 of the 2,207 passengers on board. However, the ship sailed without a full load of passengers—unusual, considering the publicity surrounding the maiden voyage of the new superliner—which may indicate that precognition saved some lives that might otherwise have been lost.

Similarly, when the *Empress of Ireland* sank in the Lawrence River in 1914, its first-class was two-thirds empty and its second-class half empty. What made people stay away from this particular voyage?

In the 1960s, W. E. Cox examined rail passenger loads on American trains that had accidents between 1950 and 1955. He compared passenger loads on the same runs on the day of the accident, each of the preceding seven days, and the preceding fourteen and twenty-eight days. He found a remarkable drop-off in passenger counts on some, but not all, accident days. One, the Chicago & East Illinois *Georgian,* was carrying only nine passengers on the day of its accident on June 15, 1952; five days beforehand, it had carried a more typical sixty-two passengers. Cox concluded that many people who had intended to travel on disaster-bound trains had unconsciously, or for some unusual reason, altered their plans or missed the trains by being late.

We may surmise that some of the people involved in the

above-mentioned cases avoided travel because they had disturbing dreams.

Many people report that precognitive dreams have made a significant difference to them personally, preventing something unpleasant happening to themselves or to someone they know. If we can be helped on a personal level, why can't we affect larger events?

TIME DISPLACEMENT

Sometimes a precognition is accurate, but timing or other crucial details are wrong. One notable example of this is a dream about the Apollo 12 moon mission in 1969 had by the gifted psychic Alan Vaughan. Vaughan was one of the principal subjects among the one hundred people tested for telepathic dreaming in the famous research conducted at the Maimonides Medical Center in Brooklyn, New York. He coauthored a book about the research, *Dream Telepathy: Experiments in Nocturnal ESP*, with researchers Montague Ullman and Stanley Krippner, two individuals well known for their work in dreams and in altered states of consciousness.

Prior to the Apollo 12 mission, Vaughan meditated on it. He had a dream in which he saw grave danger for the mission—if something in the electrical or fuel system was not fixed, there would be an explosion that could kill the astronauts. He saw an image of astronaut Neil Armstrong's footprint on the moon, with a big X crossing it out. With that came the certain feeling that the mission would not reach the moon.

On takeoff, the rocket carrying Apollo 12 was struck by lightning, causing a problem. But the mission reached the moon and returned without further mishap. It seemed that Vaughan had accurately tuned in to an electrical problem—the lightning—but had been wrong about the overall fate of the mission.

Four months later, Apollo 13 was launched for another moon mission. As the ship left the earth's orbit, there was a big explosion of fuel. Most of the ship's electricity was cut off. The lives and safe return of the astronauts were in jeopardy. Tension was high as NASA ground control and the astronauts tried to figure out a solution. The moon landing was aborted. A plan was conceived to use the moon's gravitational field as a sling-shot to help propel the crippled ship back to earth. The plan worked, and the astronauts were able to return home in safety.

Vaughan had been both wrong and right. He saw the circumstances of Apollo 13, but associated them with Apollo 12, because of his meditation on that particular mission. What if that warning prior to Apollo 12 had been reported and had persuaded authorities to alter, postpone, or cancel Apollo 12? Would the Apollo 13 events still have unfolded as they did? These are questions for which no one has a definitive answer.

The famous Aberfan, Wales, coal slide disaster was also preceded by premonitions, only a few of which zeroed in on the fateful day itself.

The disaster occurred on October 21, 1966, when 28 adults and 116 children were killed in a landslide of coal waste that tumbled down a mountain in Aberfan, Wales, and buried a school. Up to two weeks beforehand, two hundred persons experienced both premonitions and precognitions about the disaster, according to three surveys taken afterward. Premonitions included depression, a feeling that "something bad" was about to happen (some persons accurately pinpointed the day), sensations of choking and gasping for breath, uneasiness, and impressions of coal dust, billowing black clouds, and children running and screaming. One especially chilling precognitive dream was had by a young girl the night before the disaster. In the morning, she told her mother she had dreamed that everyone went to school, but there was no school because "something black had come down all over it." She also told her mother she was not afraid to die, for she would be with two children she named. She and the two children she named were among the fatalities.

The premonitions about the coal slide were reported in the media, adding to the shock and grief. So many people had had an inkling of the disaster—why couldn't it have been prevented? Perhaps those lives could have been saved.

By January 1967, a British Premonitions Bureau was established to collect and screen specific early warnings in an effort to avert other disasters. In 1968, the Central Premonitions Bureau was established in New York City for the same purpose. Both bureaus struggled along for years on low budgets and with public relations obstacles. Most of the tips they received did not come to pass; those that did often were inaccurate in terms of time, rendering them equally useless. The Central Premonitions Bureau in New York was busy collecting reports at the time of the PSA and American Airlines Flight 191 disasters, yet they still happened anyway. During the 1980s, the bureaus ceased operation.

It may be that certain events, such as deaths of important people, major disasters, and so forth, are of such large scale and momentum that they are not likely to be halted. Events in our own personal arenas are easier to alter.

I believe that all future events are mutable, not fixed. Events are the probable outcome of forces in motion, which are in constant play and flux. Those present forces in motion are created by thoughts, intent, words, and actions. When focused and sustained, they gather enough momentum to bring about "a future." Any significant change in the course of the forces in motion will change the outcome. If enough people favor a war, for example—even if only in their thinking and sentiments—then they add to the momentum for war. A precognitive dream of impending war will not be enough to go against the collective forces in motion.

A precognition is a preview of an outcome of forces in motion. If forces change after a precognition is experienced, then the precognition will not be accurate. There is a point of no return with forces in motion: The momentum toward a probability gains sufficient strength to become a certainty. So much collective momentum has built that the event cannot be diverted or stopped. This may account for the clustering of widespread precognitions close to an actual event.

We are more likely to precognitively dream about negative events than positive events. I believe this is because of the intense emotions generated by horror, shock, sadness, and anger. Big events impacting a large number of people—or likely to receive widespread media coverage—will generate a collective force of emotion that is able to penetrate through the barriers of the consciousness of many people.

Does this mean that all precognitive dreaming is unhappy? Absolutely not. If you pay regular attention to your dreams, you will discover that precognitive elements appear frequently in them—"little precognitions" pertaining to more mundane affairs of daily life. These usually get glossed over by dreamers because they do not have the emotional punch of a large-scale disaster. We can train ourselves through dreamwork to be more attuned to precognition, and we can also become increasingly skilled at having precognitive dreams.

GUILT AND RESPONSE-ABILITY

Knowing an event is going to happen and not being able to do anything about it can create distress and guilt on the part of the dreamer. If a dream tells you that there is going be a "big plane crash," what do you do? Try to stop all planes from flying? Most people who have had precognitive dreams about unhappy events feel a burden of guilt. But if they attempted to alert others, they found they were dismissed or laughed off.

Individuals who do regular dreamwork and who have had periodic precognitive dreams have learned that they may have influence over events in their personal lives, but very little influence over large or global events. That doesn't mean we should ignore precognitive dreams, however. To borrow a phrase from the seer Edgar Cayce, we can act according to our "response-ability"— our ability to take positive action. Our "response-ability" is our responsibility. At the very least, we can offer prayer, an organizing force of tremendous power. Prayer was the peace that Paul T. made with troubling precognitive dreams about deaths:

> Since I was young, I've had occasional dreams from which I've awakened with a feeling of dread, knowing that someone known to me was going to pass over soon. Sometimes I would know who it was; other times I wouldn't, but I would get the same queer feeling I had in the dream when I got the news that they'd died. I never knew exactly when or how—just had a certainty

that it would happen no matter what. For a long time I hated these dreams because I felt so powerless. I couldn't make them go away. Finally I realized that God has a plan for everyone. Even though I didn't know why I should know these things in advance, perhaps I was being summoned or called as a witness, and what I should do was pray. Maybe my purpose is to help somehow with the passing.[1]

This resolution enabled Paul to deal with distressing dreams in a positive way—it was his appropriate "response-ability."

The next dreamer succeeded in repressing unpleasant precognitive dreams, but then realized her responsibility and "response ability":

I used to have dreams that came true. I never will forget one dream: I was riding on a raft down the rapids (never been in rapids). It was so real. A dear friend of mine and my family's was on the raft with me. He fell off, and I couldn't find him. I kept going down the river, and I came upon a tree full of black birds and I heard a voice saying, "Your friend won't be coming back. He's gone." Well, he died three months later. This was when I was eleven years old.

I am now fifty-one and have developed these abilities called psychic abilities, which were there all the time. I just didn't know at the time how to deal with it. My mind would race. I would hear things others didn't hear. I would automatically "tune in" to other people's pain and hurt and problems, to the point that it was uncomfortable to enjoy anything or to go anywhere. Over the years I have learned to put this gift to use in a positive way.

At one point in my life, it interfered with just everyday happenings, so I prayed that the Supreme Being would take the power away, and he did. Then one day one of my best friends came up missing. My family and best friends begged me to "tune in" (because they knew of my power) to this person and to see if I could find them or tell them anything. I then prayed as hard as I could for the Supreme Being to give me back those powers, and again I had them back and was able to locate the friend. He was safe and sound and everyone was happy.

So I started using these powers to help others. I helped the police find a missing baby, and I found a killer. I have always kept a low profile and have never advertised. "Tuning in" is very, very mentally draining . . . I put all I have into a reading, and if I don't feel up to it, I won't read.

Back to dreams: I can will myself to go anywhere in my dreams, find out information if needed, and even meet up with souls who have passed over and gather information from them. I have also "tuned in" to souls who have just passed over and knew how they died or were killed. The trick is to write it down immediately after waking up, or else it's forgotten.[2]

All dreamers should pay attention to her last words: Write down your dreams immediately in order to preserve details.

Jean Campbell, an experienced precognitive dreamer and founder of the World Peace Bridge, was among those who had a psi dream prior to the 9-11 attacks. She awoke on the morning of September 11 at about 5:30 A.M., recalling the following dream:

> I am standing in the control tower of an airport, maybe JFK International, watching a man talk somewhat frantically into a microphone. There is a feeling of something gone wrong.

Airplanes and control towers are not common in Campbell's dream lexicon, and she puzzled over the meaning—until the events unfolded a few hours later. Realizing that of course there was nothing she could have done herself to avert the attacks, Campbell contemplated her "response-ability."

> The response I had to my own precognitive dream was to realize how unresponsive I had become to the storm clouds gathering around me. . . . Why was I in the "control tower" . . . watching someone else try to avert disaster? This was, on the one hand, quite probably a "remote viewing" of something already taking place or about to take place. But why did my dreaming self choose this particular thing to see? The image has a personal message. Part of that message is a reminder to me that I am "in control" of particular aspects of my life, not only the present moment, but all of the moments extending from it. I do not need to stand by and watch. This is what the Buddhists call "mindfulness."

As a result, Campbell increased her activities to work with dreams, educate others about the importance of dreams, encourage dream reporting and dream sharing, and especially to unite dreamers around the planet in dream activism. Said Campbell:

> I know that, if we regularly interpret our dreams, work with our dreams, pay attention to our dreams, they can be a key to clearer precognition. . . . Since the terrorist attacks, I have committed myself more fully than ever to the dream. We, all of us, can spare ourselves the guilt of precognition by recognizing that what happened in dream reality around the September 11th disasters may have, in fact, been a wake-up call. What we do, once awake, remains to be seen.[3]

Most dreamers recognize the futility of central premonitions bureaus. Dream activism, however, is an entirely different approach to establish dreams as a valid tool for shaping the future. Chapter 14 discusses dream activism and its potential.

IMPROVING PRECOGNITIVE DREAMING

A woman dreams one night that a black bird flies into her bedroom window and crashes into the bed. Two days later, she is struck by a black Firebird car, which careens and crashes after striking her.

It appears that her dreaming mind tuned in to this future event and showed it to her, but the message was so heavily cloaked in symbols and an inaccurate scenario that it was useless as a warning and interesting only as a footnote in hindsight. The dream showed *elements* of the incident but not the incident itself. Would she have been able to avoid the accident if her dream had been more specific? What if she had incubated another dream asking for clarification and appropriate action?

Are there ways that dreamers can improve the accuracy of precognitive dreaming, so that future dreaming becomes a reliable and useful tool for the waking world? As we saw in the last chapter, these questions continually perplex dreamers.

I believe that precognitive dreaming is part of our "spiritual birthright," an ability intended for us to use with wisdom and skill. We simply haven't figured out yet how to cultivate and manage this ability, in part because we still have an incomplete understanding of the full nature of consciousness. I believe we will learn how to dream the future accurately and reliably, as part of our normal range of dreaming. Significant advances have already been made by dream pioneers and dream activists.

DO WE ALREADY KNOW THE FUTURE?

One of those pioneers is Ingo Swann, a psychic of exceptional ability who led the groundbreaking research on remote viewing, established at the Stanford Research Institute in California in the 1970s. Swann's natural ability was present in childhood. At age twenty-nine, he experienced a sudden increase in *future-seeing* dreams (a term he prefers to precognitive). At first he thought the dreams were reflections of what was going on in his subconscious; but soon after the dreams, he would encounter situations that were nearly identical to those he had dreamed. He began researching future-seeing.

His research led him to conclude that we *already know the future*. (Others say we can know a *probable* future.) The future, or a probable future, foreshadows itself, and everything in the now is in the process of unfolding into the future. But we resist knowing, for a variety of reasons. One is fear—fear that we will see something we do not like and will not be able to change. One is religion—various religions teach that looking into the future is "the devil's work." One is ignorance—we think only "special" people have the gift of future-seeing.

Despite the resistance, we go to great lengths to try to learn the future, but we often go looking in the wrong places. We seek out people we think have "the gift," but we—via science—discredit and deride the gift.

According to Swann, there are exceptionally few people who are born with a gift of future-seeing who need no training. Most of those who are gifted have trained themselves through practice, practice, practice, to achieve a control over the ability. The majority of people are likely to have spontaneous future-seeing experiences that are meaningful and accurate—and perhaps frightening because they are not understood or are feared.

THE KEY TO THE PSI IS IN THE IMAGE

Future-seeing, or precognition, happens in a variety of ways in different states of consciousness. Research by parapsychologist Louisa Rhine showed that psi in general is more likely to happen in dreams than in waking consciousness. Why is that? Because our dreams are the ideal and natural medium for the language of psi.

People often wonder why dreams communicate in images that seem bizarre. If they have important messages, people say, then why can't dreams just speak to us in plain language? In other words, in words?

Dreams are formed by image—and also by emotional tone and sensory phenomena—because image is the most basic, fundamental, universal communication. Image holds more information than a word; it reaches deeper into consciousness and activates the intuition. What's more, our ability for psi perception manifests in image, senses, and emotions. Thus, our very function of dreaming is tailor-made for psi. All of us have the capacity to see the future simply because we dream.

According to Swann, the inner, mind-dynamic processes that transcend time cannot be captured by printed words, for the phenomena are nonverbal and even preverbal. "Thus, they are best understood by attempting to build images of them on paper in the form of diagrams or sketches," says Swann in his book *Your Nostradamus Factor: Accessing Your Innate Ability to See into the Future.* He advocates drawing our dreams and intuitions to enhance and manage our future-seeing capabilities.

PSI DREAMING AND REMOTE VIEWING

Another pioneer is Dale E. Graff, an experienced remote viewer, psi dreamer, and the founder and former director of the U.S. government's Stargate project of applied remote viewing. In the mid-1970s, Graff became acquainted with remote viewing research while working in aeronautics engineering and physics for the U.S. Air Force's Foreign Technology Division (FTD). The research at the Stanford Research Institute was nearly out of funding. Graff was instrumental in its continuation with FTD help and became the contract manager. Later he moved to the Defense Intelligence Agency, where he continued work in remote viewing, which led to the establishment of *Stargate*—a term he coined—the government's activities concerning the use of remote viewing for intelligence gathering. Graff also has an exceptionally sharp capability for psi dreaming, which he has explored, researched, and documented for many years.

Graff holds a high vision for the potential for precognitive dreaming:

I believe that precognitive dreams can have action potential for avoidance or prevention depending on circumstances, especially for personal situations. I also believe that they have response potential for non-personal situations, such as approaching accidents involving someone else, including terrorist attacks as the precognitive dreams prior to September 11 illustrated. But, to whom can the suspected warning be given even if they had very specific locational and timing data?

The first step is to provide a forum for people to submit their suspected precognitive dreams and a means for them to be integrated and evaluated. Patterns may emerge. Even if specifics are only fragmentary, it is my belief that with intent, specific strategies and practice, eventually the precognitive dream will become easier to recognize and will have accurate information. If several individuals—the precognitive dream team—are working together over time then the combined results should become reliable enough for action consideration in certain circumstances. These teams might be set up for specific geophysical locations.

But even if a precognitive dream team or teams becomes sufficiently proficient, similar to what I experience working with remote viewing teams, then what? How should the data be evaluated and how prepared in a combined summary? Then to whom should it be provided and how? This is a hurdle, of course, especially since the range of precognitions is vast. But I believe this: If good track records can be established, with naturally occurring situations and appropriate simulated projects, then the data users will appear. Word will get out. Even one successful and documented result will be all the advertising needed.

Of course there are many other issues. One of them is how to, or who can, take on such a coordinating and integrating role. There are challenges in such an enterprise, but the perceived difficulty should not be cause for not trying.[4]

THE PROCESSING OF PSI DATA

Research in telepathic dreaming and in remote viewing shows that individuals process psi data differently. We may be good at picking up on shapes, configurations, colors, and themes, but may misidentify these things as they are processed into impressions and images. What happens then is that we resonate with the closest facsimile in our memory, according to Graff. Some remote viewers in the Stargate and Stanford Research Institute programs could accurately see objects, but if the objects were unfamiliar to them—there were no correlates in the person's memory bank—they were likely to interpret them incorrectly. One example cited by Graff is the remote viewer whose target was the Superdome stadium in New Orleans. He sketched a huge dome, but labeled it a flying saucer.

"For some individuals, the basic psi 'signal' seems to be first processed in the brain's visual centers and then is linked with the linear, logical part of the brain that names and attaches meaning," says Graff. "For others, the psi signal may carry meaning directly to the interpretive region of the brain."[5]

This processing may account for the black bird/Firebird-dream mentioned earlier. The dreaming mind may have picked up on an actual black Firebird, but if the car brand was unknown to the dreamer, it became misidentified as a dream image of a black bird.

Graff observes differences between conscious state psi (CSP) and dreaming state psi (DSP) in terms of how visual information is presented. In conscious state psi, such as remote viewing, impressions come sequentially and are often fragmented; they must be reassembled correctly in order to be accurate. In dreaming psi—such as tuning in to a target image either telepathically or via remote viewing—the scene is scanned and the dream presents a story or movie with all sort of "psi props," which may have been assembled even before the dreamer went to sleep. Graff says that intention can help to reduce errors in psi dreaming by directing the psi portion of dreams to the finale. This technique, he says, has worked well for him. In addition, strong emotion may help to energize the psi process and improve accuracy.

Cognitive studies and split brain research are likely to help us understand more about processing of psi data. As a result, we are likely to develop entirely new ways of dreamwork. We may be called upon to consider our dream images in increasingly subjective ways, such as by sense perception rather than by rational identification. For example, a cup may not be a "cup," but be described as "a shallow container with a round opening, shiny white, apparently molded or cast, and hard like china or ceramic, smooth and cool to the touch, no obvious odor, a taste reminiscent of concrete." Think of the many ways that associations can lead you with the second type of description!

Perhaps we will also learn how to use remote viewing techniques on precognitive dreams, in order to pinpoint them more accurately in time and space.

DREAMLAB #22

Attuning to Precognition in Dreams

You've probably had at least one or several precognitive dreams in the past. Perhaps you knew upon awakening that what you dreamed was going to happen in waking life. Perhaps the precognition became apparent only after the fact.

Many seemingly precognitive dreams contain "collateral psi": dream elements that after the fact can be related to an event, but are not direct hits or are not in themselves sufficient to constitute specific psi about a specific incident. For example, two nights prior to the Columbia shuttle accident, one dreamer recorded a dream with the following scene (among others):

> I am in a park picking up litter and putting it into a big plastic bag. There seems to be lots of it laying all over the place. Other people are doing it, too.[6]

A chill ran through her when she saw on television the recovery volunteers going out to comb the countryside for shuttle debris—she was reminded of her dream. The dream scene by itself could not have been identified in advance as a precognition about Columbia; nor had the dreamer awakened feeling anything unusual or amiss. Was it just a "coincidence" that this dream occurred prior to the accident? The dreamer felt certain that she had dreamed in advance an element of the accident.

To attune to precognition in your dreaming, take these steps:

1. Identify your own precognitive signature.
If you have had precognitive dreams, revisit your description of them in your dream journal. Were there any unusual features about the dreams? Did you experience any strong or unusual emotions or body sensations in the dreams or upon awakening? Experienced dreamers soon learn that precognitive dreams have their own special signature, unique to each dreamer. There may be an unusual color or "atmosphere" in the dream, a certain emotional tone, or perhaps even a body sensation, such as an uneasy gut.

2. Examine time frames.
How far in advance of the event did you have the dream? Most precognitive dreams happen very close to an event, though some can happen weeks or months in advance. Time frames may vary, but you might see certain patterns in your own dreams.

3. Look for collateral psi.
If you recognize your dream after an event occurs, go back to your dream journal and look for collateral psi, small elements that seem to be hits. Do you see any patterns, such as in types of dream images or themes, emotions, or time frames?

4. Train your dreaming mind.
You can train your dreaming mind to receive information about the future that is meaningful to you by doing dream incubation.

Experiment with time frames, asking to see something useful about the coming week or coming month. You can also do dream incubation to ask to see an important event that will be headline news.

Asking to see the future should not be undertaken if you are easily distressed or psychologically or emotionally fragile. Remember, many events shaping up in probability will be beyond your ability to influence.

5. Maintain response-ability.
Make a commitment to use your dreams as a tool for positive change and growth. Join a dreamwork community in your area or online and share your experiences with other dreamers. Your contributions will help others validate their own experiences, and theirs will help you validate your experiences.

Alan Vaughan counseled people to learn to talk about their dreams and understand them, instead of being frightened by them. This stimulates dreams to provide helpful images. Dreams that once might have been terrifying then can be seen in a more positive light.

DREAM LAB #23
Reducing Noise

One of the main difficulties in accurate psi dreaming is "noise": day residues, psi props, and other distractions that flood dreams. Every day we are saturated with violence in the media—and that's just the news. In addition, we have violent books, violent movies and television shows, violent games, and pop songs with violent themes. How can we separate out the day residue from these stressful factors and discern true precognitive dreams of *real* disaster and violence?

One technique is to "preprocess" day residues prior to sleep. In his book *Voluntary Controls,* Jack Schwarz gives a process called "reverie," a guided daydream intended to reduce "noise" and facilitate better and deeper sleep. Dreamworkers who use this or similar "daily review" techniques report a marked decrease in day residue "noise" and enhanced precognitive and lucid dreaming.

Here's how it works:

1. Prior to sleep, take a comfortable position for meditation and use the breath, such as the Intuitive Breath, to relax.

2. Close your eyes and make a mental screen. Project onto it your day's activities. Allow impressions to arise spontaneously.

3. Objectively examine the impressions and your thoughts and emotions. Consciously release stressful and negative ones.

4. When you feel calm and centered, engage in your dreamwork for the night.

DREAM LAB #24

Wordless Dreamwork

This exercise stimulates intuitive processing of dream data. Try this for a month.

1. Instead of writing word descriptions of your dreams, record them only as images.

2. Do dreamwork by image: Record all your associations with additional images.

3. Meditate on the images.

4. To obtain more information about a dream, use an image as an incubation for dreaming.

5. After a month, review your journal of images and write a report of your experience. This will help to integrate your right-brain experience with left-brain linear thought.

QUESTIONS TO CONSIDER

1. How have you changed the way you think and process information in general?

2. What changes occurred in your dreaming? In your ability to understand a dream?

3. What changes occurred in your intuitive ability in general? Did you experience an increase or changes in intuitive perception during waking consciousness?

4. What changes occurred in terms of psi dreaming?

DREAM LAB # 25

Sensory Dreaming

Expand your ability to understand your dreams by redefining key elements in them as sensory descriptions rather than labels.

1. Take a significant dream from your journal and underline all the key nouns.

2. Redefine each one of them as a sensory experience, involving all the senses if possible.

3. Follow and write down associations that intuitively arise.

4. Do additional waking dream meditations or dream incubations as needed to gain more information.

QUESTIONS TO CONSIDER

1. What new avenues of thinking, or what new insights arise from experiencing your dream images through all the senses?

2. How do your new insights change your perspective on the present?

3. What bearing do your new insights have on the unfolding future?

CHAPTER 1 4

Dream Activism

WE OFTEN DREAM of having a better life or being in a better place. Such dreams seem more like wishes than blueprints for action, but we dream them anyway in our free time, and create in our imagination an ideal life or world. And then we let the dreams go.

But what if we could actually, literally dream a new world into being? Not through idle wishes and fantasies, but through real dreams that we create and experience during sleep?

It's not impossible. Human beings have been doing it for centuries. As we saw in the previous chapter, the terrorist events of September 11 increased interest in dreams—not only precognitive dreaming, but the use of dreams proactively for social good. Dream activism is not an idea or theory—it is fact, a growing movement in the dreaming community that is reaching out into the general population. In this post–9-11 world, it is more important than ever that we join together to use one of the most important tools of our consciousness—dreams—to change the world for the better. Dream activism builds on ancient dream wisdom and experience.

THE MANIFESTING POWER OF DREAMS

Dreams have always been seen as a direct link to the spiritual plane—a hot line to the gods or God. Since ancient times, dreams have been interpreted for messages of divine prophecy. Proactive dreaming through incubation has been used as a communications link for petitioning divine intervention in healing and problem-solving. People have used dreams to bring specific changes into the physical world.

The Greeks were terrific proactive dreamers, as we have seen in the chapters related to healing in dreams. They were not the only people, however, to engage in proactive dreaming. Programmed dreaming, or dream incubation, has been practiced around the world. Today many people use proactive dreaming for personal affairs and for creativity and inspiration. Science, invention, and the arts boast many individuals who brought something new into the world as a direct result of their dreams.

Anyone who has had a creative dream breakthrough understands that the dreaming mind has a power we do not experience during waking consciousness. It is not fettered by time or space, or self-imposed limitations. It reaches into the subtle plane of the unmanifest potential, where unlimited ideas and inspirations are born. Our dreams are filled with magic and creativity. What's more, our dreams charge us up with energy for creating what we dream.

DREAMS AND THE COLLECTIVE ORDER

Dreams are part of our soul consciousness. If we accept the idea that everything is interconnected—in accordance with the fundamentals of mystical philosophy—then the consciousness of every individual is connected to other consciousnesses, which forms a collective. Carl G. Jung was the first to recognize the collective unconsciousness and its importance in dreamwork, but it is collective *consciousness* that is important in everyday waking reality. Our thoughts and intent have the power to affect physical events that play out in the world. If enough people are angry, then war, dissension, and terrorism are created. If enough people are peaceful and loving, then harmony is created. It's order versus chaos, depending on the critical mass we create with our thoughts, emotions, and intentions.

FIELD CONSCIOUSNESS

Field consciousness provides an integrative view of the universe. It addresses the underlying unity of all things—fields held together and unbounded by space and time. These fields have the ability to organize matter on a large scale—a collective psychokinesis, or PK. "Global consciousness" and "group mind" are other ways of describing aspects of field consciousness.

Like the paranormal nature of dreams, field consciousness is not a new idea. The concept of an underlying unity of all things is part of our most ancient mystical philosophies. In quantum mechanics the universe is held together by fields of probabilities that do not exist in space and time, but keep all things interconnected in such a way that a change in one place instantly affects another place without any exchange of energy. Thus, the consciousness of a group can affect physical matter, even at a distance.

The Maharishi Mahesh Yogi, the founder of Transcendental Meditation (TM), was among the first to demonstrate this idea to a modern audience. In TM, a person achieves transcendental consciousness by meditating on a mantra. According to the Maharishi, if a minimum of the square root of 1 percent of the world's population collectively did TM, the coherence of their brain waves would result in a drop of crime, illness, accidents, and aggression. The Maharishi International University has tested this hypothesis with large groups of thousands of meditators, with significant results, including decreases in crime, accidents, medical emergencies, armed conflict, and other problems. TM researchers say they have replicated results affirming this hypothesis in at least forty-two studies. Sociologists, however, criticize the results, saying that variables are too difficult to control.

In 2002 the Maharishi announced his plan to open centers for TM meditators to practice on world consciousness in order to cancel war and terrorism. Using the theory of "constructive interference," the Maharishi hopes that local meditation centers will have a collective psi effect to bring peace and elevation to disturbed world consciousness.

THE GLOBAL MIND

Meanwhile, scientific evidence points to the existence of a global mind. The Global Consciousness Project (GCP), an international effort launched in 1998, collects random events generator (REG) data from forty continuously running monitors around the world. The random events generators (sometimes referred to as random numbers generators) produce a steady stream of unpredictable bits—sort of like electronic coin-flipping. The resulting data is measured against chance.

The working premise of GCP is that if a sufficient number of individual consciousnesses combine, they can produce a global presence. If so, then the REG data will deviate from expected random behavior. Their results do show that group consciousness seems to produce nonlocal fields. For example, major events that engage the attention of millions of people around the world—such as the death and funeral of Princess Diana, the Olympics, and even the O. J. Simpson trial—produced unusual data.

According to information published by the GCP, science hasn't yet proved the existence of a global mind; however, data collected after the terrorist disasters showed that "if there is such a thing as a global consciousness . . . it was moved by the events of September 11, 2001."

Interestingly, the shift in the REG data began *before* the attacks. This phenomenon has been observed in some other cases, as well. The GCP, however, cautions that not enough is known about this effect in order to use the data for such practical applications as early warnings.

I think this pre-event coherence of global mind also manifests in mass precognitive dreams and other premonitions, as individual consciousnesses tune in to forces in motion.

A NEW WORLDVIEW

It's only a matter of time before science acknowledges what mysticism has long known: There *is* a global mind, and we all participate in it through our thoughts, intent, will, words, actions, and dreams. Dean Radin, one of the leading scientists participating in the GCP as well as similar research at Princeton University, states in his book *The Conscious Universe:*

> These studies . . . suggest that a previously unsuspected cause of global violence and aggression may literally be the chaotic, malevolent thoughts of large numbers of people around the world. For example, the idea of a jihad, a holy war against infidels, which is fervently maintained by millions throughout the world, may not only *directly* (e.g., through terrorist acts) but also *indirectly* disrupt the social order around the world. By contrast, peaceful protests such as those embodied by Gandhi and Martin Luther King, which fostered noble intentions among groups, may have been successful not only for psychological reasons, but also for physical reasons that we are only now beginning to glimpse.[1]

Radin's book, published in 1997, foreshadows in a chilling way the state of world consciousness and events post–September 11.

If an event can affect global mind, then global mind can affect events. The GCP and other studies have significant ramifications for the responsibility each of us has about the state of our consciousness. Tomorrow's world is the direct result of today's consciousness. We see and receive what we expect. Individual thoughts collect in pools and take on momentum.

Global mind is created whenever groups of people collect to share a common purpose. Global meditation days for world peace and international prayer days use the power of collective intent to reduce chaos and establish the order of healing, peace, and harmony.

Dreaming can be part of this broad effort, too. Like our thoughts and emotions, our dreams have tremendous creative power to shape the world. Our dreams can reveal the likely outcomes of the forces in motion *and also set forces in motion.* We dream not just for and about ourselves, but in a larger "dream pool" as well. If we can use our dreams to influence the course of our personal life, then we can use our dreams collectively to influence the course of global life. Group dreaming toward a common theme, such as peace, also can establish a coherence of brain waves that in turn could affect the physical environment—perhaps by subtly altering the actions taken by individuals.

WHAT'S THE REAL LESSON?

In the past, we have sought to harness precognition as a way to manage events. But our precognitions are too often hard to recognize and not entirely on target because there is too much chaos and dissonance on the global mind level.

Instead of only trying to use precognition to identify and react to early warnings—which may or may not be on target—we should shift our attention to include a proactive use of global consciousness. If each person truly practiced the moral precepts of the world's religions and engaged in daily prayer and meditation, we would create a more enlightened global mind that would have no room for fear, hate, and violence.

Increasing global mind unity also might significantly change our ability to accurately anticipate the future, through premonitions, precognitive dreams, and intuition.

The experiments of the GCP are made possible largely because global media—especially television—can connect people around the planet quickly and simultaneously. High tech will continue to build global mind field consciousness. It's happening—and it's up to each of us whether global mind will be used for good or for ill.

DREAMING THE AWAKENED HEART

At the time of the terrorist attacks on the World Trade Center and the Pentagon, I was preparing lectures and workshops based on my book, *A Miracle in Your Pocket,* which explores the subject of miracles and how to cultivate "miracle mind consciousness." The untapped power of global mind was very much on *my* mind. I also saw dreams as an important force in global mind.

As early as 1982, global experiments were being conducted in dreaming. One notable experiment that year was developed by Bill Stimson, then editor of the *Dream Network Bulletin.* Nine groups in the United States and Europe incubated dreams on the topic of a World Dream and then met on the winter solstice to share results. Author Linda Lane Magallón reported in her book *Mutual Dreaming*:

> The similarity of images in the networking process was impressive. Themes included a recognition of the importance of the era in which they lived, a realization of the choices they faced, and great hope for the future. There were three mentions of animal and intercultural themes, four references to water, five to transformations or new beginnings, and five to flight or upward movement.[2]

Nineteen years on, it seemed to me that it was time for dreamworkers around the world to unite again, this time in a sustained effort to dream a new and better world into being—to realize the "great hope for the future" envisioned in 1982.

After the terrorist attacks, I contacted my friend Rita Dwyer, a cofounder and the former executive director of the Association for the Study of Dreams (ASD), the leading international organization for the study and education of dreams, to discuss how the dream community and dreamworkers could create a global mind to manifest healing and beneficial change. Together we developed the idea to present at the annual ASD conference.

Our plan was the creation of a central dream affirmation to be meditated on and incubated on the same night every month by as many dreamworkers as possible. The affirmation would be directed to benefit something on a large scale—the collective good. It would stimulate thought on a collective level to inspire people with ideas, initiatives, and drive to manifest real and positive change in the world.

At the next ASD conference at Tufts University in Medford, Massachusetts, in 2002, a group of ASDers convened for our workshop. We discussed many affirmations that were good, such as for peace, for healing, for the end of poverty and hunger, and so on. One thing quickly became clear: While people may generally agree in their desire to help make the world a better place, they want to go about it in different ways. We all have causes to which we feel drawn.

The solution to this proved to be a general "activation" affirmation that would unite many people in dreams toward a common goal—improving conditions in the world—while allowing individuals to emphasize specific priorities.

The dream activism affirmation that we created is:

*Tonight I dream the awakened heart . . . Today I awaken
the dreaming heart.*

In recognition of the impact of the terrorist events of September 11, we set the night of the eleventh every month as the time for dreamworkers everywhere to incubate this affirmation with the focused power of the collective dreaming mind. However, on the first practice the following month, many in the group felt that the night of the tenth is more appropriate, for it allows the healing messages to come forth on the day of the eleventh. Dream activists can use either or both nights, as well as any other time that seems appropriate.

The affirmation is used in the following manner. Sometime during the day of the tenth, or prior to sleep that night, focus on the affirmation and set your intent for the dreaming mind to provide a meaningful dream. If you desire, also think of a specific goal for the common good that you would like to help realize. It may be for freedom, for the relief of hunger, for education, for cessation of war—whatever powerfully moves you. Intensity of emotion is important in order to create and manifest, so choose something that generates strong feelings within you.

Prior to sleep, concentrate on the affirmation, "Tonight I dream the awakened heart," inviting guidance, inspiration, and ideas to be presented in your dreams. The following day, record your dreams and interpret them with the help of meditation on the second part of the affirmation, "Today I awaken the dreaming heart."

In this fashion, your dreams—one of your best connections to the spiritual realms and to our own inner wisdom—will show you what you need to do, as individuals and as part of humanity, in order to bring about the harmonious world we envision.

It is important to be open and to have no set expectations about results. Major change can take place with many small steps. You may be guided to do small things in your own personal spheres of life. The awakened heart affirmation assumes a faith in spiritual guidance as it needs to be given. The affirmation is like a dream prayer.

Don't be surprised if you dream the affirmation dream a night or two before or after the tenth. Members of the ASD Dream Activism group experience a range of dreams before and after the actual night of incubation. Dreams are outside of time and space.

We report our dreams and discuss them on-line. It's always amazing how our individual dreams mesh together. The sharing of insights stimulates breakthroughs of awareness.

THE EFFECTS OF DREAM ACTIVISM

For our first effort, the dream activism affirmation stimulated a lot of dreaming among the participants. Some themes that emerged concerned group cooperation, the assertion of people for their rights, renewal and rebirth, identification of global needs, sharing of abundance, the overcoming of fear, funding for peace, and the emergence of new projects of a healing nature. Discussion of our dreams in turn stimulated more dreaming.

Dwyer dreamed of a process called "The Tree of Life":

I am at a meeting with many others, and there is a place where on a table people leave food as if in offering to others. Much of it is fruit or single portions of finger food, and I pick up a beautiful luscious peach and place

money in a container, sort of an honor-system arrangement. We can take what we want and pay what we
want, or nothing at all, for what is left is with no expectation of monetary return. It's just left as a gift to the
others. Those who have funds to pay leave something
for the privilege of eating what is there, and that money
in turn is used for those in need in some way in which
money is essential. A kind of loop . . . the process is
called The Tree of Life.

Curtiss Hoffman reported several dreams over several
nights, including the following:

I am with a group of esoteric workers, very possibly this
group, in a city (possibly NYC). We are discussing ways
of alleviating conditions of political repression in various parts of the world. One of our number shows us a
political cartoon which they have drawn and had published in a newspaper. It shows four people representing
the oppressed rising up and demanding their rights. One
is a Tibetan; one is a Chinese peasant in a coolie hat
who was displaced by the Three Gorges Dam Project;
one is a central Asian peasant displaced by a trans-
Asian gas pipeline project, and the fourth is a tall blond
American with arms folded over his chest, with a sign
around his neck which says, "Victim of Fear, 9/11."
There is a strong sense of courage as the group views
this scene.

As the group evolved, some themes recurred, as noted by
scribe Janice Ryalls: survival, self-defense, joy, and spiritual heal-

ing. The emergence of strong spiritual figures entered many dreams, guiding, healing, and awakening dreamers to the higher truths of love, charity, faith, and inner peace. Understandably, many of the dreams have dealt with the threat of violence or violent acts carried out in the dreams; the activism forum has provided ways to examine how we consciously and unconsciously perpetuate the cycle of violence, and steps we can take to heal it.

On a brighter side, many dreams have portrayed beautiful images: a "Peaceable Kingdom" where all creatures peacefully coexist, a sacred site in the woods, spiritual symbols, meditating monks, and so on. These images contain healing energy, and they hold the "great hope for the future," to paraphrase Magallón once again.

Perhaps the most outstanding continuing themes are self-discovery and introspection. Said Ryalls, "Though many of the dreams have global settings, they still seem centered in dealing with self finding Self, reminding us all to continue our own inner work in an effort to create peace within which will then expand to peace throughout . . . our families, communities, countries, the world. . . . We all seem to agree that for any peace to emanate outward, there has to be peace within. As we search for this peace, there is a sense that this will be an ongoing project for us all."

The establishment of inner peace and harmony in order to have outer peace and harmony is one of the hardest lessons to learn. It is far too easy to blame disharmony on an adversary and maintain the attitude that when the adversary is eradicated, disharmony will vanish and harmony will take its place. Dream activism has made the powerful point to participants that change must happen first within.

In one of Ryalls's dreams, a sickly white dove flies in

through the window. She tries to feed it, but it doesn't want what is offered. She and the dove have a conversation, in which she learns the dove's name, Baronca. In commenting on this dream, Curtiss Hoffman noted that Beruchah is the Hebrew word for blessing. This resonated with Ryalls, who realized the importance of reevaluating and adjusting her own attitudes and centering herself in prayer and meditation, which will feed the white dove and nurture her own inner peace.

A few months later, Ryalls had another white dove dream that was significantly different:

THE PEACE BOX

This dream is an image. A white bakery box with its lid open. Beautiful white doves fly out and upward one at a time. The sense is that the doves will keep on coming out one at a time without end.

Comments: This image gave me a great sense of peace just with the beauty of it. In writing it, I thought of all the individuals who are sending out peace everywhere. Each prayer, project, ribbon, meditation is sending hope out into the universe. I think this does definitely depict some healing that has taken place within my psyche. I think it is so amazing how a dream can be both personal and universal!

WORLD DREAMS PEACE BRIDGE

One of the charter members of the ASD Dream Activism group is Jean Campbell, a longtime ASD member who launched another important international dream activism program, the World Dreams Peace Bridge. Campbell is an experienced precognitive dreamer—her precognitive dream about September 11 is detailed in the previous chapter—and believes in the creative power of dreams. Her work in group dreaming, which she conducted in her capacity as former director of the Poseidia Institute, a consciousness research organization, produced dramatic results in dream synchronicities and mutual dreaming.

At the time of the attacks, she was developing the ASD's On-line Guide to International Dreamwork and was moderating the ASD on-line bulletin board.

The first wave of reaction came in reports of precognitive dreams and dreamers' anguish and guilt over not being able to prevent the tragedies. In the second wave of reaction, dreamers expressed frustration at seeing but not changing events. Campbell reflected back on her precognitive dream about being in the control tower of an airport. She was further inspired by a dream of a single, lighted candle reported by ASDer Victoria Quinton in Australia. It reminded Campbell of a childhood memory of watching Bishop Fulton J. Sheen stride onto his television program, while offstage a chorus sang, "If everyone lit just one little candle, what a bright world this would be." What if these dreams were urging dreamers to become proactive instead of reactive—to literally take control and light a candle against the darkness?

Campbell sent out one hundred e-mails worldwide asking dreamers to participate in an experiment "to dream up some world peace." The response was immediate and enthusiastic. Since then the World Dreams Peace Bridge has served as an online international dream lab and dream journal, logging more than one thousand e-mails a month. And though the focus is on creating peace, the dreaming touches other areas as well. At the suggestion of Rita Hildebrant, the group adopted as their informal theme song, "Let there be peace on Earth," a church hymn familiar to many.

Part of the World Dreams Peace Bridge is the Peace Train Project, which came into being as a result of a dream had by Jeremy Seligson on July 26, 2002, in Korea:

> I am traveling with a group of friends in the countryside in the middle of nowhere. We're near a village. I've wandered off on my own, but a responsible young man fetches me and says, "A train has come."
>
> I am in line with the group for lunch at a cafeteria. While in line, Ada Haroni (the founder of IFLAC—International Forum for Literature and Culture of Peace) comes over to me and smiling, says, "We are more successful than the other peace group because it is not so well organized. Our group always gets together on time when it's time to move on."
>
> Our long black locomotive travels across the country to Washington, D.C., where outside the Capitol steps it is applauded by President Gore and many others dressed in suits. A large white banner around the smokestack reads, PEACE TRAIN. This makes me joyful. I leap high in the air and float partway down a hill, landing on my feet. Others around me are surprised I could do that.

The Peace Train Project stimulates art, creativity, and discussion on the theme of world peace and includes an outreach to children.

BENEFITS OF DREAM ACTIVISM

Participants in dream activism experience telepathic dreaming, precognitive dreaming, lucid and OBE dreaming, and mutual dreaming. These occur in any group that dreams together, but when played on an international stage for world peace, the interconnections of mind, dream, and heart take on a new significance and power.

Other benefits are:

• *Our dreams show us what we as individuals can realistically do to make positive change for the world.*

The creative process initiated by dreams continues in the intuition and waking consciousness. Changes can include shifts in attitudes and social consciousness; greater identification with, and empathy for, peoples around the planet; and specific ideas for action.

The World Dreams Peace Bridge conducts special meditations in response to participants' dreams, especially of a possible precognitive nature. "We may change the future without knowing it," said Campbell.

• *Our dreams inspire us to act, and without action there is no manifestation. Dreams also help us feel empowered in a good process.*

The following dream reported by Curtiss Hoffman has a bearing on dream activism:

I turn on the TV news in my car, at the intersection of I-495 and Route 140 in Franklin, Massachusetts. Evidently, Bush has recently given a speech about the need

for funding peace projects in the Middle East. A series of
young reporters repeat sections of this speech, alternat-
ing male and female, one after another. Bush said that he
was so concerned about the prospect of young Americans being sent off to war—his own sons included—that
he has donated $500,000 of his own money to this
cause, and he urged all Americans to do likewise. I react
to this with a mix of cynicism and hope: I know that
very few Americans, after all, could afford to give that
much; but it is an "act of international wonder!"

Hoffman commented: "It is obvious to me that little knots
of people are forming all over the world who are bringing
forth a transformed consciousness, getting together in groups
to share dreams and other activities, generally leaderless and
independent, almost like al-Qaeda cells, with one crucial difference: It is our mission to perpetrate acts of international
WONDER!!!"

> • *The collective dreaming lifts collective consciousness up to
> a nobler level, which in turn influences the level of waking
> consciousness and shifts more weight toward the positive
> critical mass, a point at which physical reality shifts in re-
> sponse.*

The ASD dream activists quickly saw how the group's
dreams related to their own dreams and also influenced
their dreams. The dream shared by Hoffman was an influence on Janice Ryalls's "awakened heart" dream, which occurred about three weeks later. "I was thinking about
Bush's contribution and request for each of us to give
$500,000," said Ryalls, the scribe for the dream activist

group. "To me the number five is the number for 'change,' and zeroes are like exclamation marks. So, if it were my dream, I would be realizing that for peace to take place in the Middle East, there has to be major change and we are all invited to be a part of it!" Here are the highlights of Ryalls's dream:

I'm with a group of people who are showing President Bush around a house. Bush does not look like Bush—he is taller and more handsome, definitely charismatic. Amongst the people are reporters and others who feel like family. We are now in the basement, which is a family room set up with chairs for everyone to sit in. Three chairs are set up at the head of the room, and then there are three rows of other chairs along one wall for everyone else.

Everyone there has been asking him question after question during the tour, all politically oriented, which is something he puts up with day in and day out. I have had an opportunity during the tour to speak with him also, but rather than ask him political questions, I have spoken with him more heart-to-heart, as if he were a friend.

I now take a seat at the end of the front row of chairs. [There follows a scene with puppies and baby sea turtles whose hairy spider-like legs look like three stairs from the sides.]

Now I look up to see President Bush looking right at me. He is gesturing for me to come sit right next to him on his right side, which surprises me! I feel honored and accept his invitation.

Once I'm next to him, he looks at me and says, "I've sent peace to three people here, and you are one of them." He has sent the peace to us through his eyes. I feel a lot of healing energy in my heart when he tells me this! He then gestures with his head towards a coworker of mine, intimating that he is one of the others he has sent peace to. He doesn't share with me who the third person is.

In the last part of the dream, Janice shares the Bush dream with Rita Dwyer. The number three is prominent in it; three occurs frequently in Rita's dreams, too.

BECOME A DREAM ACTIVIST

Sigmund Freud's book *Dreams: The Royal Road to the Unconscious* guided dreamers of the twentieth century into explorations of their own inner spaces through personal dreamwork. In the twenty-first century, we will push beyond our personal spheres to use dream activism as a force for social change. If enough of us unite in consciousness, we can make dramatic changes. The collective is only as powerful, as strong, and as good as the contributions made to it by individuals. Whether we unite to create chaos or order—terror or wonder—depends on each one of us.

Information on ASD Dream Activism, the World Dreams Peace Bridge, and the Global Consciousness Project can be found in the appendix.

DREAM LAB #26

The Awakened Heart

On the night of the tenth of every month, join dream activists around the world by incubating the following affirmation:

Tonight I dream the awakened heart.

In the morning, use this affirmation as you do your dreamwork on your results:

Today I awaken the dreaming heart.

Join the on-line forum—see the appendix—to contribute to a global sharing.

This affirmation can be used any time for individual dreamwork or for your own local dream groups.

CHAPTER 15

PK Dreaming

OUR PRECOGNITIVE DREAMING and dream activism to create change will unfold a new level of visionary dreaming: "PK dreaming."

PK dreaming, or psychokinetic dreaming, is the use of dreams to effect change in the material world. Psychokinesis, the ability to use mind to influence matter, has been well demonstrated in psychical research. Through precognitive dreaming, we will be able to alter circumstances and change forces in motion. Through dream activism, we will be able to create a group mind dynamism to establish a more harmonious field consciousness, which in turn will affect the playing out of events. We will be able to do these things personally and also participate in a larger, more global force.

Actually, we are already engaging in PK dreaming simply by paying attention to our dreams and making changes as a result:

changes in attitudes, activities, decisions, and so forth. All of these alter the course of unfolding events.

Now we stand on the threshold of something far more significant: the use of, and contribution of, our dreams to the greater whole of humanity.

WHAT IS PSYCHOKINESIS?

We tend to think of PK as the exaggerated abilities of fictional characters to mentally throw people and large objects about and exert mysterious forces upon things. PK actually is part of daily life. It's a force behind healing, miracles, and manifestation. It's one of our "abilities of the future"—we are learning more and more about how PK operates and what it affects.

Psychokinesis literally means "to move at a distance by soul or lifebreath." Essentially PK is the use of your thought and will to make some sort of changes in the physical world. In scientific experiments, researchers have studied subjects who can affect the roll of dice, the sequence of numbers in a random generator machine, the temperature in a room, the physical properties of water, the movement of compass points, and so on. Some research investigates the ability of the human mind to affect subatomic particles and time itself.

PK happens both spontaneously and deliberately. It has been recorded since ancient times. The acts of shamans, such as bringing rain, are PK events. Many of the miracles of the saints, such as bilocation, levitation, controlling the forces of nature, and manifesting food, have PK elements. Healing at a distance involves PK. Real magic involves PK.

Some people are born with extraordinary PK ability, just as

some people are born with extraordinary artistic talent. For example, Ted Serios could look at something and apparently create an approximate photographic image of it on film. A healer named Ted Owens also seemed to have remarkable PK ability and could influence the elements.

PK can be cultivated deliberately through training concentration and intent. There are many ways, and techniques vary. Thought and will are at the basis. One of the fundamentals of both magic and mysticism is that thoughts are things, and thoughts create reality. You become what you think and believe. Your life reflects what you think and believe. The universe orders itself around you according to your thoughts.

Thought powers the Law of Attraction, setting forces in motion that draw to us the people and circumstances that match our beliefs and expectations. If you believe deep inside of you that you are creative, that you are talented, that you are a winner, you will consciously and unconsciously fulfill those thoughts. The same follows if you think negatively. If you go around thinking that you "always" fail, then you will. Mental power in the form of concentration, self-belief, ambition, goal-setting, intent, and visualization is incredibly strong. Just ask any athlete, artist, or business superstar. You don't get to the top without mental focus.

But thought isn't everything. To be truly effective, it has to be united with action. Your thoughts have the power to magnify your action. You can do more, accomplish more. Thought without action becomes wishful thinking. Harnessing the power of your thought takes effort. Thousands and thousands of thoughts, many of them conflicting, pass through our minds every day. The majority of our thoughts do not come to pass in reality because they are not organized into sufficient energy, powered by will and intent.

The cultivation of PK works best when we call upon higher powers. The universe is a dynamic, living thing with constant forces in motion. The people who develop their powers are in touch with a higher reality. They understand that the ideal state of all things is harmony and wholeness, and that love is the strongest force of all. Shamans, mystics, and healers call upon higher powers—whether it's God, the gods, or the forces of nature—in their PK. They become instruments for higher powers to work through them.

Magnified PK power is generated in groups that unite their thoughts and wills together. This is why rituals are done in groups and why people pray in groups and why teams have a collective spirit and force. History is the outcome of a complicated play of united group consciousnesses interacting with each other.

MONEY MATTERS

People ask, "If PK is real, then why don't more people win the lottery on purpose or make a killing in the stock market?" It is possible to influence the roll of dice and the arrangement of numbers in machines—this has been demonstrated scientifically in the laboratory. Chance is 50-50, and overall study results fall barely above chance. Statistically, this is very significant, though it doesn't seem so from a what's-in-it-for-me-perspective.

Also, there are subtle group factors involved. When you enter a lottery, for example, you are going up against the hopes and intents of potentially millions of people. That's a lot of wills mixed together. The stock market is a complex entity involving global events and a large group psychology, of which a single person is a tiny part.

Nonetheless, there are cases of psi dreaming enhancing lottery wins and investments. Some of the dreams come in the form of spontaneous precognition. In his book *Your Nostradamus Factor,* Ingo Swann relates that in the early 1960s, he had a dream that repeated three nights in a row that he should buy Madison Square Garden stock. Swann was not an investor and had no background or interest in the financial markets. He had no idea that Madison Square Garden even issued public stock, but he looked it up in the financial pages of a newspaper and found that indeed the stock existed, and it was selling for 33 cents a share. He consulted a woman who he knew made investments and was told that according to her broker, the stock hadn't budged in value in years and probably never would. Swann had no money to invest. He might have borrowed $1,000 from his credit union, but opted not to do so.

Six weeks later, Madison Square Garden stock suddenly shot up in value to a high of $35 a share. Had Swann borrowed the $1,000 and invested it, he could have grossed $35,000!

It was, he said, a shattering experience—he had been caught completely unaware and unprepared to act. Try as he might, he could not coax his "NostraFac," his future-seeing mind, to provide another stock tip. "This has led me to the conclusion that our NostraFacs are very stubborn and are not easily pushed around by our mere intellectual desires—another testament to their autonomy," he said.

I had an experience with a lottery dream in the 1980s that also went amiss, but not because I did not act on the dream. I had a dream that consisted only of three huge black numbers flashing on a white background. I was not a lottery player, nor did I have any money matters going on at the time. The only way I could make sense of the dream was to relate it to lottery numbers, so I ran down to the store and bought a pick-three ticket. None of the numbers was drawn in the next round. I didn't track subsequent draws, so I don't know if my dream was a case of "psi missing"— being a little off on timing or a number or two.

A little while later, I thought I'd try another game, and I bought a six-number ticket. I can't recall if I picked the numbers or got a random draw, but there were no dreams involved. To my astonishment, five of the six numbers were winners. I was quite excited, but my husband at the time dismissed it all, saying the ticket was worthless without all six numbers. I knew nothing about lotteries, and so I threw it away! I had no idea one could win on several numbers.

I'm not certain how much money got tossed away that night. But I have never had another lottery dream. I do believe the dream was precognitive, in that it prompted me to pay attention to the lottery and to follow two urges to buy tickets.

I find it interesting that three was significant in both cases of my dream and Swann's dream: Mine involved three numbers, and his was a dream that repeated three nights in a row. My personal experience has been that significant, visionary dreams often involve the number three.

A lottery win reported in Sweden in 2002 concerned a man who dreamed he got his pants filled with money. Upon awakening, he had a strong feeling of winning and bought a scratch-off lottery ticket. He won 10 million kronas, about one million dollars. Note the strong emotion correlation to the psi data; the feeling also helped to urge the dreamer to action.

But most interesting of all is the stock market dreaming experiment conducted by a group of inventors who also are interested in the work of Edgar Cayce and are members of the

Association for Research and Enlightenment (ARE). Their experiment involves intentional psi dreaming to make money in the market.

The Precognitive Stock Market Dream Group, which has members around the globe, was formed by Walt Stover, a research engineer whose interest in dreams began after hearing a lecture on them in the late 1970s. In 1983, Stover had his first spontaneous psi dream involving the market. The messages were clear, but he hesitated to act on them—as many people are hesitant to act on dreams. In 1987 he had two dreams warning him to sell all of his stocks. He did, and thirty days later, the market fell more than five hundred points in one day, the biggest drop to that time since the big crash of 1929. Since then, Stover has experienced financial dreams about five or six times a month. In 1998, he connected with other ARE members who were having similar dreams and formed the group.

The dreams vary considerably among dreamers. Some are highly specific, mentioning names of companies and market sectors, while others are more symbolic and tone-oriented. For example, a woman dreamed of a building falling down, but not all at once. She was very cold. She interpreted the dream to mean she should sell all of her investments in mutual funds. She did, and avoided serious losses. A man dreamed of a long group of orange houses extending as far as the eye could see and winding up in high hills. He associated the image with the Home Depot chain of do-it-yourself stores, which has a bright orange corporate logo. He bought its stock, which increased sixfold. Some of the dreamers have fared better than others. In general, the stock market dreamers have fared much better than the markets themselves.

Timing is a continuing difficulty, Stover says; the precognitions have occurred in dreams weeks and months ahead of the market activity, and in a few cases one to two years in advance. The participants must develop their own sense of interpretation. Stover says he has learned through trial and error to ignore stock dreams that are not highly specific and to wait for one that is.

The mission statement of the group states that "we are cocreators with God in the area of prosperity and abundance and use the principles of universal spiritual laws to guide our decisions." This statement expresses the ideal of PK dreaming: to use one's natural, inborn ability to create a better environment. There is nothing "unspiritual" about using psi to make better investments.

The Precognitive Stock Market Dream Group demonstrates that with sufficient intent, focus, attention, and research, it is possible to cultivate dreams for money-making purposes. I think market investments are more conducive to this type of psi dreaming than are lotteries. Markets have trends, reactions, forecasting, facts, and figures mixed into the blend; lotteries are a different type of gambling.

PRACTICAL PK

We will continue to advance our understanding of how mental power works and be able to adapt it in practical and reliable ways. Already researchers are working on computers that respond to thought. Sci-fi scenarios in which we use thought to operate a variety of machines will someday come to pass. Will we be able to flip objects through space like fictional characters do today? To do so would require some sort of interaction with the law of gravity. We know that defying gravity seems possible at least to some extent because we have historical testimonials of saints, yogis, and spiritual masters levitating in altered states of consciousness. (For saints, these experiences usually came during raptures brought on by intense prayer and meditation and by a lifestyle totally devoted to spiritual study and practice.) Most of these experiences seem to happen spontaneously. Whether we will learn how to make them happen on cue and to manage the experiences themselves is another matter.

Research also will help us understand how other forces affect PK. For example, studies show a relationship of PK to electromagnetic forces. There are even studies that suggest—note I say suggest, not prove—that lunar cycles may indeed be a factor as well. Since the dawn of history, humankind has believed in the power of the moon to affect all areas of life. Some gambling studies show a slightly better hit rate during full moons than during new moons. I stress that these studies are inconclusive, but they do show that we have a lot to learn about the complex dynamics of the universe.

Our emotions and expectations are factors in the process, too. It's been well established in scientific research that believers in psi generally have a higher hit rate in experiments than do disbelievers. Studies have also shown that people who are generally happy and relaxed have a higher psi hit rate than people who are tense, anxious, and self-doubtful.

I also believe that we will increasingly learn how fluid time is, and that it can be expanded and contracted. Athletes in "the zone" know this. And some scientific experiments attempt to examine "retro-PK," or influencing the outcome of events that have already happened in linear time.

As with any advancement, there is always the potential for

abuse. There are always people who seek to turn things to their own selfish or negative interests. Ultimately you experience the consequences of your actions. If you use your abilities for good, you will experience good. If you use them to manipulate or harm, you will experience the fallout of that, too. Always take the high road!

DREAM LAB #27

Harnessing PK

How can you harness PK? Know yourself and your purpose and set goals. Visualize, affirm, meditate, and pray daily; pay attention to dreams and learn how to dream proactively. Follow with action in the material world. Develop your intuition—it is a power related to PK. Above all, put yourself in partnership with your Higher Power and make love the center of your life.

CHAPTER 1 6

Dreaming with Others

WORKING ON YOUR own dreams is rewarding, but only part of the richness of dreaming. Dreaming with others—family, friends, groups, business associates, and others—yields results that many times are astonishing to the participants. Sharing the same dreams, precognitive dreams, creative breakthroughs, emotional healing, astral traveling, and shared lucid dreaming can occur anytime two or more people set their intent to dream together. In fact, I believe we share the dream landscape with others more than we realize— we simply don't know about it until we talk about our dreams.

MUTUAL DREAMING

Mutual dreaming is the term for dreams that two or more people share, especially on the same night. There are different levels of mutual dreaming:

- Same general theme

- Similar theme, not quite the same

- Same elements and images

- Comparable elements and images

- Same emotional tones

- Recognition of the other person or people in the dream

- Sharing lucidity: Both or all persons are aware of being in a dream together while dreaming

Mutual dreaming happens spontaneously, especially among people who share a close emotional bond. It also occurs among people who share the same mental focus, such as a project or problem at work, a personal cause, or even a class devoted to a particular subject. In Chapter 14, the participants in dream activism for peace experience frequent mutual dreaming.

Here is an example of mutual dreaming experienced between my husband, Tom, and myself:

My dream: Islamic terrorists have a space station in orbit around the earth. We send up a craft like the Space Shuttle to destroy it. The craft has long tractor arms. I see it reaching out to grab the space station. Just as it grabs the station in its pincers, I am awakened from sleep by Tom making a loud sound, "Ummmph!"

Tom's dream: He has a false awakening, waking up in bed and hearing intruders downstairs in the house. He tries to make a sound to let them know there is someone in the house. He succeeds in making a sound.

The dreams are similar in theme and have to do with invasion by an enemy. Tom's dream is about personal space and private home, and he is actively trying to prevent it. In my dream, invasion is on a global scale, and I am a passive witness to it.

Mutual dreaming also can be incubated with intent. Two or more persons can set a particular night to dream together.

Sometimes mutual dreaming is displaced a little in time, such as separated by a night or two. The mutual aspect of the dreams is valid if they occur before you discuss them. Otherwise, one dreamer might be influenced by suggestion.

The benefits of mutual dreaming are new insights into your own dreams. A person who shares the dream landscape with you may dream images that add dimension to your own experience or have a dream interpretation that places yours in a completely new light.

DREAMING FOR OTHERS

A variation on mutual dreaming is dreaming for another person in order to obtain guidance on a question. The exercise, called the "Dream Helper Ceremony," was developed by Henry Reed and Robert Van de Castle. Popular and effective, it is used in many group dreamwork settings.

The subject focuses on a question on which they need guidance but does not reveal it to the dreamers, in order to avoid influencing dream content. For example, the question might be, "Should I take the job and move?" The helpers set their intent to dream for the subject and then relay their dreams without interpretation to the subject. First-time helpers usually are skeptical that their dreams could have any bearing on the subject; they are surprised and astonished to find out they have had hits. Sometimes the hits are uncanny in their precision and accuracy. Helpers also often discover elements of mutual dreaming among them. Subjects receive validation of their feelings and intuition and also get fresh ideas for problem-solving.

DREAMWORK IN THE WORKPLACE

If dreamwork is productive on a personal level, could it also be of benefit in the workplace?

Dream education courses are offered in a variety of institutional settings. For example, dreamwork is used in corporate and organizational settings as a way of accessing the intuition for problem-solving and enhanced creativity. The dreams of individuals can contribute to the dreams, or aspirations, of the collective. An organization is a living entity, made up of the souls and consciousnesses of its members or participants. In her book *Daring to Dream,* management trainer and corporate consultant Anjali Hazarika says:

> To rekindle the "spirit" of the organization or to set the organizational "soul" on fire, fresh dreams need to be incubated. When a dream is shared by many people it has a profound effect on the quality of their lives. It has been observed that when we dream together we can become contributing parts of a larger whole. People who share a common sense of direction and community can achieve their goals far more quickly than people who do not. . . .
>
> It is therefore not surprising to find that, although participants have important individual concerns and personal

dreams, there is a great deal of convergence when they dream together for a corporation.[1]

A tremendous amount of creativity emerges when coworkers incubate dreams to address specific questions or needs.

Dream educator Rosemary Watts has taught court social workers how to work with children's dreams. Businesses have used dreamwork seminars as ways to stimulate creativity among employees. And dreamwork has proved a valuable therapeutic tool in prisons, helping inmates to deal with anger, frustration, self-esteem issues, abuse issues, and so on.

I have given courses on dreamwork to health care professionals, so that they can better understand their own dreams and also those expressed by patients. Perhaps because of the empathetic nature of their relationship to patients, health care workers sometimes have precognitive dreams about patients, diagnoses, or treatments they soon will see in their practice.

Attitudes towards dreams as viable professional tools still have a long way to go, but nonetheless have changed dramatically, as we have shifted from an industrial age to an information age.

SOCIAL DREAMING™

Social dreaming is a trademarked term for a particular method of organizational dreamwork developed in 1982 by W. Gordon Lawrence, a senior consultant at the Tavistock Centre in London. Since then, it has been taught in businesses and organizations around the world. In social dreaming, dreams are discussed within a "social matrix" consisting of a group. The

group may be employees of a particular company or participants in a conference who come together from diverse places.
The process begins with someone offering a dream. Others respond as they choose, perhaps offering a dream of their own
that seems related, or an association or interpretation. The
group explores the social meanings of the material offered; the
dreams are seen less as relating to an individual and more to the
life of the group as a whole. A facilitator guides the process,
looking for emerging themes.

Lawrence drew some inspiration for social dreaming from
other cultural perspectives on dreams as being within us, not of
us, and also from a book by Charlotte Beradt, *The Third Reich
of Dreams*. Beradt collected hundreds of dreams of Germans between 1933 and 1939, which demonstrated a link between
dream image and reality. The dreams could be seen as a rehears-
ing and foreshadowing of political events leading up to World
War II. If dreams could reveal social and political realities, then
they also could illumine social dynamics in the workplace.

Lawrence holds that dreaming has been an essential part of
humankind since our very beginnings, and is essential to our
evolution. A form of "protodreaming" existed in the first
cynobacteria. Protodreaming and then dreaming became the
means by which living entities adapt to the outside forces that
cause them to evolve.

DREAMS AND THE EVOLUTION OF THE HUMAN SPECIES

Dream researcher Montague Ullman has long spoken on the importance of dreaming to human evolution and the survival of
the species, and on the social referents that appear in dreams:

From birth on we are faced with the task of finding our own way in an ever more complex social order. The survival task we face ultimately comes down to the way individuals in a society relate to each other and this, in turn, influences the way different cultural groupings relate to each other. The task goes directly to the heart of the adaptive function of dreaming consciousness.[2]

Dreams reflect our disconnects to one another, according to Ullman. Besides personal referents, they contain social referents that metaphorically depict how social issues affect us, not only in work, but in the broader context of life. In dreams we see ourselves more from a global perspective. If more of us would recognize the social importance of dreams, we might "open up one more pathway to a more human social order," Ullman says.

If you participate in group dreaming for a purpose, you will soon have great appreciation for the force and power of collective dreams. Encourage dreamwork to be introduced to your work environment.

DREAM LAB #28
Dream Sending

Dream sending demonstrates the link of consciousness that operates during dreaming sleep, enabling people at a distance to communicate via their dreams. It is an ancient practice and was used to send messages quickly, or even to attempt to influence others. In this exercise, a simple target is sent out on the "dreamwaves" directed to specific recipients.

You will need to work with a partner or a group. Twosomes can work productively together, but results become much more interesting in a group setting. Initially, you may have more success with people you already know and therefore have a link to, but the exercise also works among people who are acquaintances, even first-time ones, and also among people you don't know, such as dream groups that form on the Internet.

Decide who will be the dream sender, and set a designated night when full attention can be devoted to the process.

The target should be a simple message, such as a word, a single image, a color, a number, or a feeling. More complicated messages can be transmitted, but it's best to keep things simple in the beginning. Recipients may have long and involved dreams, and it may be difficult to judge how well a complex message was received.

The sender should not decide the target in advance. If you choose a target early, you will carry it around in your consciousness, raising the possibility for unconscious telepathy with the recipients.

- **Everyone:** On the designated night, have a light meal and avoid stimulants and alcohol, which can interfere with sleep. Prior to retiring for the night, set your intention to remember your dreams.

- **Receivers:** In addition to intentions to remember dreams, tune in to the sender at bedtime. Visualize the sender and say his or her name, reinforcing this with the affirmation that you will be linked in dreams *on this night*. It is important to set time parameters; dreaming by its nature roams about outside of time.

- **Sender:** At some point during the night when all recipients should be asleep, make a spontaneous and random choice of the target. Concentrate upon this with the intent of conveying it into the dreaming consciousness of the recipients. Put as much intensity and energy as you can into the target. Convey sensory impressions: sight, sound, touch, taste, smell. Visualize the recipients and say their names. Imagine them receiving your target. Try imagining the transmission itself; for example, waves of energy going out from you to the receivers. Try to sustain sending for fifteen minutes.

If you don't know what participants look like, use their names, if you know them. If you do not, or the group is very large, imagine that you are transmitting to everyone who is participating in the experiment. One helpful image that works well for me is to see lines of light connecting around the globe.

- **Receivers:** In the morning, write down whatever you recall, even if it's only a fragment, an impression, or a feeling. Do not try to analyze whether or not you've had an accurate hit. Record as much detail as possible. Draw the dream images and note colors.

- **Sender:** Like the recipients, record all of your dream impressions. The experiment may result in mutual dreaming as well as transmission of the target.

- **Everyone:** Meet or confer to evaluate results. Receivers should first report their dreams. The sender then reports the target. Some receivers may have partial hits, getting some, but not all, details right. For example, if the target is a red vase with yellow flowers, a receiver might have a red container or a vase-shaped object in an otherwise unrelated dream. Consider other elements, such as emotional tones, both in the dreams and upon awakening, and any "feelings" that the dream is in some way different from "ordinary" dreams.

One product of dream sending is the aforementioned mutual dreaming: Two or more people will share the same dream, the same elements in a dream, or the same dream theme. The mutual dreaming may have nothing to do with the target. However, it reveals a "meeting of the dream minds" as a result of a deliberate effort to do so.

• **Tip:** In addition, pay special attention to recalled dreams on one or two nights immediately before the designated sending night. Receivers may experience "displacement," a precognitive reception of the target.

The more you practice dream sending, especially with the same people, the more proficient and accurate will be your results. Dream sending is a skill, and like any other skill, becomes more polished with practice.

DREAM LAB #29

Dreaming Guidance for Another

This exercise demonstrates the powers of intuition and the links of consciousness that operate during dreaming sleep. It is based on the "Dream Helper Ceremony" developed by Henry Reed and Robert Van de Castle. You can do this with one partner or in a group.

Decide who will be the subject. The subject will decide on a question to be answered in dreams. The question must be about a personal matter and be of importance to the subject. *The question will not be disclosed to the group.*

You will do a circle meditation in which you will focus your intent upon helping the subject and making an empathetic connection to her or him. Direct your Dreaming Mind to answer the subject's question in a dream that night.

Allow time and space in the morning to remember and record dream material. Do not disregard anything, and do not attempt to fit anything to the subject.

If you do not recall a dream on the designated night, try again the following night. Keep your intent on dreaming for the subject.

When the group reconvenes, the subject listens to all dreams. The subject will then reveal the question. Do group dreamwork on how the various dreams addressed the question.

You may also discover how others' dreams answered your own questions as well, even though the dreams were intended for the subject.

DREAM LAB #30

Mutual Dreaming

Discover the ways you share the dreamscape with others. Work with a partner; in the beginning, you will have the greatest success with a friend or family member with whom you share a close emotional tie.

Set your intention to share the dreamscape with each other for a week. You may wish to conduct a ceremony together, or compose a mutual dream affirmation that you both will use as an incubation every night. For example, "_____ and I will share the dreamscape tonight."

Record your dreams, but do not discuss them with your partner until the week is finished. Otherwise, you might influence dreaming in each other.

At the end of the week, compare your dreams. Look for common themes, images, and emotions.

QUESTIONS TO CONSIDER

1. Did you dream of each other on the same nights?

2. Did you dream the same dreams?

3. Did your dreams share identical or similar images or themes?

4. Were any of your dreams lucid?

5. Can you identify any patterns or make any conclusions based on your results?

6. Did your dreams answer or illuminate anything for your partner, and vice versa?

APPOINTMENT TO DREAM

As a variation, set an appointed date in the near future with your partner to dream together. On the designated night, incubate your intention prior to sleep. Follow up with a comparison of results.

APPOINTMENT TO LUCID DREAM

Set a dream intention with your partner that you will share a lucid dream with him/her on an appointed night. Your affirmation for incubation might be, "Tonight _____ and I will share the same dream, and be aware that we are dreaming while we are in the dream."

MUTUAL DREAM TRAVELING

Set your intention to go dream traveling with your partner. Decide in advance on a desired destination. Your affirmation for incubation might be, "Tonight _____ and I will visit _____ in a dream we will share together."

GROUP MUTUAL DREAMING

Do the above exercises with an entire group.

DREAM LAB #31
Dreaming the Rainbow

The rainbow is a symbol of the bond between heaven and earth. It is the bridge to heaven and a symbol of God's covenant with humanity. It shows the way to the treasures of the heart. It denotes happiness, peace, prosperity, and good fortune. It is a sign that all is well.

In this exercise, the image of a rainbow is used to incubate an open-ended, meaningful dream. It can be done individually, but is very effective in group dreamwork.

Prior to sleep, hold a vivid image of a rainbow in your mind. Choose either a nondirected or a directed incubation. A nondirected incubation is:

Tonight I dream a rainbow.

A directed incubation is:

Tonight I travel the rainbow to _____.

Follow through with dreamwork.

QUESTIONS TO CONSIDER

1. Where does your dream rainbow appear?

2. Are there dream images that embody the symbolism of a rainbow, regardless of whether or not an actual rainbow is present in the dream?

3. What emotions arise in the dream concerning the rainbow? Upon awakening?

4. How can you relate the rainbow dream to yourself? To waking life?

5. What can you view differently from the perspective of a rainbow?

6. How does your rainbow compare to the rainbows of others in the group?

7. What themes and images emerge among the group's dreams?

CHAPTER 17

Dreaming of Past Lives

IF DREAMS TRANSCEND time and we can dream of the future, then can we dream of the past—not just of this life but of previous lives? Yes, we can, and there is ample evidence of past-life content in dreams in the literature of scientific investigations into reincarnation. In many such cases, dreams have provided factual information previously unknown to the dreamer that can be validated, such as information about a place or even family members from a previous life.

I have experienced dreams that I have interpreted as past-life. Shortly after I met my husband, Tom, I had several intense, vivid, and lucid dreams that I could only interpret as glimpses of past lives. I was somebody distinctly different from the person I am now, but I was very much "me." I could not explain these portrayals of myself as symbolic representations of the "me" now. Instead, it was as though I had stepped through a doorway in time. Admittedly, the interpretation of these dreams as past-life is very subjective, perhaps even more subjective than regular dreamwork. Identifying dreams as past-life can be an uncertain process. However, I think many people have dreams that seem to them past-life, and they wonder if it is possible to dream in this fashion.

My past-life dreams came in the early stages of my relationship with Tom. As the relationship became more cemented, the past-life dreams gradually decreased in frequency, and even stopped for a long period of time. It seemed as though their initial purpose was part of a reestablishing of contact. We do feel we have shared other significant lifetimes together, and so it makes sense that dreams—which can access any records in the vaults of cosmic time—would serve as a way of soul remembering.

In *Dreamwork for the Soul,* I describe a dream of a life as a Polynesian woman who is pregnant. In another dream, Tom is bringing boxes out of our basement, and one is labeled "Memories of the Past."

One night I had this lucid dream, which had a very "heavy" atmosphere:

> Tom and I are in New Canaan, Connecticut [where I lived during my previous marriage], and I take him to see my old house. We arrive, only the house has been transformed into a huge castle (this seems to be the norm, i.e., I am not surprised in the dream). We walk in. The floors are stone. It seems to be a mix of eras and places. There is a Renaissance-type white marble fountain with a cherub in the middle in the entrance. One huge room is decorated like a German hunting lodge, with stuffed trophies and large beer steins. The rest of the place looks medieval.

When I related the dream to Tom, he told me of a lucid hypnagogic dream he had had about a month earlier. He had a vision of being in a castle and walking on a winding staircase. It seemed a past-life scene, and the vision lasted quite awhile. He kept going through the castle. Tom said he felt that some of our past-life connections were during medieval times in Europe. I thought my dream was interesting with its mix of eras and cultures.

In a later dream, I found myself in a setting that seemed medieval, though the details around me were not distinct. The central part of the dream was that my body had large, painful sores on it, and a large boil on my abdomen that looked ready to burst. Tom was concerned about taking me to a doctor.

In that dream, I do not recall clothing or surroundings. But the boil reminded me of the black plague that swept through Europe in the fourteenth century, killing about 25 percent of the population. One of its distinctive hallmarks was large boils or carbuncles on the abdomen. I tried to do traditional dreamwork on the body afflictions and boils, but could find no resonance in the context of my present life.

CHARACTERISTICS OF PAST-LIFE DREAMS

Many dreams judged to be past-life are lucid, and carry the characteristics of lucidity discussed in Chapter 4. The dreams feel very "real" and different from ordinary dreaming. We may be entirely different than who we are in the present, gender-wise and racially. It's as though we are suddenly dropped into another timeline or another universe, where another life that belongs to us is playing out. We participate in a scene or two, and then our dreams ferry us back to the present life.

Past-life information also can surface in the borderlands of sleep, in the jumbles of voices and faces. Some of these reveries may contain psychic or past-life information that is not filtered out by the conscious mind—as Tom believed in his hypnagogic vision of the castle.

Many past-life dreams are recurring, especially those that replay scenes of trauma. For example, Rabbi Yonassan Gershom, author of *Beyond the Ashes* and *From Ashes to Healing,* has collected many past-life memories of people who feel they died as victims of the Holocaust. Many had repeating nightmares of being tortured or killed in Nazi concentration camps, or of being shot in their homes and villages.

TRIGGERS OF PAST-LIFE DREAMS

SPONTANEOUS RECALL

Some past-life dreams seem to have no particular trigger, but happen spontaneously, perhaps in childhood. We have distinct knowledge of ourselves as someone else in an earlier time and life, and the memories lie close to the surface of waking consciousness. Dreams can shed more light on our knowledge and provide information for further exploration and research.

Dr. Ian Stevenson, one of the world's leading experts on cases of reincarnation, has collected thousands of cases, many of which involve spontaneous memories in both waking consciousness and dreams. Not surprisingly, most of them originate in non-Western cultures, where beliefs about reincarnation are stronger. In many of the cases, the information about the deceased person is specific and can be verified, thus contributing to a growing body of what scientists call "evidence in support of reincarnation."

A famous Western case of spontaneous past-life dreaming concerns an Englishwoman, Jenny Cockell. In her childhood during the 1950s, Cockell had a vivid, recurring dream in which she saw herself as a grown woman named Mary, who was lying in a bed in a large white room and was dying of fever. Upon awakening, Cockell would sob about the eight children she was leaving behind.

Cockell drew maps and pictures of the village where she believed this Mary had lived, and also somehow knew the village was in Ireland. Her spontaneous recall was so specific that she was able to identify the town, a village north of Dublin, and locate records of a Mary Sutton, a woman who had had eight children and who had died of fever. This case was especially intriguing because Mary Sutton's life had been recent and her grown children were still alive and could be located. Cockell's knowledge of Sutton's life, including details she could not possibly have known, were confirmed by her surviving family. But not all of the children accepted her as the reincarnation of their mother.

In her book *Children's Past Lives,* Carol Bowman describes a dream that recurred from childhood:

Ever since I was very young, I had a recurring dream of a woman with medium-length brown hair wearing a maroon coat, a black hat, and carrying a shoulder bag, walking down a boulevard with a stone wall in the background.

The image was bright and clear, so vivid that I could never forget it. I remember thinking as a young girl that I was going to be that lady when I grew up.[1]

The dream remained the same, until much later in adulthood, when Bowman became interested in reincarnation and past-life memories. The dream changed; Bowman knew she was the woman in the dream. The woman went into a large building. Speaking in German—a language Bowman could not speak—the woman angrily addressed a man behind the desk. She was escorted out. Humiliated, she wondered how she could care for her children alone. Bowman came to discover that the dream came from a past-life in Germany during World War II.

MEETING SOMEONE

More often, past-life dreams are triggered by something that happens in the present life. My meeting of Tom seemed to trigger past-life dreams for both of us.

VISITING A PLACE

Visiting a place for the first time can trigger a past-life dream, especially if that place had been meaningful to us. In the following example, a woman's first trip to a city in Belgium had both precognitive and past-life elements. The dream preceded her actual visit, and she later discovered its possible past-life connection:

One of my dreams was in Bruges, Belgium. I had never been there. The night before I traveled there by train from Brussels, I dreamt about the city in exquisite detail. However, the time frame was off. I dreamt I was watching bodies go down a canal which was burning on all sides. Fires.

When I visited the place I had dreamt about, it was exactly as I had seen it in my dream. Interestingly enough, I learned later that day that the canal had been used during the plague in the Middle Ages to transport the dead away from the city—where they were then burned. Thousands were dying everyday during the plague. Very strange.[2]

PAST-LIFE REGRESSION

Undertaking past-life recall, such as in a workshop or in one-to-one sessions with a regressionist, can stimulate past-life dreams. Deborah, an administrator on Carol Bowman's Internet Web site forum, "Children's Past Lives," had spontaneous memories of being "Clara," a black slave girl who lived around the time of the American Civil War. Deborah learned more about Clara in regressions. Then came the first past-life dream:

> It was *very lucid* and seemed so real. I was in the 1860s; I was a young black woman. I was in an area where several black people had been hung for "crimes" they did not commit or that did not require such a terrible sentence. I saw four black men carrying a coffin, and they were singing "Come on, Come on, It's time ta go down to da Mojo, cause someone here's been killed . . . Keepin on . . . keepin on . . ."
>
> The men wore brown pants, suspenders, funny

round hats, and black, worn boots. An old man was digging through the black peoples' possessions, the ones left in the holding area. I saw used bullets, broken chains, copper pennies, rags, nothing of real value. But, when I looked in one woven box—inside was a man's pocket watch, oval in shape, with elongated numbers. There was engraving on the back. I saw an *L* and *M*.

Also inside was a cloth wrapped around four forks. Two metal ones and two engraved silver ones. The silver ones had the date 1864 on the back. Then I saw a music box/jewelry box that was made of china and painted with flowers that could fit in my hand. On one side it was a clock, the other a music box, the bottom a drawer for earrings and rings. A black man rode up on his horse and snatched the music box from me and took it to his wife. I only had the watch left, the cloth and the forks.

I wore a long dress, with a white apron. I was barefoot. I could smell the dirt on the ground, everything was in full color. I could hear the singing in a southern accent, I could feel the dirt on my toes.

I told my mother my dream (she is very clairvoyant). I told her everything except the engraving part. Funny, she asked me if I could see the back of the watch. I said only part of it. She said, "It has engraving on it, yes?" I said, "Yes." She said, "*L. M. S.*, right?" I said, "I saw the *L* and the *M* but not the *S*."

She suggested I work on it and find out the significance. She could see my whole dream before I told it to her—like a movie. She says [dreams] are her "favorite movies."

I hope to find out who *L. M. S.* is. Also I had to look up "Mojo" at the college library because my dictionary had nothing listed; I thought I made it up. But it is indeed an African form of witchcraft, pertaining to magic, and Voodoo in South Africa. I am sure the black slaves in America brought some of their religion with them.

I know much about this past life, but all in the dream was new.[3]

Deborah had other dreams about Clara, although the meaning of the initials *L. M. S.* remained elusive. She painted a portrait of her past-life self. The exploration of this past life has been an ongoing journey of self-discovery.

The famous novelist Taylor Caldwell believed she had a past-life connection to the fabled lost continent of Atlantis. From childhood, she seemed to "know" the place and wrote a surprisingly mature novel about it at age twelve. The novel was not published for some sixty years; meanwhile, Caldwell underwent regression to learn of her past lives in Atlantis.

In the novel, *Salustra*, the empress of Atlantis, faces the aggression of the neighboring nation, Althrustri. She falls in love with Althrustri's emperor, Signar. Both lands are destroyed by earthquakes and tidal waves, save for a handful of inhabitants and the two leaders, who manage to escape to a new land.

Caldwell, working with Jess Stearn, a journalist and author interested in reincarnation, published the novel as *The Romance of Atlantis*. She then experienced three vivid, exceptionally intense dreams about Atlantis, in which she was Salustra. The dream left her weeping for Atlantis and yearning for Signar, whom she knew in her present life, but whose identity she never disclosed.

It can be argued that the dreams were the products of her novel. The past-life view is that the dreams validated the real past life, which the novel expressed.

Other triggers of past-life dreams are unfinished business, phobias, and affinities. An event, a meeting or a trip may stimulate dreams in which we feel compelled to do something in order to bring a closure to an unhealed wound from the distant past, or finish something we started long ago and never completed.

ILLNESS AND INJURY

Sometimes illness, especially involving fever, or trauma to the body, acts as a trigger to release past-life recall in various forms, including dreams. In 1986 Bowman fell seriously ill with respiratory troubles that left her weakened and fatigued. One afternoon she fell into a much-needed nap. In the borderland stage of sleep, she had a vision of a frail, middle-aged man whose brown eyes looked steadily into hers. She then saw him lying in bed dressed in a white gown, having great difficulty breathing. A middle-aged woman sitting beside the bed looked worried.

Bowman felt she had been the man in the dream. He had died at about the same age she was, and of a respiratory ailment. Initially, she thought the dream might be due to medication or to anxieties about her condition. Much later, after her recovery, she underwent a regression in which she learned that the man had been a pianist, whose talent had left him isolated from others.

PHOBIAS

Phobias can be explained by past-life dreams. For example, an inexplicable extreme fear of water may surface in recurring past-life dreams in which one has drowned, as in this example:

> From my earliest memory, I have been terrified of being out on any kind of open water. I do not like riding in boats, or even walking out onto a pier. I have also had recurring dreams of drowning. There is only one scene in these dreams, which are really nightmares, because I wake up frightened and shaking and gasping for breath. In the scene, I am in deep and cold water, and I feel myself losing strength and going under. I seem to know I am going to drown.[4]

The dreamer, a young woman, assumed that the dreams reflected her fear of water. After becoming interested in reincarnation, she underwent a regression to explore the phobia and found herself revisiting a dream in which she, as a young man, had drowned in a shipwreck.

UNFINISHED BUSINESS

I have had a number of past-life dreams that seem to explain unfinished business and also interests of mine. In them I am a monk or cleric in settings that look like medieval churches, abbeys, or monasteries. In some of these dreams, I am toiling away, copying religious manuscripts—a task performed by many monks. Wherever I travel, religious sites top my list of must-see places, and I can spend many hours and days prowling about the cold halls of old cathedrals and abbeys. Though I did not feel compelled to enter into the life of a religious, I devote much of my writing to spiritual topics, including several encyclopedic books on saints and mysticism.

The monk dreams came long before my book projects. I feel that in this life I am concluding some unfinished business. Perhaps there was something I wanted to record and did not have the chance—or the freedom—to do so. In this life I have resisted aligning myself with any particular religious school. Perhaps I am engaged in looking at the "full story," rather than at a narrow viewpoint.

DREAM LAB #32

Looking into the Past

Through incubation, we can ask our dreams to show us a past life or past lives. Before you undertake this type of visionary dreaming, be aware that reentering the past may involve bringing trauma and intense emotions to the surface. Many people who work with past-life memories experience great healing, but must deal with traumatic events in order to achieve the healing.

Compose an incubation that directs dreams in a constructive way. For example, here are some possible incubation intentions:

- Show me a past life that is meaningful for me now concerning my talent for _____.

- Show me a past life that helps me improve my relationship with _____.

- Show me a past life that explains why _____ and provides me with helpful insights.

- Show me a past life that will help me heal _____.

- Show me why I have a recurring dream about _____.

Follow through with dreamwork. It may be advisable to conduct these dream labs with the help and supervision of a qualified regressionist.

CHAPTER 18

Dreams of Pets and Animals

OUR DREAMS EXPLORE not only our relationships with people, but also our relationships with animals: our pets and creatures of the wild. Dream animals sometimes are symbols of characteristics and behaviors. Sometimes, however, dream animals are themselves, communicating something about themselves or their relationship with us. They may "speak" in symbols, imagery, and emotional tones, or in direct communication with the magical ability of speech.

TUNING IN TO PETS VIA DREAMS

Many devoted pet owners know that they communicate with their pets via telepathic impressions. Dreams have been established as a domain for telepathy among humans; it stands to reason that we also have the capability of communicating tele-pathically with animals in dreams. In fact, dreams may be one of the best ways in which animals can make themselves under-stood to us, as in the following experience of Val Bigelow:

In reality I have just inherited an adorable Burmese cat—tan with grey points, six pounds of personality and a total of 25 toes (due to a little too much inbreeding). I love her dearly. My son had to give her up after having her for 5 years, because his fiance is allergic to cats.

My dream was: I was at my son's wedding and *very* sad that he was getting married, to the point of tears.

When I woke up this dream surprised me very much since I'm very *happy* that he has found a real soulmate, and we all get along very well. Then I spotted our new Burmese who sleeps in my room, and realized that I was tuning into the *cat's* feelings—being sent away from her "daddy" because daddy is getting married.

As the result of this dream I have lavished even more love and attention on this cat to make up for the heart-break I feel she is going through. I think I was helped to this conclusion by watching Sonya Fitzgerald, The Pet Psy-chic, on Animal Planet, a show I really love. The show em-phasizes the reality of our pets' emotions and how we do tune into them.[1]

Animals have emotional responses to changes in their lives. The most dramatic way they can communicate their feelings may be in dreams, through an empathetic link with the people who care for them.

DEPARTED PETS

We grieve the loss of our pets as deeply as we grieve the loss of loved friends and family. We can have closure dreams of our pets. The following dream marked a closure for the dreamer, who felt her pet had come to her in a dream to reassure her that he was well, and was also in the company of her dead father:

> I had to put my old dog to sleep. I had a dream in which my father and the dog were in a hall with steps going up. The dog was young and his tail was wagging. At the time of the dream my dad had been dead for a long time, and I hadn't had a dream about him in a long time, either.[2]

Sometimes dreams of departed pets are unhappy or disturbing, especially if we have had to make the difficult decision to put a pet to sleep because of illness or injury. Such was the case for Tracy Duncan, who had repeating unhappy dreams and asked me for help:

> I had to put my beloved miniature schnauzer, Oscar, to sleep. He was fourteen, deaf, and had trouble seeing. The reason I put him down was due to internal bleeding. (He ate a rabbit—bones and all). I dream of him at least once a week, and each time, we are in a dangerous situation and I can't get him to hear me when I try to warn him of the danger. Other times, I'll dream he's back, and I'm not sure I can go through the loss again that I know is inevitable. Do animals

make contact through dreams? I feel I made the only choice that I could, so I don't believe guilt has anything to do with it.[3]

I told Tracy:

My heart goes out to you, for I've been in the same position of losing beloved pets (dogs), one to cancer who died at home, and one to old age who had to be put to sleep. I do believe animals can make contact through our dreams. There are probably a lot of messages going on in these particular dreams of yours. I consider dreams one of our best interfaces to the afterlife. Because dreams are unfettered by time and space and the limitations of waking consciousness, we can indeed have real experiences in our dreams with people and animals who have passed on. Not all dreams of the dead are "real experiences," however; they can reveal our emotions about the person or pet who has passed on. The circumstances surrounding Oscar's death—eating the rabbit—are likely to create feelings of guilt and remorse: "If only I had . . ." You may be experiencing some of this inner conflict in your dreams.

You are likely to have two kinds of dreams about Oscar. I certainly experienced them myself. One kind is where you are with him again and he is healthy and happy and full of vibrancy. I think these dreams express our soul's wish for the well-being of those we love. They also serve as messengers from beyond—a communication that all is well. I do think our pets try to assure us so.

The second kind of dream is more about unresolved guilt and remorse. In these dreams, pets may start out healthy and then fall ill and die, or nearly die, or become seriously injured, often through our own actions or neglect. These dreams are a sign of need to come to terms emotionally with the events that took place. Of course you followed the right course of action for Oscar, given the circumstances. What may be at work is a subconscious feeling or desire that something could have been done to prevent the episode in the first place.

After my own dogs died, one naturally to cancer and one being put to sleep, I had both types of dreams frequently. In the second kind of dream, a typical scenario would be I would find my dogs languishing away nearly to death without food or water because I'd forgotten to feed them.

In the case of the dog who had cancer, I suffered a lot of remorse because the cancer was well advanced before it was diagnosed. I couldn't help but feel that if I'd been more on the ball, more observant, it could have been caught early and she could have been saved. Even the assurances of my vet didn't help. He told me that animals often don't show obvious symptoms of illness until it's very far along. This is especially the case with cancer, which progresses much faster in an animal than in a human. I simply had to acknowledge to myself that my husband and I had done the best we ever could for them throughout their lives.

In the case of the second dog, I was second-guessing whether or not I had ended her life too early; was there anything else I could have done. Again, veterinary opinions didn't matter—I still felt that way.

Over time, the guilt/remorse dreams diminished, and now when I dream of them it is usually a happy dream of reunion with them when they were in their prime. This I feel is what our pets wish to convey to us from the Other Side. I do believe that Oscar would like you to feel good about where he is now.

I think if you convey in your prayers how much you loved Oscar and cherished your time together, this will help to heal the emotional wounds. Remember that our dreams tell us how we are feeling emotionally about events in our lives. Emotions often have little to do with "rationality" (for example, the circumstances of Oscar's fatal meal may have been entirely out of your hands), but nonetheless they are powerful and must be honored.

It may be helpful to invoke some angelic help, or perhaps the intercession of St. Francis of Assisi, the patron saint of animals.

Soon I heard again from Tracy, who told me, "Since you gave me an explanation, the dreams have mostly stopped."

My communication with Tracy prompted me to revisit my own dream journals concerning my two dogs. More than a decade after their deaths, I still dream about them, but less frequently. The following is one particularly happy dream:

I am with Tessie and Honey Dog again. Even though I seem to know that they are dead, I am really with them. They are healthy and full of energy. We go for a walk in the woods.

When I lived in Rye, New York, our house was near the marshes. I used to take the dogs for walks in the woods there and let them run off leash. They always loved it.

I felt this dream was a reunion dream. It came as a welcome change from guilt dreams, which were similar to this one:

I find Honey Dog in a closet. I think she had been in there at least two weeks. She is very weak, maybe dying. I don't know if I can save her. Why wasn't I paying more attention to her? I run around looking for food to feed her, but I can't find the right stuff.

Whenever I had one of these neglected pet dreams, I would awaken feeling very sad and distressed.

The next dream, however, seemed to speak on two levels to me. One was a replaying of old "did-I-do-the-right-thing?" guilt feelings. The second level was a message pertaining to where I was placing my attention:

While I am getting my hair done, I let Tessie and Honey Dog out. They do not come back. I get concerned. After two weeks, they still have not come back. I go out into the neighborhood calling for them. Other dogs answer, but they do not come. I am afraid they are gone for good.

The dream could be rewritten this way:

While I am distracted with superficial activities, I let something very important go out from me. When I discover it missing, I try to get it back, but it doesn't return.

Dogs are symbols of guardianship, protection, faithfulness, and friendship. Tessie and Honey Dog can also be seen as guardians of something important, which I let get away.

ANIMALS AS SYMBOLS RELATING TO
OTHER AREAS IN LIFE

We have great emotional attachments to our pets, and thus in dreams they can symbolize strong emotions or attachments. The next dream was very distressing to a woman who adored cats and owned several:

> I don't even have the slightest idea of where to go with this dream.
>
> I was myself (a female) and a new male friend that I seemed to have known for a good length of time. We were outside my house, and we noticed my cat seemed to be dying painfully. So I suggested that we put it out of its misery. He shot it, and it did not seem to affect it. I shot it in the head for what seemed many times (not all at once—but a space of time in between each shot), and it still did not die. It finally awoke me in terror.
>
> I love cats. I have seven in my house and four semi-wild ones (from a stray cat) in my barn. I just simply love them. Why would I have dreamt of killing one and more importantly why did it *not* die? It frightened me badly.[4]

Dream images are symbols, something important to keep in mind especially when a dream is disturbing. In the above case, the dream was not about cats, but was conveying a message about deep feelings that need to be examined or changed about an old issue that resisted being put to an end. To a person unfamiliar with the language of dreams, such images can be quite upsetting.

Dreams are messengers of healing. When they bring us painful images, it is because something painful needs to be healed.

PETS WHO ANNOUNCE THEIR COMING

The phenomenon of "announcing dreams" is documented in different cultures around the world, especially where beliefs about reincarnation are strong. In announcing dreams, the soul of a baby-to-be announces its coming or its identity in a dream to one or both parents. Women are more likely than men to have announcing dreams.

Animals also make themselves known in announcing dreams. Shawn was contemplating getting a puppy. She loved huskies. She also felt drawn to adopting an unwanted pet from the local shelter, even though she might not find a husky there. She had this dream:

A new puppy comes to stay in my house. It's a boxer, brown, and it jumps up and down on my leg like it's happy to see me. It's a female, and I start calling her Happy.[5]

Several days later, Shawn decided to visit the animal shelter "just to see what was there." She did not anticipate making a decision. At the shelter, she asked to pet and see several dogs outside of their cages. Her breath caught when she saw a little boxer puppy. It was a female. Out of its cage, it jumped up and down on her legs, just like the dream puppy had done. She took it home and named it Happy. "I feel she came to visit me in my dream so that I would notice her at the shelter and choose her," Shawn said. "She was meant to be with me, even though she's not a husky."

Two weeks after Judi's beloved black cat, Miranda, died, she had a dream:

> I had this weirdly realistic dream that Miranda had come back. I could literally feel her in the dream. I was so glad. It all seemed so real that when I woke up, I was very disappointed to find out it had all been a dream.[6]

When Judi felt ready for another pet, she acquired a cat. Lucy was much different in personality than Miranda, but Judi loved her just as much. A little more than two years after Miranda's death, Judi opened her back door one morning and found a kitten huddled on the porch. Its fur was ratty-looking, and it was thin. It was evidently lost or abandoned and somehow had landed on her doorstep. Judi took it in, and within a few weeks, the kitten was back on the road to health. No one answered her ad about a lost kitten. There was no question that she would keep it—she couldn't imagine turning the poor little creature over to an animal shelter after it had found salvation. More important, the kitten reminded her of Miranda in odd ways. It was a different color and was male, but Judi couldn't get over the unusual feeling that maybe Miranda had reincarnated. She was drawn repeatedly back to her dream. "I think

Miranda did come back," she said. "The bond we have with our pets is stronger than death."

TUNING IN TO WILD ANIMALS

Wild animals also communicate with us in our dreams—if we attune ourselves to them and their world. As we saw in Chapter 7 on calling dreams, wild animals are important elements in Native American visionary and dream experiences involving acquiring skills and spiritual power; this reflects the important relationship shared with nature and animals in those cultures.

In many cases, animals in dreams are symbols of qualities, behavior, and characteristics; they also serve as divine messengers. But in some cases, the animal realm and the human realm can speak heart to heart in dreams; two worlds can come together.

CALLING IN THE WHALES

One spring, my husband, Tom, and I took a vacation out to the Oregon coast. The rugged coastline and coastal mountains full of emerald timber provide fine hiking with some breathtaking views. Shortly after arriving, I had this dream:

> I am standing on the edge of a cliff, looking out to sea. I know there are whales out there in the distance. They seem to know I am looking, for suddenly there are several whales very close. They are enormous. I can see them clearly under the water, as though I am looking

through glass. They swim in slow motion. I am shot
through with a feeling of awe.

The dream had a certain "tone" I experience from time to
time in dreams. These dreams are distinguished from ordinary
dreams, as though I am in another dimension having a genuine
experience that is also a dream. I awakened with the feeling of
awe still strong, as though I were saturated in some heavenly
perfume.

It was a lovely dream. I had never been on a whale watch or
seen whales in the wild up close—only as little water spouts way
in the distance.

One morning we got up early to take an especially long hike
out to the promontory of a headland that jutted out into the
ocean. The views were supposed to be good. We wanted to get
out on the trail before many other hikers were about. It was a
beautiful morning, with shafts of sunlight penetrating the tall
evergreens. The air was cool and crisp. We were entirely alone
on the trail. About halfway there, we encountered a man coming from the opposite direction. "There are a lot of whales out
today," he informed us. It was migrating season for the Pacific
blue whales, and they passed by the Oregon coastline in large
pods. The man told us that they were some distance off the
coast, but could be spotted by their spouts. Excited by the
prospect of seeing the migrating whales, we hurried on.

We arrived at the promontory, a small piece of rock perched
high above the water. The beach line actually was some distance
behind us. The headland ended in a cliff that plunged straight
down into the water. The view more than lived up to its billing.
And we had the entire place to ourselves.

We scanned the distant water looking for spouts, but the gray waters were empty. Where were all the whales? Had we missed them? Some time passed, and still there was no sign of them.

I thought about my dream, where the whales had been so close. I had stood on a similar cliff. "I'm going to try to call in the whales," I announced, somewhat surprising myself. I sat down to meditate. I held in my mind a picture from the dream and attempted to reconnect with the emotional feeling I'd experienced.

Still nothing happened for what seemed like a long while. Then Tom said, "Spouts!" I jumped up. Way off in the distance, we could indeed see spouts. "It worked!" I exulted.

Seeing the spouts of the passing whales seemed reward enough. Then we noticed that the spouts were getting closer. We could glimpse some shapes above the water. This was even more thrilling—but we still had no idea what was about to happen.

The spouts came closer and closer, until there were two enormous whales right in front of us down below, swimming very close to the cliffside. The water evidently was quite deep. Shortly they were joined by two seals. The whales and the seals cavorted in the water. The whales would roll in the water, breach, and spout. The water was not crystal clear like my dream, but it was almost like looking down into a large swimming pool. It was breathtaking beyond description, and I was shot through with awe.

The whales and the seals swarm round and round in the water in front of us. They didn't seem to be in any hurry to leave. I felt that all of us—humans and sea creatures alike—were fully present in the moment. I wanted to freeze the moment forever. I didn't think I would ever see anything like it again.

It wasn't long before a young man arrived. He, too, was astounded by the scene below us. He said he'd often seen migrating whales far offshore, but never this close. He said there were now lots of people coming on the trail—he had passed them on the way in. Soon others arrived. The magic was broken, and the whales and the seals moved on.

The memory of that experience remains sharp and vivid, years later. Was my dream a precognition of events that were to come? Or did my dream provide an instruction so that I could bring a possible event into being? Would it have happened anyway, without the meditation?

It's impossible to answer those questions with any certainty. I think the dream was both precognition and instruction. Perhaps *preview* would be a better term than precognition. The dream previewed a possible event. Although I did not feel the dream was precognitive—it left no mark of feeling that it portrayed an event that was going to happen—I probably would not have had the inspiration to meditate had it not been for the dream.

Even so, without the dream and meditation the events might have transpired, anyway. We certainly would have felt blessed. But because of the dream, I took a specific action. The resulting experience was powerful and affected me in a deeper way than I think I would have been affected otherwise. I experienced in a profound way a link to the animal kingdom and shared with other creatures a moment of joy. Perhaps it was the whales reaching out to me in a dream. Perhaps the only purpose was a mutual celebration of life in the glory of creation.

In the wake of a profound experience, we are often tempted

to project onto it a big meaning. I did not feel this dream and experience were a calling to do any work with or for whales. In fact, I do not know if I will ever have another significant encounter with whales. The calling of this dream was personal, a revelation of a new dimension of my spiritual growth. It was a peak experience, a mystical, magical moment that defies words and brings change that is understood, intuited, and felt.

THE CROW AND THE HAWK

I would like to share one other personal story about wild animals and dreams.

Several years ago, Tom and I acquired a family of crows. They came into our lives as an unexpected bonus of a bird feeder on the back deck. We became quite fond of them.

We've always enjoyed wild birds, and we set out the feeder so that we can bird-watch while we eat our meals. We read up on the different species that come to visit and appreciate learning more about them by watching their behavior.

A pair of crows began making regular visits to the feeder. At first we thought them rather piggy, as they would scoop up large quantities of whatever food was present and make off with it. This, however, is the crow way, to stash food. Later, puzzled friends would ask us how we knew it was the same two crows, and how could we distinguish even between the two which was which. The answer to us was obvious: No two creatures are the same, and if you are observant you see the uniqueness of each.

We knew crows mated for life, and we named the pair Mork and Mindy. Over time, Mork and Mindy became quite friendly. They were aware of us as their food benefactors, and they interacted with us. We began putting out special tidbits just for them, in their own little dish, which we laughingly referred to as Café Corvus. In the mornings, we would find them waiting in the trees for us. They probably thought they had us pretty well trained: Every day we came out of our boxes to give them food. We learned some nuances in their cawing. Mork policed his territory with great vigor against poachers such as cats and other crows. He especially did not like the little sharp-shinned hawks that came around every now and then looking for a songbird meal.

The crows allowed us to get quite close to them—Mork more so than Mindy. Every breeding season they brought their new fledges to the dish. We named them, too; they would stay a year or so and then go off to their own territories.

Mork and Mindy taught us a lot about crows. Through observation and reading, we learned crows are exceptionally canny and intelligent and have one of the most sophisticated societies in the avian world. When a story broke in the news in which crows demonstrated intentional problem-solving abilities, we were not surprised.

Also not surprising to me was the introduction of crows to my dreamscape. Whenever crows appeared in my dreams, it was a sign to pay special attention. They became a dream power animal.

Mork and Mindy and their offspring visited us for several years. Then one day Mork came no more. Mindy and the fledges showed up, very distressed. We knew Mork had somehow met his end, and we grieved for him. We even went out into the woods with the crazy idea that maybe we would find his remains but of course there was no trace of him. As we returned to the house, Tom felt a presence alight on his shoulder, and then it seemed to pass right through him. He knew it was Mork.

We hoped Mindy would find a new mate and the little crow family would keep going, but about seven months later the fledges went off, and then Mindy did, too.

About a month after Mork's passing was the full moon that Native Americans call the Full Crow Moon, a harbinger of spring. Prior to sleep I meditated on the spirit of the Full Crow Moon and wished Mork well wherever he was. That night I had this dream:

> I am handed a feather. It is long and brown and cream in color, and has been in the earth. It is pulled out from under dead autumn leaves. It has some beads attached to it. At first I think it is an eagle feather. Then I think it might be a falcon feather. Whatever, I feel that the feather comes from a bird who has passed on into spirit, like Mork.

I felt greater resonance with falcon, rather than eagle, and associated the dream feather with Horus, the falcon- or hawk-headed god who is the son of Isis and Osiris. I have always had an interest in Horus, and often wear a Horus pendant that I acquired in Egypt. Visiting Edfu, the temple devoted to Horus, was one of the highlights of our trip to Egypt.

I felt that in the dream I had been given a gift from the realm of spirit, especially the realm of animal powers. The feather resurrected from the earth, from under dead leaves, seemed a rebirth of Mork and the Crow Spirit.

I also associated this dream with creativity and a project I wanted to bring into being concerning Egyptian mythology. It had been on my back burner for a long time, and I knew I needed to move it forward. But with a press of other commitments and deadlines, it had continued to languish in the shadows.

Nine months after the dream and two months after the departure of Mindy and the fledges, a new visitor came to the bird dish: a red-shouldered hawk. It was enormous and spectacular to behold at close range: brown and russet with cream, and a brown and white banded tail. Never before had a hawk landed on the bird feeder. We had seen red-shouldered hawks up in the air, and sometimes we spotted the little gray sharp-shinned hawks holding vigil in the trees nearby, waiting for prey.

We thought it was a fluke—an extra-hungry hawk spying an easy meal of dinner scraps. But the hawk returned again and again, almost on a daily basis. We named him Horus, since Horus is described both as falcon-headed and hawk-headed. We wondered if it were Mork reincarnated. Tom opined that Mork gave the hawk a nudge from the spirit world and told him where he could get a good meal.

I had forgotten my dream, however, until one day I was perusing my dream journal and rediscovered it. Here was my dream manifest in the physical world in the hawk, making the connection to Horus and the Egypt project. And yet on another level, it was our crow friend Mork giving us a wink from the spirit realm.

There was magic to the dream that I had yet to discover. I could do so only by moving forward on the Egypt project.

Communicating with Animals

Incubate dreams to receive a real message from a living pet or a wild animal.

Compose a question, for which the answer is not obvious, to pose to your pet or to a favorite wild animal. Incubate the dream and follow through with dreamwork. Validate the answer by taking action based on the dreams, or by research.

QUESTIONS TO CONSIDER

1. Did your answers/results surprise you? In what way?

2. Were you able to take action in accordance with the dream?

3. What did you learn about yourself? Your dreams?

Communicating with Pets
Who Have Passed Over

Prior to sleep, hold an image in your mind of your pet and summon loving feelings and thoughts. Hold the image of your pet in light. It may also be helpful to hold in your hand something that belonged to the pet, such as a toy or collar.

Ask for a dream with your pet that will be meaningful, healing, and helpful. If you have a message that you would like to convey to your departed pet, ask for this to be communicated in your dreams.

Follow through with dreamwork.

QUESTIONS TO CONSIDER

1. How was your message communicated in the dream?

2. What message was communicated to you? In what way?

3. Did you receive any message or information that was unexpected?

4. How did the dream resolve emotional concerns?

CHAPTER 19

Haunted Dreams

A NIGHTMARE IS any dream that is unsettling or frightening to the dreamer. Nightmares can vary from dreams in which we are in unpleasant circumstances to truly terrifying and vivid experiences in which we are threatened, harmed, or in great danger. Some persistent nightmares are part of psychological stress syndromes and require therapeutic help. For many dreamers, the occasional nightmare or repeating nightmare deals with unhappy circumstances that need attention in waking life; they cease when the problem is rectified.

Certain nightmares may have paranormal origins. The dreamscape may be invaded, such as by a haunting presence in a specific locale. If we accept the premise that we can encounter other people and beings in our dreams, we cannot assume that all of them are benevolent. One must consider the possibilities discussed in this chapter with great caution, however. I believe that our dreams generally are protected space, as is the personal boundary around us. It is important not to leap to conclusions, but to eliminate all other possibilities through traditional dreamwork.

WHEN A NIGHTMARE ISN'T "JUST A BAD DREAM"

"Adene" (a pseudonym) is a woman who has experienced a certain nightmare periodically throughout her life. An invisible but palpable evil presence suddenly makes itself known beside her bed and then sexually molests her. There are no sounds or smells, but the bedroom takes on a heavy, unpleasant atmosphere.

To Adene, the nightmares are not "just bad dreams" but strange and very real experiences that involve dreams. Sometimes she isn't certain whether she is awake or dreaming. The attacks are unpredictable, and she has never been able to link them to anything in particular; however, she acknowledges she carries a lot of internal anger and frustration and has never had a good sexual relationship. She refers to the invading presence as "It." In the past, she had tried to send It away, but It always came back.

When Adene's husband died, she was frightened that It would increase Its attacks. On Its next return, she screamed at It to go away and leave her alone for good. Perhaps her intensity of emotion made the critical difference, for It left without molesting her and never returned.

A psychologist might regard these dreams as caused by repressed sexual tension and emotions that were relieved by the death of the husband. This explanation has never satisfied Adene, who regards "It" as an external force that somehow managed to invade her dreams.

She is not alone in this experience, or in this conviction.

SOME DREAMS ARE "REAL"

As noted in earlier chapters, modern dream researchers regard dreams as subjective and distinguish between "dreams" that reflect our internal states and "reality" that is the outside world. But according to more universal and ancient beliefs, dreams can serve as a medium for visitations by otherworldly beings and the dead, some of whom may cause mischief. The ancient Egyptians, Greeks, and Romans—as well as other cultures—believed that a person could be visited in one's sleep for healing or receiving a message, or to be plagued by demonic beings who wished to molest the dreamer or suck off his life force.

Numerous cross-cultural accounts exist of dream visitations by ghosts, poltergeists, vampires, demons, and nightmare hags, as well as helpful and benevolent beings such as angels, fairies, religious figures, and spiritual guides. Dreams of ghosts can be either pleasant or unpleasant.

Visitation dreams are distinctly different from ordinary dreams. They are intense and vivid in imagery and sensory experience, and the dreamer often is not certain of being awake or asleep. The dreamer may awaken certain that the "dream" was a real event.

Let's look at some of the darker aspects of visitation dreams.

HAG ATTACKS

The dreams experienced by Adene are a well-documented universal and ancient phenomenon known as the "hag attack." The hag attack has been documented around the world. It intermingles with lore about vampires, witches, incubi, and succubi. Our term *nightmare* comes from the Old Hag syndrome: *Mare* is Old English for incubus. In medieval lore, nightmares, or bad dreams, were caused by witches (hags) sitting upon one's chest, riding the victim to exhaustion.

The dominant characteristic of a hag dream is an unpleasant entity or presence that invades the room. Sometimes, but not always, it comes up on the bed and may press upon or sexually assault the victim. Other characteristics of hag attacks are awful smells; grunting, shuffling, scraping and unpleasant sounds; grotesque dark shapes, which may have red eyes; and a pervasive atmosphere of fear. The victim may feel as though he is having a lucid dream, or may be uncertain whether he is awake or dreaming, or may feel completely awake. The victim often awakens in the morning feeling drained and exhausted, as in this example:

From time to time I have these dreams in which a horrible "something" is trying to get into me to take possession of me. I never see it, but I can "feel" it—I know it is there. I always feel like I'm awake when this happens. I try to make it go away, but just when it seems that it's going to get me, I wake up for real. I am always exhausted all day long after one of these dreams.[1]

In this book *The Terror That Comes in the Night,* folklorist David J. Hufford describes different hag attacks, including this one had by a man:

The first thing that occurred to me was that I was dreaming. When it [the hag] got into the room it sat down on the floor and it looked to me like an elephant of all things! Just a blob, but white. I was—ah—I knew I wasn't dreaming! I thought I was dreaming but I knew I wasn't dreaming! And I broke out into a sweat and was just forced onto the bed.[2]

From my case files is the account of S., who had a history of related haunting and hag dreams from childhood. S. described herself as "a really happy, outgoing person. I love life and I make a conscious effort every single day to thank God for something that he has shared with me or the experiences that I have had. I have prayed every night since I was a little girl because I used to hear my grandparents whispering prayers in their room before they went to sleep. I knew it must be important." The nightmares were hard for her to understand:

These have continued into my adult life. They are recurrences. They are both nightmares. The majority of my nightmares take place in this house. It is a mansion out in the country, very old Southern style. I have never seen this house, been to anything like this house, nor have I any relatives that lived in such a house (as far as I know; I have a large family). This is my nightmare house. Sometimes it is in its day, grand and beautiful, but the majority of the time it is almost demolished, overgrown with weeds, et cetera. It has a horseshoe driveway; there are more trees and such on the right side of it. It also had a big front yard. It is always haunted and only on a few occasions has someone I've known lived in it. I am always trapped in it. Usually I am either trying to open or close a door, but some force won't let me. It's very cold, and I usually get a strange smell. I can't describe it. If fear had a smell I am sure that would be it. I don't associate it with anything pleasant. When I get it I know that something bad is going to happen.

All kinds of different things occur in these dreams, but the house and its surroundings are basically the same. This house has been with me for as long as I can remember. I am trying to figure out what it means.

The other dream that I have is similar in nature, in that I have had it since I was a child. The first one that I really remember was when I was about eight or nine. I was dreaming that I was lying in bed and I heard someone enter my parents' room and then my brother's room. I heard heavy breathing and got that weird smell that I mentioned before. Suddenly, this man (because that is what I sense) comes into my room. I wake up just as I see the silver blade of a knife coming right down at me. I literally woke up screaming and drenched. You could have wrung my clothes out.

I don't really remember many of those types of dreams for a few years until I got into my twenties. At one time I was having them about every two to three months. These dreams were always the same. I'd be sleeping, I'd hear someone come into my room, I'd hear breathing, I'd even feel the pressure on the bed. At this point I'd start telling myself to open my eyes, that it was just a dream, but they are so heavy that it is nearly impossible. Later in life they did not include the knife aspect. I just awaken with no one there and my heart beating out of control. On one weird occasion, I think it was a cat. I felt a cat-like creature walking on the bed and even felt its whiskers on my nose just before I woke up. (I don't have a cat.) Only once did I actually get a vision of a man's face as I woke up. All of these dreams took place in the morning. Usually after I would kiss my boyfriend good-bye and drift back to sleep. These dreams are so realistic that I feel like I am being haunted. They have occurred in many different places that I have lived.[3]

S. acknowledged that other psychic experiences had occurred to her mother and to herself: visions of the Virgin Mary and also of the dead and ghosts. In dreamwork, she acknowledged that the house could represent circumstances in her life in which she felt trapped; however, the dream had recurred since childhood, and it stood out as distinctly different from her other dreaming.

Modern attempts to explain hag dreams arrive at no definitive cause. They have been linked to psychological stress, mental disturbances, sleep disorders, physical discomforts, sexual repression, repressed anger, and even diet, but there are many cases that simply have no obvious explanation. An average person is likely to experience at least one hag dream in life, and some people have them periodically or frequently.

Just as there are no satisfactory explanations for hag attacks, there are no certain "cures." Some people who experience them frequently have successfully repressed them through sheer will by telling the invading presences to go away, or invoking Divine help. Others endure them. Medical help and counseling may or may not offer any relief. The following dreamer was able to banish a hag attack dream by praying to her guardian angel:

> The first time I remember having this happen to me was when I was five years old. I remember the feeling of not being able to speak or talk; I remember trying to call my mom, but nothing came out, and I remember the feeling of the presence of something with me in the same room, and it was hard to breathe, and I was very wide awake. This has happened five or six times in my life so far. The last time this occurred, I remember feeling the presence of something there in my room like I was being watched, so I knew it [the choking presence] was going to happen, so I said the guardian angel prayer and the feeling slowly went away.[4]

Another of the cases described by Hufford involved three college girls who shared a lonely country house. One of them had a history of being sort of a psychic lightning rod: Wherever she lived, weird things happened, such as poltergeist and haunting phenomena and hag attacks.

Soon after they had moved in, the "lightning rod" girl began experiencing nightmares. The nightmares spread like a virus to the other girls, increasing in unpleasantness and violent, bloody imagery. They were visited by a hag presence. Poltergeist phenomena occurred in the house. They called in a priest to bless the house, but that only made things worse. Finally they had no resource but to leave the house and they went their separate ways.

The two secondarily affected girls experienced relief. Whether or not the "lightning rod" girl continued to have problems is not known.

PSYCHIC ATTACK

Can the living invade dreams? Magical rituals exist in many cultures for causing a sleeping person to have a certain kind of dream or get a certain message in a dream. A person might be deliberately psychically attacked by wild or supernatural animals or demonic beings in dreams.

A vulnerable person might also be "dream-attacked" by another person who harbors anger and intense dislike for them. Such dream attacks may occur without conscious effort, due to intense negative emotions finding pathways in dreamtime.

The great occultist Dion Fortune wrote extensively on psychic attack. In her book *Psychic Self-Defence,* Fortune says that "characteristic dreams" are the first sign. She goes on to describe the features of hag attack dreams—a weight on the chest, foul smells—as well as other features, such as the precipitation of slime, mysterious footprints, poltergeist effects, and most important, a severe weakening of the victim. Fortune herself was the victim of psychic attack from a hostile superior at work and learned on her own how to neutralize it. She stresses that though psychic attack can occur, the average person has natural auric barriers of protection against it and is unlikely to encounter it.

EXTRATERRESTRIAL ENCOUNTERS

Many extraterrestrial abductions are said to occur while the victims are asleep. John Mack, Harvard psychiatrist and ET expert, reports in his book *Abduction: Human Encounters with Aliens* that typical of abductions are "frightening dreams that seem more real than ordinary nightmares." The victim may recall the "dream" upon awakening, or may need hypnosis to remember. Mack divides ET dreams into three types: 1) abductions distorted as dream experiences; 2) dreams that relive abductions; and 3) ordinary dreams that contain UFO material. Many ET dreams are recurring. Says Mack:

> When abductees call their experiences "dreams," which they often do, close questioning can elicit that this may be a euphemism to cover what they are sure cannot be that, namely an event from which there was no awakening that occurred in another dimension . . .
>
> Allow for the time being that there is little knowledge about the domain from which the alien beings derive—perhaps not even language or concepts to describe it. Yet acknowledge too that something going on that cannot be dismissed out of hand.[5]

ET experiencers say they are sexually assaulted in medical probings, and some feel they are being used to propagate a hybrid race. These attacks bear a resemblance to old accounts of demonic dream invasions and may be a modern version of "high strangeness" in a multidimensional universe.

Not all dreams are unpleasant, however. Some ET experiencers feel they are contacted in dreams for special instruction and to cooperate with aliens in benefiting the earth.

I conducted an informal survey of ET and UFO dreams with Carol D. Warner (see Chapter 10). We advertised for participants in a variety of magazines and Web sites, and received numerous replies. Our purpose was to gain insight into these dreams that would benefit dreamers, therapists, and other dreamwork facilitators. Many of these dreams are vividly realistic to the dreamers and seem like waking events rather than dreams. Do dreams of ETs and UFOs automatically imply an invasion of our dreamscape by alien beings? Or are they more symbolic, like most of our other dreams?

Here are three things to consider in interpreting ET and UFO dreams:

1. *ETs and UFOs have become common dream symbols.*

   Our dream imagery reflects our waking environment. For decades, ETs, UFOs, alien beings and space travel have been a significant part of our popular culture, appearing in our literature, mass media and advertising. It's only natural that these subjects and images should appear in our dreams—just as the automobile, once an "alien" machine, now dominates our dreaming.

   As dream symbols, ET and UFO images convey personal associations within the context of the dream. For example, if a dreamer considers ETs and UFOs to be threatening or frightening, these associations take on symbolic meaning in the dream, representing those feelings about something else in waking life. Similarly, if a dreamer associates ETs and UFOs with excitement, mystery, awe or even salvation, then these would also be related to the dreamer's waking life situations.

The context of the dream is important. Perhaps the dreamer has no negative associations with UFOs, but in the dream a UFO seems sinister. In that case, the dreamer might ask why something that is not normally frightening to him is a threat, and then try to relate that to waking life.

Thus, from this perspective, ETs and UFOs are ordinary dream symbols, just like houses, cars, buildings, animals, and so on.

2. *ET dreams are modern versions of ongoing collective otherworld contact.*

Ancient beliefs about dreams held that dreams were genuine intersections with other realms that were populated by gods, demigods and hosts of nonworldly beings who coexisted in parallel but invisible realms. In fact, some of our experiences with such entities could take place only in the special state of consciousness of dreams.

Many dreamers believe this to be the case today, too. I do. I think that in addition to our personal dreams, we have dream encounters in other realms. It's possible that the beings we encounter reflect our cultural conditioning. For example, dreams of fairies are far outstripped by dreams of ETs—yet centuries ago the reverse would have been the case. ETs may be but the latest "clothing" or "framework" for certain otherworldly experiences that are part of the evolution of collective human consciousness.

There are interesting parallels between ETs—especially the abducting variety, which I will focus on here—and other entities from myth and folklore. Let's look at three of them: the fairy, the vampire, and the angel.

First, what are the dominant characteristics of abducting ETs? They usually strike at night while the victims are asleep. They can be invisible if they choose, and they have supernatural powers over humans and animals. They have the power to shapeshift. They come in brilliant light, passing through walls, and creating poltergeist-like disturbances. They paralyze their victims and levitate them to their world, a spaceship, where time passes much differently. The victims are subject to medical procedures and sexual assaults. The ETs are intensely interested in human mothers and babies, for their own are sickly, as are the hybrids with unusual eyes that they create with humans. The human victims sometimes are returned to locations other than the place where they were abducted; they are exhausted and often bruised. Or, they wake up in their own beds exhausted. The ETs often have apocalyptic warnings about the end times and the dire fate of the earth. Some abductees are shown star maps or are taken on cosmic tours, and are given special information for humanity, which may be presented to them in mysterious books or couched in strange symbols.

ETs have long been compared to fairies. In 1987, folklorist Thomas E. Bullard examined ET reports and opined that ETs were not fairies per se. However, the comparison to fairies cannot be dismissed out of hand.

In his exhaustive work *The Fairy Faith in Celtic*

Countries, W. Y. Evans-Wentz wrote about the great dread of fairies. They were considered to be evil spirits who lived in another dimensional world. They visited the realm of humans at night, and were quite dangerous for either man or beast to encounter. They could be invisible if they chose. They had supernatural powers over people and animals, and they could shapeshift. If you were in the wrong place at the wrong time, they attacked you while you were sleeping, paralyzed you, and carted you off to their world, inside the earth, where time passed much differently. If you were "taken," it meant you had been abducted by fairies while you were sleeping or dreaming. You might be abducted physically, or you might be taken in spirit, with your shell of a body left behind. You might be forced to stay with the fairies forever, or you might escape back to the world, perhaps returning to someplace other than where you had been seized. You felt much worse for the wear, tired and exhausted. Fairies were intensely interested in human mothers and babies, for their own were sickly, with unusual eyes. The fairy realm of the inner earth, just like outer space, was a place of mystery and uncertainty, and to be feared. Fairies issued no apocalyptic warnings about the fate of the earth; however, they had associations with salvation. The "gentry" fairy folk of Ireland claimed to have the power to destroy half of the human race, but would not do so because humans were "expecting salvation."

Other interesting similarities exist between ETs and vampires. Forget the Bram Stoker or Anne Rice variety of vampires—those are fictional creations. The real vampire of folklore originated in Slavic lore as the restless dead who returned from the grave to attack the living— both man and animal—while they slept. The grave, just like inner earth and outer space, inspired fear and dread. Vampires usually were invisible, but sometimes could be seen by their victims. They possessed supernatural powers over humans and animals, and they had the power to shapeshift. The vampire sexually assaulted their paralyzed victims and drained away their vitality, causing them to have wasting-away illnesses. Like ETs, their entry into a household was through mysterious means, and was often accompanied by poltergeist-like disturbances: movements of objects, banging noises, and so forth. Vampires subsisted on the blood of their victims. There are UFO cases—mostly from South America—in which victims reportedly were drained of blood or fell mysteriously ill of wasting-away diseases after being attacked by red lights from *chupa-chupa* UFOs. (*Chupa-chupa* comes from *chupacabra,* or "goatsucker," a blood-sucking entity that chiefly attacks animals.) Some of these *chupa* cases are questionable, but others are an enigma.

Vampires, of course, had no save-the-world agenda. For that aspect we find similarities between the ET and the angel. Apocryphal literature—sacred texts outside the canon—is full of dream visions recitals or prophets who were visited by angels in their sleep. The Book of Enoch is the best known of these texts. Back then, angels were not the saccharine creatures presented to us in the media today. They were fearsome beings of great power, who—despite their obedience to God—were not necessarily kindly disposed towards inferior humans. The angels came in brilliant light and levitated the prophets into their world, heaven. The prophets were taken on guided cosmic tours and given special information about creation and the fate of humanity, along with dire warnings about sin, judgment and the end times. They sometimes were given mysterious books, or were dictated books. They were returned to earth with the instructions to disseminate the information.

We have considered here a few examples of both negative and positive encounters with otherworldly beings. The dominant medium for these encounters is the dreamscape, as well as altered, dream-like states of consciousness. The ET embodies both positive and negative features. Like the vampire, the ET is a soul stealer. Like the fairy, the ET is a trickster. Like the angel, the ET is a messenger of salvation. The ET both terrifies and fascinates us.

Carl G. Jung died before the emergence of the abduction scenario but he did consider the reality of UFOs and the significance of UFOs in dreams. He thought them to be a modern myth of projection from the unconscious, of salvation from the sky, largely in response to the deep collective fear of nuclear annihilation that developed after World War II.

Perhaps the ET is part of our inner struggle of opposing forces of good and evil. The forces are personified by different beings and projected onto the landscape of our consciousness, especially our dreams, in ways that make sense to us in our time and place. From this perspective, ET dreams may say more about the collective of human consciousness than about personal matters.

3. *ET dreams are real experiences.*

Modern ET experiencers firmly believe that their dreams of ETs are genuine encounters, in which events take place that are as real as waking life. This especially applies to abduction dream experiences. As I mentioned earlier, ancient beliefs about dreams considered them to be real experiences in other realities. I believe this to be the case, too, although I think that most of our dreaming takes place in a reality where we work out inner material in the form of symbolic imagery. Nonetheless, I have had startling dreams in which I have felt I really was in the presence of nonworldly beings. If people can dream of really being with an angel or a god of healing, for example, why not an ET?

Unfortunately, the field of abduction research has been fraught with controversy over dubious hypnosis, which is often the only way abduction dreams are recalled. Many experiencers are not well versed in dreamwork, and once they feel they are being abducted, they interpret all of their dreams accordingly so. One experiencer opines in her book that dreams of flying and being examined by doctors and nurses—among many other ordinary dream themes—are really ET "screen" dreams— which would make *all* of us abductees!

4. *How to approach ET dreams.*

It is unlikely that we will ever be able to make definitive statements about what ET dreams are and what they are not. We can consider only the sense they make in each context. Clearly, ET dreams share striking similarities to different kinds of otherworldly dream encounters that cannot be ignored, even if we interpret ET dreams literally. Jung envisioned a "psychic reality" in which we accept our experiences in both inner and outer worlds equally. From this perspective, we can find truth and validity in ET dreams in all three of the areas covered here: as ordinary dream symbols, as part of our ongoing otherworldly experience, and as real experiences in the full spectrum of consciousness.

To understand your own ET dreams, look first for ordinary dream symbolism with personal meaning, and then consider if and how the dreams fit the theme of humanity's contact with other realities. Certain dreams may speak to you as real encounters. Many encounter dreams reported to us were benevolent in nature, in which the ETs were helpful figures who might be interpreted as angels by others. Abduction dreams recovered by hypnosis must be approached much more carefully, and taken to a *qualified* therapist.

GHOSTS

The ancients regarded dreams as a halfway house to the land of the dead. In dreams, the dead lament their deaths, give burial instructions, and provide warnings. The Greeks in particular believed that the unburied dead would haunt the dreams of the living until they were properly interred.

Ghosts also appear in dreams to reenact their own violent deaths or traumatic events in their lives. A person can spend the night in a haunted place, not knowing it was haunted, and be visited in dreams by the resident ghost.

A case in my files concerns a woman who had strange dreams while vacationing in a cottage; no one else she knew who had stayed there had similar experiences. She woke up in the middle of the night choking, to find a strange man with his hands around her neck; she was looking right at him. The only man present in the cottage was her husband. The next night, she woke up to see a semitransparent woman with a pillow in her hand in the bedroom. The woman went away.

In another case, a ghost seemed to be reenacting a violent event. During a vacation in England, Carol and her husband, Jack (pseudonyms), stayed overnight in an old pub. They settled into bed with expectations of a comfortable sleep. But during the night, Carol experienced a vivid and terrifying dream in which a man dressed in a bloody soldier's uniform charged into the bedroom swinging a knife. The experience was so real that she thought she was fully awake and that they were under some bizarre attack. But just as the figure reached the side of the bed, it vanished. Jack slept peacefully throughout the entire episode.

Carol shrugged off her experiences as "just a bad dream." The next morning, she learned from one of the employees that the pub was haunted by a ghost of a soldier from England's Civil War during the mid-seventeenth century. She was not the only guest to have that or a similar dream.

Carol hadn't known anything about the history or haunting lore of the pub prior to the dream. The probable explanation is that her dreaming mind tapped into a ghostly recording imprinted in the psychic space of the pub. Her husband did not share the dream, because his dreaming mind did not, or could not, attune to the presence; perhaps he was occupied doing other things in the dreamscape.

A recurring haunting dream was reported to me by a young woman:

The first time I ever had the dream I was just walking around this big, old white house. I remember thinking to myself it felt familiar; like I had been there before. I was walking through the house feeling the walls as I walked. When I reached the stairwell I heard something and a little door, a panel in the wall opened. I went through, I was in pitch black. I walked down the hall. Nothing but black. Before I knew it there was this girl. A beautiful little girl with long blonde hair. She is wearing a white dress or sleeping gown. She is probably about six or seven. I was so scared, I started running. I went down black hall after black hall, I couldn't find my way out. I was crying. Then I awoke. The next couple of times I would fall asleep I would end up looking for the panel on the stairwell. I could always hear my friends telling me not to go, it was dangerous. I always went over.

Despite my fear I was drawn to her. The more I had the dream, the more I began to enjoy it. You see, I am scared to death of this little girl, because every time I see her I think she is trying to kill me. On the other hand, I like the mystery. The house isn't like a black maze anymore. I can now recognize rooms I have "been in" before. One room in particular. It's a bedroom with an antique barber chair in the corner. The room and everything in it has an iridescent glow. It's my safe room. She doesn't follow me in. I have only been in there once. Some rooms I run into are full of people. I beg for help, but no one listens. It's like they don't even see me. I feel like I know the house. I just needed to familiarize my-self with it again. If I wake up, I always fall back into where I left off.

At this point, one might speculate that the little girl in the dream is symbolic of an aspect of the dreamer. However, the ex-perience gets much stranger:

The most confusing thing for me is my uncle and my dad have the exact same dream. The only difference is, my dad has gotten chased to the attic. He said the ceil-ing is low, and there are statues of gargoyles.

I haven't had the dream in about a year. Since the last time I had it, I have built a house on my dad's prop-erty. I live in front of his big, white farmhouse that was built in the 1700s. I have since found out it has tunnels in the basement and was used to move slaves under-ground. There are also two doors that will not open and look as if they lead outside. If you go outside and look, you don't see a door. We tried to bust the doors in with a fifteen-pound sledgehammer. No luck! Both my dad's house and mine are haunted. The previous owners and neighbors have told us that a young woman and her child walk the house. There have been many sightings, but that's another story.[6]

In the American Civil War, the "underground railroad" was a network of antislavery people who aided slaves in their escape to northern, non-slavery states. Slaves were hidden and moved in underground tunnels. Many homes and buildings where these tunnels are located have haunted histories. Perhaps the intense emotions of fear and anxiety, combined with deaths that surely occurred in tunnels, have imprinted the spaces with ghostly presences.

HOW CAN WE EXPLAIN HAUNTED DREAMS?

Non-paranormal explanations advanced for haunted dreams are sleep paralysis and normal hypnagogic, or "near sleep" visions. It's normal for the body to experience a certain degree of "paralysis" during sleep; otherwise we might act out our dreams. In cases of sleep paralysis, people can wake up feeling paralyzed, choked, and confronted by ghosts or presences. Experts say that the dreamer hasn't entirely awakened; the effects of sleep paralysis and lingering dreaming create misleading impressions about supernatural attacks.

Many cases of presences and ghosts seem to occur in the twilight stage of near-sleep, a state of consciousness that is well known for its fleeting, jumbled images of faces and snatches of voices.

These explanations can account for some cases of haunted dreams, but not all of them. They especially do not explain situations in which diverse people have similar dreams in the same place, without prior knowledge of a place's "dream history."

Why do some people have visitation dreams and others not? In my book *Dreamspeak: How to Understand the Messages in Your Dreams,* I tell about a woman whose dead mother-in-law explains in a happy visitation dream that she cannot appear in the dreams of her son to deliver messages to him because "of the way that he dreams."

Our visitation dreams are influenced by many factors: emotions, physical conditions, auric fields, and natural psychic channels and abilities. Parapsychological studies show that most of our psychic episodes—up to 70 percent of them—occur in dreams rather than in waking consciousness. Some of us may be more naturally receptive to the "unusual" when in the dream state. Emotional links can play a significant role in dreams of the dead. Emotions seem to provide a "psychic electricity" for dream connections.

Place also may be important. Paul Devereux, an expert in ancient mysteries and earth energies, has researched dream patterns at sacred sites in the U.K. If certain patterns occur at certain places, that might demonstrate that earth energies—perhaps electromagnetic forces—influence dreaming consciousness. Such patterns then might be linked to other phenomena reported at sacred sites, such as mysterious lights, hauntings, UFOs, fairy folk, and so on.

Perhaps the most important but unknown factor is our "consciousness DNA"—something within us that affects states of consciousness and psychic receptivity, and which is evolving within us on a collective level. This may be the most significant factor explaining why, for example, two people can sleep in the same haunted place and only one of them will have a disturbed dream.

IF YOU EXPERIENCE A HAUNTED DREAM

Don't rush to assume that a nightmare is more than symbolic. Look for natural explanations first before assuming the supernatural. Nightmares and troubling dreams may need to be scrutinized in dreamwork with a qualified therapist or practitioner, as they are likely to carry symbolic meanings pertaining more to the dreamer than to any outside agents.

If you do feel vulnerable, give yourself an affirmation of protection and light prior to going to sleep. The vulnerability itself must be dealt with, for fear can help to create the very dreams one wishes to avoid. Only by thoroughly understanding dreams through dreamwork can we sort out their true meanings.

CHAPTER 20

Forming a Dreamwork Group

ONE OF THE most rewarding ways to deepen your understanding of dreams and work with them proactively is to participate in a dreamwork group. Lay dreamwork groups are popular and can be found in just about every community. If one does not exist near you, consider starting one. Most dreamwork groups meet in private homes.

DREAMWORK GROUP STRUCTURES

There are numerous ways to structure a dreamwork group. What you do will depend on the interests of the participants and how many people are in the group. Here are things to consider:

LEADERSHIP

Some groups have a single leader who directs the sessions. Others are leaderless, and still others rotate the leader position.

PURPOSE

The group may wish to have an organized purpose and mission. Most groups are general in purpose, but some have a specific focus, such as experimentation in lucid dreaming, precognitive dreaming, dream activism, and so on. It is important that participants understand that the group is a *lay* group and that its meetings do not constitute therapy or a substitute for therapy.

TECHNIQUES AND FORMAT

A wide variety of dreamwork techniques exist, and groups gravitate to the ones that appeal to them most. The group may wish to experiment before settling on a few favorites. Some groups are devoted to, and organized around, the techniques taught by a particular individual.

Will you just do dreamwork, or will you engage in study and discussion of dreams? Will you have presentations? In the dreamwork group I belong to, we initially began every meeting with a short presentation on a dream topic by one of the group members. This fell by the wayside, as we decided to spend all of our time on actual dreamwork. Nonetheless, group members bring articles and resource information that they think will be of interest to the group.

ETHICS

Dreams take us deep into personal privacy, so it is of paramount importance that a dreamwork group have clear requirements about ethics. In general, participants should not be required to divulge personal information. After working on a dream, a dreamer might simply wish to say that he or she now under-stands the dream, without volunteering additional information. The group should maintain confidentiality—what occurs in the group should stay in the group.

It also is not considered ethical to tell another person what his or her dream means. Interpretation is strictly up to the dreamer; the dream is personal territory. The ideas of others are offered as projections—possibilities they would consider if a dream were theirs. It's a good idea to keep language couched in that way: "If that were my dream, I would make these associa-tions . . ."

Participants should be willing to take responsibility for follow-ups necessary to their dreamwork and for finding the appropriate professional avenues to deal with their personal is-sues.

The Association for the Study of Dreams has a good ethics statement, given at the end of this chapter.

GROUP MAKEUP AND SIZE

Will your group be open to anyone, or will it be limited to ex-perienced dreamworkers? You may wish to limit the size of your group. Size will depend on how you decide to conduct your meetings. For example, if everyone will be able to work on a dream at every meeting, then your group will be very small. The dreamwork group I belong to is women only, and we have ranged from three to six people. This enables everyone who wishes to work on a dream to do so each time we get together. We are a leaderless group.

If you have a larger group, set some parameters for ensur-ing that everyone gets a chance to work on a dream at certain intervals. It may be a good idea to limit the time the group spends on a dream. Dreamers should always feel a sense of completion, but without time guidelines, it is all too easy to spend the entire meeting on a single dream. The group must be flexible in order to deal with the needs of each situation, however.

SEATING

For work with groups, the most productive seating arrangement is a circle. The circle is a mandala for wholeness, oneness, and the endless cycle of time and energy. It has been used in sacred traditions around the world since ancient times as a means of communicating with a consciousness deeper than conceptual thought—our everyday thinking. The circle prepares the mind at ordinary levels of consciousness for what will be perceived at deeper levels.

Everyone is equal in a circle. Everyone has a unique place and yet is part of the whole. The circle holds a sacred space for support and sharing.

The center of the circle can be used as a focal point for the purpose of the experience. Placing something special in the center of the circle, such as a candle, helps to create a special atmosphere.

PERSONAL ETIQUETTE

A few rules of etiquette are:

- **Speak your Truth.** Be honest about your views. Speaking one's Truth does not mean making someone else wrong or being undiplomatic.

- **Everyone has something important to say.** What someone has to share may not seem important to another, but may lift a tremendous weight or open the door to inspiration.

- **Listen without judgment and interruption.** Respect the integrity of another person's viewpoint.

- **Be fully present.** Thoughtful consideration given to the dreams of others ensures that you will be given thoughtful consideration when it is your turn.

ASD DREAMWORK ETHICS STATEMENT

Here is the statement of dreamwork ethics from the Association for the Study of Dreams. Whenever I conduct a dreamwork class or workshop, I distribute and discuss these ethics in advance:

ASD celebrates the many benefits of dreamwork, yet recognizes that there are potential risks. ASD supports an approach to dreamwork and dream sharing that respects the dreamer's dignity and integrity, and which recognizes the dreamer as the decision-maker regarding the significance of the dream. Systems of dreamwork that assign authority or knowledge of the dream's meanings to someone other than the dreamer can be misleading, incorrect, and harmful. Ethical dreamwork helps the dreamer work with his/her own dream images, feelings, and associations, and guides the dreamer to more fully experience, appreciate, and understand the dream. Every dream may have multiple meanings, and different techniques may be reasonably employed to touch these multiple layers of significance.

A dreamer's decision to share or discontinue sharing a dream should always be respected and honored. The dreamer should be forewarned that unexpected issues or emotions may arise in the course of the dreamwork. Information and mutual agreement about the degree of privacy and confidentiality are essential ingredients in creating a safe atmosphere for dream sharing.

Dreamwork outside a clinical setting is not a substitute for psychotherapy, or other professional treatment, and should not be used as such.

ASD recognizes and respects that there are many valid and time-honored dreamwork traditions. We invite and welcome the participation of dreamers from all cultures. There are social, cultural, and transpersonal aspects to dream experience. In this statement we do not mean to imply that the only valid approach to dreamwork focuses on the dreamer's personal life. Our purpose is to honor and respect the person of the dreamer as well as the dream itself, regardless of how the relationship between the two may be understood.

Best wishes, and may your dreamwork open new vistas of self-discovery and fulfillment.

APPENDIX:
ON-LINE RESOURCES

BELOW ARE WEB sites that offer information of interest to visionary dreamers. Please note that URL addresses are subject to change.

The Alchemical Egg
http://www.thealchemicalegg.com
Author and artist Robert Michael Place's Web site with articles on the tarot and dreams.

Association for the Study of Dreams
http://www.asdreams.org
E-study groups (Dream activism, psi, healing, spirituality, lucidity, and more), Psiber Dreaming Conferences archives, bulletin boards, chat, articles, bookstore, ethics statement, and more.

Children's Past Lives
http://www.childpastlives.org
Author Carol Bowman's site on reincarnation and past-life memories.

Dream Network
http://www.dreamnetwork.org
Articles, networking, and more.

Global Consciousness Project
http://noosphere.princeton.edu
Research results on global mind.

The Great Tomorrow
http://www.thegreattomorrow.org
Author Nick Bunick's site on angels, reincarnation, spirituality, and more.

Mugwort and Dreams
http://www.nauticom.net/www/netcadet/EDPAPER.htm
"Sleeping with Plants: A Low Tech Approach to Dream Enhancement," by Ed Wirth. Paper presented to the Association for the Study of Dreams annual conference in Washington, D.C., July 7, 2002.

Stock Market Dreaming
http://www.webspawner.com/users/stockdreams
Information on investment dreaming experiences.

Visionary Living, Inc.
http://www.visionaryliving.com
Rosemary Ellen Guiley's Web site, with articles on dreams, intuition, and other topics, and an Angel Dream Forum.

World Dreams Peace Bridge
http://www.worlddreamspeacebridge.org
Jean Campbell's international dream activism group for peace and social causes.

NOTES

Chapter 4: Lucidity and Dream Traveling

1. Patricia Garfield, *Pathway to Ecstasy: The Way of the Dream Mandala* (New York: Holt, Rinehart and Winston, 1979), 44–45.
2. Correspondence to author.
3. Correspondence to author.
4. Posting on asd-PsiDreams on-line listserv forum, March 25, 2003. Used with permission.

Chapter 5: Experiencing God in Dreams

1. James H. Charlesworth, ed., *The Old Testament Pseudepigrapha*, Vol. 1 (New York: Doubleday, 1983), 106.
2. Correspondence to author.
3. Correspondence to author.
4. Correspondence to author.
5. Correspondence to author.
6. Correspondence to author.
7. Correspondence to author.
8. Correspondence to author.
9. Correspondence to author.

Chapter 6: Spiritual Turning Point Dreams

[1.] Correspondence to author.
[2.] Correspondence to author.
[3.] Correspondence to author.
[4.] Correspondence to author.
[5.] Correspondence to author.
[6.] Correspondence to author.
[7.] Used with permission of Roberta Ossana.
[8.] Correspondence to author.
[9.] Correspondence to author.
[10.] Correspondence to author.

Chapter 7: Calling Dreams

[1.] Correspondence to author.
[2.] Kathleen Sullivan, *Recurring Dreams: A Journey to Wholeness* (Freedom, Calif.: The Crossing Press, 1998), 5.
[3.] Ibid., xii.
[4.] Emily L. VanLaeys, *Dream Weaving: Using Dream Guidance to Create Life's Tapestry* (Virginia Beach, Va.: A.R.E. Press, 2001), xiii.
[5.] Ibid., 166.
[6.] Ullman, Montague and Nan Zimmerman. *Working With Dreams.* Los Angeles: Jeremy P. Tarcher, 1979.
[7.] Lee Irwin, "Sending a Voice, Seeking a Place: Visionary Traditions among Native Women of the Plains," in *Dreams: A Reader on the Religious, Cultural, and Psychological Dimensions of Dreaming,* ed. Kelly Bulkeley (New York: Palgrave/St. Martin's Press, 2001), 94.
[8.] Joseph Epes Brown, *The Spiritual Legacy of the American Indian* (New York: Crossroad, 1987), 79.

Chapter 8: Calls from the Goddess and the Ancestors

[1.] Correspondence to author.
[2.] Correspondence to author.

Chapter 9: Dreaming for Creativity

[1.] Excerpted from Robert Michael Place's introduction to *The Alchemical Tarot,* by Rosemary Ellen Guiley and Robert Michael Place (London: Thorsons/HarperCollins, 1995), 1–7. For a fuller account, see "It Starts with a Dream," by Robert Michael Place, on his Web site, The Alchemical Egg, http://www.thealchemicalegg.com

2. Correspondence to author.

3. Tom Crockett, *The Artist Inside: A Spiritual Guide to Cultivating Your Creative Self* (New York: Broadway Books, 2000), 42.

4. Richard Russo, "Dreams and the Spirit of Place," *Dream Time,* Winter 2002, 27.

Chapter 10: Healing Power in Dreams

1. Marc Ian Barasch, *Healing Dreams: Exploring Dreams That Can Transform Your Life* (New York: Riverhead Books, 2000), 2.

2. Ibid., 3.

Chapter 12: Dreams about the Dead and about Dying

1. Correspondence to author.

2. Correspondence to author.

3. Correspondence to author.

4. Fraser Boa, "Dreams, Dying and Beyond: A Conversation with Marie-Louise von Franz," in *Dreamscaping: New and Creative Ways to Work with Your Dreams,* ed. Stanley Krippner and Mark Robert Waldman (Los Angeles: Lowell House, 1999), 275.

5. John Sanford, *Dreams: God's Forgotten Language* (San Francisco: Harper & Row, 1968, 1989), 60.

6. Marie-Louise von Franz, *On Dreams & Death* (Boston: Shambhala Publications, 1984), ix.

Chapter 13: Precognitive Dreaming

1. Correspondence to author.

2. Correspondence to author.

3. Jean Campbell, home page of the World Dreams Peace Bridge, http://www.worlddreamspeacebridge.org

4. Dale E. Graff, posting on asd-PsiDreams listserv forum, February 2003.

5. Dale E. Graff, "A Closer Look at Dream Telepathy," *Dream Time,* Summer 2001, 42.

6. Correspondence to author.

Chapter 14: Dream Activism

1. Dean Radin, *The Conscious Universe: The Scientific Truth of Psychic Phenomena* (San Francisco: Harper Edge/HarperSanFrancisco, 1997), 174.

2. Linda Lane Magallón, *Mutual Dreaming* (New York: Pocket Books, 1997), 88–89.

Chapter 16: Dreaming with Others

1. Anjali Hazarika, *Daring to Dream: Cultivating Corporate Creativity through Dreamwork* (New Delhi: Response Books/Sage Publications, 1997), 48–49.

2. Montague Ullman, "A Note on Social Referents of Dreams," *Dreaming* 11(1), March 2001, 1–12.

Chapter 17: Dreaming of Past Lives

1. Carol Bowman, *Children's Past Lives: How Past Life Memories Affect Your Child* (New York: Bantam Books, 1997), 39.

2. Correspondence to author.

3. Correspondence to author.

4. Correspondence to author.

Chapter 18: Dreams of Pets and Animals

1. Val Bigelow, archives of 2002 ASD PsiberCon, http:\\www.asdreams.org

2. Correspondence to author.

3. Correspondence to author.

4. Correspondence to author.

5. Correspondence to author.

6. Correspondence to author.

Chapter 19: Haunted Dreams

1. Correspondence to author.

2. David J. Hufford, *The Terror That Comes in the Night: An Experience-Centered Study of Supernatural Assault Traditions* (Philadelphia: University of Pennsylvania Press, 1982), 33.

[3.] Correspondence to author.

[4.] Correspondence to author.

[5.] John E. Mack, *Abduction: Human Encounters with Aliens* (New York: Charles Scribner's Sons, 1994), 405–406.

[6.] Correspondence to author.

BIBLIOGRAPHY

Barasch, Marc Ian. *Healing Dreams: Exploring Dreams That Can Transform Your Life*. New York: Riverhead Books, 2000.

Barrett, Deirdre. *The Committee of Sleep: How Artists, Scientists, and Athletes Use Dreams for Creative Problem-Solving—and How You Can Too*. New York: Crown, 2001.

Barrett, Deirdre, ed. *Trauma and Dreams*. Cambridge, Mass: Harvard University Press, 1996.

Bergquist, Lars. *Swedenborg's Dream Diary*. Translated by Anders Hallengren. West Chester, Pa.: Swedenborg Foundation Publishers, 2001.

Bowman, Carol. *Children's Past Lives: How Past Life Memories Affect Your Child*. New York: Bantam Books, 1997.

Brown, Joseph Epes. *The Spiritual Legacy of the American Indian*. New York: Crossroad, 1987.

Bulkeley, Kelly, ed. *Dreams: A Reader on the Religious, Cultural, and Psychological Dimensions of Dreaming*. New York: Palgrave/St. Martin's Press, 2001.

Charlesworth, James H., ed. *The Old Testament Pseudepigrapha*. Vol. 1. New York: Doubleday, 1983.

Crockett, Tom. *The Artist Inside: A Spiritual Guide to Cultivating Your Creative Self.* New York: Broadway Books, 2000.

Evans-Wentz, W. Y. *The Fairy-Faith in Celtic Countries.* Secaucus, N.J.: University Books, 1966. First published 1911.

Freud, Sigmund. *The Interpretation of Dreams.* New York: The Modern Library, 1950. First published 1900.

Fortune, Dion. *Psychic Self-Defence.* York Beach, Me.: Samuel Weiser, 1982.

Garfield, Patricia. *The Healing Power of Dreams.* New York: Simon & Schuster, 1991.

———. *Pathway to Ecstasy: The Way of the Dream Mandala.* New York: Holt, Rinehart and Winston, 1979.

Gershom, Rabbi Yonan. *Beyond the Ashes: Cases of Reincarnation from the Holocaust.* Virginia Beach, Va.: A.R.E. Press, 1992.

———. *From Ashes to Healing: Mystical Encounters with the Holocaust.* Virginia Beach, Va.: A.R.E. Press, 1996.

Graff, Dale E. "A Closer Look at Dream Telepathy." *Dream Time* (summer 2001): 42.

———. *River Dreams: The Case of the Missing General and Other Adventures in Psychic Research.* Boston: Element Books, 2000.

———. *Tracks in the Psychic Wilderness.* Boston: Element Books, 1998.

Guiley, Rosemary Ellen. *The Encyclopedia of Angels.* 2nd ed. New York: Facts on File, 2003.

———. *The Encyclopedia of Saints.* New York: Facts on File, 2002.

———. *Dreamspeak: How to Understand the Messages in Your Dreams.* New York: Berkley Books, 2001.

———. *A Miracle in Your Pocket.* London: Thorsons/HarperCollins, 2001.

———. *Breakthrough Intuition: How to Achieve a Life of Abundance by Listening to the Voice Within.* New York: Berkley Books, 2000.

———. *Dreamwork for the Soul: A Spiritual Guide to Dream Interpretation.* New York: Berkley Books, 1998.

———. *Harper's Encyclopedia of Mystical and Paranormal Experience.* San Francisco: HarperSanFrancisco, 1991.

———. *Tales of Reincarnation.* New York: Pocket Books, 1991.

Guiley, Rosemary Ellen, and Robert Michael Place. *The Alchemical Tarot.* London: Thorsons/HarperCollins, 1995.

Hall, James A. *The Unconscious Christian: Images of God in Dreams.* Edited by Daniel J. Meckel. New York: Paulist Press, 1983.

Hazarika, Anjali. *Daring to Dream: Cultivating Corporate Creativity through Dreamwork.* New Delhi: Response Books/Sage Publications, 1997.

Hufford, David J. *The Terror That Comes in the Night: An Experience-Centered Study of Supernatural Assault Traditions.* Philadelphia: University of Pennsylvania Press, 1982.

Ingram, Julia, and G. W. Hardin. *The Messengers: A True Story of Angelic Presence and the Return of the Age of Miracles.* New York: Pocket Books, 1998.

Jung, Carl G. *Memories, Dreams, Reflections.* New York: Vintage Books, 1989.

Krippner, Stanley, Fariba Bogzaran, and Andre Percia de Carvalho. *Extraordinary Dreams and How to Work with Them.* Albany: State University of New York Press, 2002.

Krippner, Stanley, and Mark Robert Waldman, eds. *Dreamscaping: New and Creative Ways to Work with Your Dreams.* Los Angeles: Lowell House, 1999.

LaBerge, Stephen, and Howard Rheingold. *Exploring the World of Lucid Dreaming.* New York: Ballantine Books, 1990.

Lawrence, W. Gordon, ed. *Social Dreaming @ Work.* London: Karnac Books, 1998.

Mack, John E. *Abduction: Human Encounters with Aliens.* New York: Charles Scribner's Sons, 1994.

Magallón, Linda Lane. *Mutual Dreaming.* New York: Pocket Books, 1997.

Neihardt, John G. *Black Elk Speaks: Being the Life Story of a Holy Man of the Oglala Sioux.* New York: Pocket Books, 1973.

Radin, Dean. *The Conscious Universe: The Scientific Truth of Psychic Phenomena.* San Francisco: Harper Edge/HarperSanFrancisco, 1997.

Russo, Richard. "Dreams and the Spirit Place." *Dream Time* (winter 2002): 27+.

Sanford, John. *Dreams: God's Forgotten Language.* San Francisco: Harper & Row, 1989.

Sullivan, Kathleen. *Recurring Dreams: A Journey to Wholeness.* Freedom, Calif.: The Crossing Press, 1998.

Swann, Ingo. *Your Nostradamus Factor: Accessing Your Innate Ability to See into the Future.* New York: Fireside/Simon & Schuster, 1993.

Tick, Edward. *The Practice of Dream Healing: Bringing Ancient Greek Mysteries into Modern Medicine.* Wheaton, Ill.: Quest Books, 2001.

Ullman, Monague. "A Note on Social Referent of Dreams." *Dreaming* 11(1) (March 2001): 1–12.

Ullman Montague and Nan Zimmerman. *Working with Dreams.* Los Angeles: Jeremy P. Tarcher, 1979.

Van de Castle, Robert L. *Our Dreaming Mind.* New York: Ballantine Books, 1994.

VanLaeys, Emily L. *Dream Weaving: Using Dream Guidance to Create Life's Tapestry.* Virginia Beach, Va.: A.R.E. Press, 2001.

von Franz, Marie-Louis. *On Dreams & Death.* Boston: Shambhala Publications, 1984.